Human Values in Critical Care Medicine

HUMAN VALUES IN CRITICAL CARE MEDICINE

Edited by
Stuart J. Youngner

PRAEGER

New York
Westport, Connecticut
London

Library of Congress Cataloging-in-Publication Data

Human values in critical care medicine.

Includes bibliographies and index.
1. Critical care medicine — Moral and ethical
aspects. 2. Critical care medicine — Social
aspects. 3. Long-term care of the sick — Moral
and ethical aspects. 4. Medical ethics.
5. Humanistic psychology. I. Youngner,
Stuart J.   [DNLM: 1. Critical Care.   2. Ethics,
Medical. WB 105 H918]
RC86.95.H86   1986   174'.24   86-22569
ISBN 0-275-92264-2 (alk. paper)

Library of Congress Catalog Card Number: 86-22569
ISBN: 0-275-92264-2

First published in 1986

Praeger Publishers, 521 Fifth Avenue, New York, NY 10175
A division of Greenwood Press, Inc.

Printed in the United States of America

The paper used in this book complies with the Permanent
Paper Standard issued by the National Information Standards
Organization (Z39.48-1984).

10 9 8 7 6 5 4 3 2 1

Contents

Human Values in Critical Care Medicine

Introduction
William A. Knaus

Daniel Bell, Professor of Sociology at Harvard University, published a book in 1973 entitled, *The Coming of Post-Industrial Society: A Venture in Social Forecasting*.[1] Bell's effort has stood up well to the test of time. Read today, a decade after publication and two decades or more after the ideas initially appeared in the sociological literature, the phrase "postindustrial" society and the concepts that underlie it seem more relevant than ever.

In this introductory chapter, I will briefly review the major new dimensions that Bell attributed to a postindustrial society, and illustrate how they have direct relevance to current discussions of medical policy and medical practice. I will then describe how I believe the seven chapters in this volume illustrate aspects of the larger themes described by Bell. My purpose is to place the discussions contained in each of the chapters into a larger societal context. Knowledge of this larger societal and historical perspective has helped me to better understand why discussions of ethical, moral, legal, and social values have such large and far-reaching implications for the practice of medicine, especially critical care. But first, the big picture.

Bell contends that all societies can be described as being in one of three broad categories: preindustrial; industrial; postindustrial. Preindustrial means their economy is based on agriculture, mining, fishing, timber, or other natural resources. Many African, and some Latin American and Asian, countries remain preindustrial societies.

An industrial society is primarily concerned with the fabrication and manufacture of goods using energy and machine technology. The

Soviet Union, Japan, and most countries in Western Europe are industrial societies. Finally, there is Bell's concept of a postindustrial society, in which the development of new theoretical knowledge, the processing of information, and the production of services, as opposed to goods, dominates. The United States is currently the best example of a postindustrial society.

More important than labels, however, are the characteristics, dimensions, or trends which Bell ascribes to the United States postindustrial period—trends that succinctly describe what is happening to the world in which we live. Bell listed 11 dimensions in an expanded 1976 foreword to *The Coming of Post-Industrial Society*[2]; I have chosen six that I believe have direct relevance to critical care medicine and the topics discussed in this volume.

1. *The central importance of theoretical knowledge.* The first dimension describes how the codification or development of new theoretical knowledge has become the basis of technological innovations. For society in general, the best examples are the new science-based industries of computers, optics, and electronics. In medicine, fundamental breakthroughs in our understanding of molecular biology have already led to new technologies that alter natural genetic patterns. The future is sure to bring more discoveries in genetic engineering that will expand many of our fundamental concepts of science.

Within critical care, the growing influence of theoretical knowledge can be seen in our increased understanding of immunology and its impact on organ transplantation. The frequency and ease with which we use new devices such as pulmonary artery catheters, which were developed in direct response to our increased theoretical knowledge of cardiovascular physiology, also illustrate the impact of new theoretical knowledge.

Indeed, within the microcosm of critical care, we can already see the beginnings of the transition from new technology, discovered serendipitously and extended because it met a need (for example, the positive pressure ventilator), to new technologies that could emerge only from established theoretical principles (for example, the adequacy of circulation, as estimated by mixed venous oxygen saturation).

The contrast between these two technologies also illustrates the increased complexity associated with new theoretical knowledge. In its initial application, the adequacy of the ventilation provided by positive pressure breathing machines was determined largely by observing the patient's color and feeling his/her skin. Full interpretation of a mixed venous oxygenation saturation requires a complicated knowledge of interacting variables (such as, oxygen demand, consumption, the extent of organ or peripheral arteriovenous shunting) that can make simple observations or intuitive judgments dangerous.

2. *The creation of new intellectual technology.* This dimension of our postindustrial society describes how new mathematical and analytic techniques are altering the nature of scientific inquiry. Linear programming techniques, multivariate analysis, computer modeling, simulation, and other newly developed techniques are rapidly changing the way engineers and scientists approach their research and their work.

It is difficult to read any general or subspecialty medical journal without confronting an article that uses one or more of these new mathematical techniques. Prior to initiating or publishing a study, most authors seek statistical advice. Alfred Sofer, one of this country's prominent medical authors, commented recently that the submission of many large-number clinical studies employing advanced statistical methods is progressively pushing individual or small-number case reports from the pages of medical journals.[3] There is now a medical journal (*Medical Decisionmaking*) devoted exclusively to quantitative medical decision making. Decision theory is increasingly being taught to medical students. Computer literacy has become a requirement for graduation in some medical schools.

These same trends are apparent within the field of critical care. I, my colleagues, and an increasing number of critical care professionals are concentrating on prognosis and prediction of outcome research that would have been impossible 20 years ago[4]; it would have been impossible to analyze information on such large numbers of patients without advanced statistical techniques. As a result of these techniques, however, medical research, and especially critical care, is entering new areas that will, in turn, increase our ability to describe the incremental value of new medical techniques for both society and individuals. These projections would have been impossible using individual case-reporting techniques.

3. *The change from goods to services.* Along with the increase in theoretical knowledge, this is the most important characteristic of a postindustrial society. As evidence, Bell cites the statistics demonstrating an increasing proportion of the U.S. workforce employed in delivery of services (70 out of 100), as opposed to manufacture of goods (30 out of every 100 workers). He also points out that in a postindustrial society the concept of services is concentrated on human services,

primarily education and health. As the percentage of life the average citizen spends working decreases and the opportunities for good jobs are increasingly linked to higher education, access to the good life increasingly becomes a matter of education and health. The reduction of the impact of disease and the corresponding gains in life span (we have extended the average life expectancy more in this century than in the previous nine) have resulted in growing numbers of people who want to enjoy the full length of that increase.

This has helped to make medical services such a large and consistently growing sector of our economy. Beyond the often-quoted statistic that medical care now accounts for over 10 percent of our gross national product is the reality that it is the local hospitals, rather than traditional manufacturing industries, that are now the main source of employment in many previously industrial and manufacturing areas. The continuous expansion of these services, however, prevents the use of our labor and economic wealth for other areas of growth, thus constraining future progress and leading to persistent inflation.

If rapid growth in medical, especially hospital, services has been a characteristic of the past three decades in U.S. society, critical care medicine has been at the cutting edge of the movement. Unknown 30 years ago, critical care alone now accounts for over 10 percent of all medical expenses, enabling it to claim a full percentage of our GNP.[5] On a more easily recognizable level, critical care units concentrate machines and a growing number of skilled professionals (physicians, nurses, monitoring technicians, respiratory technicians, physical therapists, dieticians, pharmacists, laboratory technicians) in the service of a small number of increasingly elderly, increasingly ill patients.

4. *A change in the character of work.* In a preindustrial society, according to Bell, life was mainly a game against nature, men making their living from the land. In an industrial society, work was defined by the interface between man and machine. In a postindustrial society, however, work is primarily a "game between persons." As our world becomes more complex, each of us has to learn how to live and work closer together than ever before. Because cooperation between men is substantially more difficult than the management of industrial production, this raises new challenges.

Medicine has also been influenced by this shift in the nature of work. The most obvious single sign is the trend toward increased specialization. Because of the growth in both theoretical and applied knowledge, each physician now cares for an increasingly small portion of the human body, or is responsible for a limited portion of an overall episode of illness. The ability of one physician using his own tools to treat an entire episode of illness has virtually disappeared in the United States. Today, even the diagnosis and management of a malady as common as arthritis frequently involves consultation with experts and sophisticated laboratory testing. The same is true for more acute life-threatening illnesses. There is an increasing recognition that the best medical care available today is the result of a team effort, involving the patient as well as diverse members of the health care team. Organizing and coordinating that care, however, is a talent we have yet to learn; so far, no specialty has established firm leadership in the area.

We still have a physician-dominated medical system in which a single doctor can, regardless of ability, control much of what happens during an episode of illness. There are, however, signs of possible change. The unopposed dominance of the physician is being challenged by both patients and other medical professionals. Fewer patients are willing to accept a physician's decision at face value, and other health care professionals are demanding and receiving privileges to use their special expertise to treat patients, both in private offices and public hospitals. Because physicians have not fully accepted many of these challenges to their authority, many of these changes are associated with bitter debates and calls for a return to simpler times.

Critical care medicine, perhaps because of its early and heavy reliance on teamwork, has been somewhat less torn by inter- and intraprofessional struggles than other subspecialties. There has long been an informal acknowledgement that Intensive Care Units (ICUs) are best managed by physicians and nurses working together. A direct comparison of ICU care given at 13 tertiary care hospitals resulted in the initial recognition of the direct relationship between the quality of interpersonal care and the probability of a patient's surviving an acute illness.[6]

This is not to conclude, however, that the ability of critical care to properly manage the crucial "game between persons" is unhampered by problems. Acceptance of a team approach is far from universal, as we will see when we discuss the subsequent chapters in this volume.

5. *The substitution of location of work for professional groups.* This dimension of the new postindustrial society may be the most controversial because it threatens to upset traditional class and interest groups. Bell's argument, as I understand it, is that professionals, technicians, and administrative classes are becoming more and more iden-

tified with their work environments than with their individual classes. Thus, scientists and engineers can work for economic enterprises, government, universities, nonprofit research institutes, or the military. In the future, each of these political or social organizations will serve as the source of public power or influence, rather than individual professional organizations.

Within medicine, there is early but distinct evidence that a transition in this direction has begun. First, the American Medical Association, the professional organization that once represented most of this country's physicians, now accounts for less than half. There are also fewer and fewer physicians in private fee-for-service practice; more and more of them are joining groups or becoming employees of institutions, to which many of them are beginning to claim primary loyalty. Academic physicians, for example, are increasingly responsive to the unique needs of their university hospitals, even if these demands run counter to those that are supported by organized medicine.

Critical care physicians and other professionals have always been closely associated with institutions. Their professional association, the Society for Critical Care Medicine, has traditionally welcomed physicians, nurses, and paraprofessionals. Because the Society for Critical Care Medicine does not have a credentialing function, however, its ability to demand primary loyalty may be limited.[7] If institutions and hospitals progressively develop as centers of professional and public interest, critical care professionals could build on existing strong loyalties to form an important and natural part of their constituency.

6. *Development of new scarcities.* From long waiting lists for the first commercial moon shuttle trips to the increasing competition for spaces in rush hour traffic, we have created new scarcities that previous generations never imagined. This new dimension of Bell's post-industrial society is very closely related to the practice of critical care.

Because of the progress in immunology, molecular biology, and other areas of both theoretical and practical knowledge, we now have a range of new medical scarcities (organ transplants, immunosuppressive drugs, highly skilled open-heart surgery teams) that were unknown a few decades ago. Some of the scarcities exist because the supply is so limited (organ transplants), or because our ability to organize complex services (such as open-heart surgery) is haphazard. Regardless of why these shortages exist, however, they are raising new questions of resource allocations and rationing that are not being answered well, and are creating substantial individual and societal confusion. Part of the reason for this chaos in our medical system is that there is, as yet, no widely accepted public agreement on how to face these issues, and no mechanism for accomplishing our objectives—even if we could agree on common goals.

Another reason we have so much trouble with these questions is our strong tradition, or ethos, of individualism. In this century, we have developed an absolute reliance on the fee-for-service doctor-patient relationship as the major safeguard for ethical and moral decision making. While this approach has served us well (the quality of U.S. medical care is unsurpassed in the world), it is not able to meet the challenge of the distribution of scarce new medical resources. If an individual physician is obligated to do everything possible for his patient, he will have difficulty considering the relative needs of others. But if he is *not* his patient's advocate, then how do we ensure full consideration of each individual's right to treatment?

One possible answer is that in a postindustrial, knowledge-driven society, information describing the relative ability of individuals to benefit from advanced medical care may become more important; the individual's right to demand therapy, irrespective of prognosis, will, consequently, become less absolute. This change in emphasis may be unavoidable because the decision to treat one individual increasingly has direct consequences for other patients; in addition, our elderly population will demand more medical treatment than society will be willing or able to provide.

The difficulty of facing a possible transition from an individual-physician, individual-patient society to one that more explicitly incorporates public values into individual medical decisions cannot, however, be underestimated. What sort of public decision-making structures are we going to establish to promote societal consensus? Who is going to be responsible for implementation on a local institutional level? Will physicians continue to provide leadership as we move into new areas of decision making, or will they become more scientific, technical, and narrow in their expertise, participating in, but not leading, discussions concerning allocation and rationing? What new social organizations will be necessary to provide the patient protection now found in the private physician-patient relationship? Can we make the transition without reducing our scientific leadership? Can we avoid the stifling of innovation found in most bureaucracies? For me, these are the fundamental questions that will dominate public medical policy well into the next century.

Clearly, we need help in addressing these questions. So let us turn to what the contributors to this volume have to tell us about how we might handle these and other future challenges within the field of critical care.

In Chapter 1, Stuart Youngner presents his view of the current state of Do Not Resuscitate (DNR) orders. He tells us that DNR orders have become a very visible symbol of the new ethical dilemmas facing critical care practitioners. Youngner also points out that CPR is a technology only partially based on new theoretical knowledge (defibrillation). We still do not know exactly how other components of CPR work, and recent scientific investigation even suggests that certain aspects, such as closed chest compression, may be doing more harm than good. Despite these concerns and the rather dismal outcome record for most in-hospital resuscitation attempts, we have made CPR standard practice in all acute care hospitals. Every patient whose heart stops is now resuscitated, unless an order is written specifically prohibiting CPR. In his chapter, Youngner provides guidelines that institutions could use to evaluate and update their use of DNR orders.

One of the reasons institutional guidelines are needed is that the decision to institute or withhold resuscitation involves more than the patient and physician; it involves the entire health care team, as well as the institution. Thus, decision making concerning DNR orders is one example of the complex "game between persons" that now characterizes much of medical work. Youngner gives us some clear practical advice on how to play the game in ways that can reduce human suffering, while respecting the rights of the patient and members of the health care team.

In Chapter 2, "The Role of Burden/Benefit Analysis in the Orchestration of Death in the ICU," Mayo and Bennett take on many of the misperceptions that they feel make the team management of critically ill patients more complex than necessary. They contend that the use of the terms "slippery slope," "extraordinary," "ordinary," and the concept that there are substantial ethical and moral distinctions between withholding and withdrawing life-supporting treatment create confusion. For Mayo and Bennett, the central issue is not whether we are limiting, not beginning, or stopping life support, because in their view we are already on that slippery slope. For them, the central question is whether the potential benefits of treatment outweigh the burdens—a determination that should be based on the patient's values. Mayo and Bennett argue that a focus on any other considerations may draw us too far away from the moral questions created by our new life-sustaining technologies.

A similar concentration on beneficence toward the patient appears as the central theme in Chapter 3, "Ethical Decisions in Neonatal Intensive Care" by Mary Mahowald. She emphasizes that the physician, in combination with responsible family members, must clearly keep the best interests of the newborn at the forefront of decision making.

Both of these chapters illustrate the strong influence of individualism recognized by Bell as dominating U.S. society for most of its history. While these three authors agree that absolute patient autonomy is not an appropriate moral position (especially for the newborn), it is also clear that they give questions of social justice only passing mention.

But what happens when the "best interests" of the individual newborn or adult may not be in the best interests of society? Mayo and Bennett tell us that no procedure is inherently extraordinary, and that it would be inappropriate to withhold a potentially beneficial therapy merely because it is unusual. Unfortunately, many extraordinary and unusual treatments are also expensive. As we increase the amount of our national wealth that goes to provide medical care, it is likely that issues of societal allocation will become more prominent.

Claudia Coulton makes this point in "Resource Limits and Allocation in Critical Care," Chapter 4. She contrasts the amount of money we spend on high technology rescue treatments, such as end-stage renal disease and less visible, but more fundamental, nutritional feeding programs for pregnant mothers and newborns. She concludes that in the not-too-distant future continued growth of intensive care will eventually restrict our choices in other areas of society, thereby forcing us to establish formal rationing mechanisms for its use. How we will do this, however, is far from clear. These macroallocation decisions will force us to recognize more explicitly that the amount of money we spend on advanced medical care reduces the amount available for other social support systems. In addition, questions of individual rationing are likely to be brought into sharper focus.

The increasing competition among individual patients for scarce resources, such as organ transplantations, is an example of the new scarcities associated with scientific progress. In her discussion of how we might go about distributing these newly scarce resources, Coulton describes various theories of rationing. All present dilemmas for intensive care, especially in light of the strong tradition of individualism that characterizes almost all of U.S. medical practice.

The importance of the individual patient-individual physician relationship as the main protector of patient rights is inherent in the discussions of Mayo and Bennett, as well as that of Mahowald, in which the physician is clearly identified as the newborn's advocate and protector. If the individual physician is charged with doing everything possible for an individual patient, however, who is going to take responsibility for leading society, hospitals, and individuals into the difficult areas of allocation and rationing that Coulton contends are unavoidable?

"Society must decide," is a response commonly heard from physicians and other health care providers in discussions of painful ethical and rationing decisions. But aren't physicians considered leaders in our society? Shouldn't we be taking the lead in questions of allocation and rationing? Should we not be assuming broader responsibilities in the area of medicine and public policy?

How far away the medical profession is from actually demonstrating such leadership is illustrated in Chapter 5 by Jackson and Annas. They describe the development of organ transplantation policies in Massachusetts and Ohio. From Annas' description of the Massachusetts program, it is obvious that political and personal interests took precedence over the larger cost and quality of care concerns. "Thus, Boston now has more hospitals performing or ready to perform transplants than any other city in the world, and is the only city with more than two such hospitals," is the pessimistic conclusion to Annas' discussion. And while it can be argued that Boston's concentration of medical talent is unique in the world, the experience in Massachusetts does not bode well for the future of physician leadership in these different areas.

The Ohio initiative led by former critical care physician David Jackson appears to have a better chance of meeting the larger goal of social justice. Jackson's tale of the state legislator who knew of a single patient who wasn't receiving a transplant because of "bureaucratic red tape" clearly illustrates the difficulties inherent in maintaining this objective. The director of the Ohio Department of Health was pressured into finding an institution that would immediately place the patient on a transplant list. The larger goal of building a fair and just transplant allocation system in Ohio was temporarily threatened.

The rights of the individual to demand all medical care necessary, and the need for society to set limits on the amount of its wealth used to treat the desperately ill, will be major public policy issues in the decades ahead. Considering the legacy of individualism in the United States, it is very unlikely that the United Kingdom's system of explicit and implicit rationing practices, described by Coulton, would be acceptable. In fact, some observers of the U.S. political system are concerned that our society will never be able to directly face the need to balance individual requests against the common good. As a result, prominent economist Lester Thurow believes we may soon develop a three-tiered medical care system.[8] The poor and the uninsured will have access only to a basic set of services available in a limited number of health care institutions. The middle class will have broader coverage, but only the wealthy will be able to enjoy the full range of medical services. Such a system would restrain costs, but at the expense of access.

Fighting against this future are a few groups of involved professionals and citizens who are attempting to make the difficult initial transition from rhetoric about social justice to public policy. Most notable among these efforts is that of the Oregon Health Decisions, a group of professionals and community leaders that has provided a clear public statement of the need to ensure access and justice in health care decisions, even if such decisions run counter to individual demands for advanced medical care.[9] In a pluralistic society such as ours, it is likely that such local initiatives, based on community organizations and institutions, stand the best chance of shaping public policy in health care rationing, cost containment, and allocation.

While we are waiting to see how well we face these difficult issues, the final two chapters in this book contain some practical guidance for providing current levels of intensive care.

In Chapter 6, Barbara Daly expands on the concept that much of modern medical care is a game between persons by describing the current relationship between physicians and nurses. Daly believes there are substantial problems in nurse-physician relationships, and that a wider acknowledgement of these difficulties is an essential step toward resolving them. A key element of improvement is better communication among physicians and nurses. Communication is also a key feature of Joel Frader's chapter in ICU visiting (Chapter 7). As the world in which we work becomes more complex and more dominated by theoretical knowledge that is rapidly transformed into practical applications, it becomes more and more difficult to maintain a human perspective.

Chapters 6 and 7 build on a theme emphasized by Bell in *The Post-Industrial Society*—that is, that the management of people is substantially more complicated than the management of production; certainly the challenges of managing a multidisciplinary intensive care unit demand constant attention to communication. Being a good manager is a new role for physicians, and a responsibility we are unlikely to accept until the current system of reimbursement is altered to reward directly such efforts. Change, however, is in the wind—not only for reimbursement of critically ill patients, but also for other aspects of public policy influencing critical care. Indeed, the very fact that money is now so closely linked to public discussions of medicine is the best evidence of the nearness of change.[8]

In this time of rapid societal change, there will be opportunities to examine, alter, or reaffirm our basic values. Do we wish to maintain the current concentration on the individual patient described in the chapters by Mayo, Bennett, and Mahowald? If so, how are we going to address the critical allocation and rationing issues raised by Coulton? If, on the other hand, we want to change to a more consequentialist approach that more explicitly acknowledges the common good, how should we proceed?

How do we want to organize and distribute complex services like organ transplantation? It is clear that not all hospitals are equally proficient in performing these operations. But will the inferior ones stop? Do we really want to improve communication within our ICUs? If so, physicians and nurses will have to learn to be better managers and listeners. Do we want to extend these leadership roles beyond the hospital and into society?

Whatever our answers, it seems clear that critical care practitioners, physicians, nurses, and related professionals must deal more forthrightly with these issues; this book is a step in that direction. Only by broadening our knowledge and leadership skills will we be able to ensure the preservation of human values in our specialty, and thereby improve the treatment of future patients.

REFERENCES

1. Bell D: *The Coming of Post-Industrial Society: A Venture in Social Forecasting*. New York, Basic Books, 1973.
2. Bell D: Foreword. *The Coming of Post-Industrial Society: A Venture in Social Forecasting*. New York, Basic Books, 1976.
3. Sofer A: Personal communication, 1984.
4. Knaus WA, Draper EA, Wagner DP, Zimmerman JE: APACHE II: A severity of disease classification system. *Crit Care Med* 1985, *13*: 818-829.
5. Berenson RA: Intensive care units (ICUs): Clinical outcomes, costs and decision making (Health Technology Case Study 28), prepared for the Office of Technology Assessment. US Congress. OTA-HCS-28, Washington, DC, 1984.

6. Knaus WA, Draper EA, Wagner DP, Zimmerman JE: An evaluation of outcome from intensive care in major medical centers. *Ann Intern Med* 1986, 104: 410-418.
7. Grenvik A: Subspecialty certification in critical care medicine by American specialty boards. *Crit Care Med* 1985, *13*:1001-1003.
8. Thurow L: Medicine vs. economics. *N Engl J Med* 1985, *313*:611-614.
9. Crawshaw R, Garland MJ, Hines B, Lobitz C: Oregon health decisions: An experiment with informed community consent. *JAMA* 1985, *254*:3213-3216.

1   Decisions Not to Resuscitate

Stuart J. Youngner

The use of do not resuscitate (DNR) orders as a paradigm for decisions to forego a variety of life-sustaining treatments has made them the focus of much discussion and debate. Although DNR is generally understood to be an order to withhold cardiopulmonary resuscitation (CPR), a specific life-saving medical intervention, its exact meaning is often misunderstood. The treatment of cardiopulmonary arrest with CPR involves external chest compression and some form of artificial respiration. CPR was introduced in the 1960s, and did not have the approval of the American Heart Association until 1974.[1] The exact physiologic mechanisms by which CPR works are still the subject of study and debate.[1,2]

While CPR is unique in many ways, it is just one of a myriad of possible life-saving interventions. Under the right circumstances, the withholding or withdrawal of any of these interventions will result in death.

Unique Character of CPR

CPR is an extremely dramatic intervention because it actually brings the patient back to life after the traditional signs of death have already appeared. Thus, it may symbolize either the wonders of modern medicine—snatching precious human life from the jaws of death, or its horror—a cruel refusal to recognize the inevitability and naturalness of death.

In the absence of effective intervention, cardiopulmonary arrest is a sudden and uniformly fatal event. Unlike the failure of other vital organs—for example, the kidneys or liver, there is no time for reflection and discussion. Failure to act immediately means certain death.

Almost every person who dies is a potential candidate for CPR, because cardiopulmonary arrest is almost always the final common pathophysiologic event in the dying process. Eighty percent of the 2 million people who die in the United States each year die in acute or chronic care facilities.[3] Thus, approximately 1.6 million persons are potential candidates for CPR each year. Indeed, with the increasing number of "rescue squads" and community training programs for lay persons, even those who die at home are no longer immune to the benefits and burdens of CPR. In an article entitled, "Prehospital Cardiopulmonary Resuscitation, Is it Effective?", Cummins and Eisenberg note, "teaching and learning the skill of CPR has moved out of the hands of medical personnel and has achieved, with the lay public, the status of a virtual national institution."[1]

A fourth characteristic of CPR, which is a direct result of the two just mentioned, is that it is routinely performed in almost all hospitals and nursing homes. In fact, it is the only medical intervention that can be performed by nonphysicians without a physician's order; a physician's order is required only *if CPR is to be withheld*, even in the patient's home. A paramedic expressed his concern about the pressure to perform CPR once the rescue squad has entered the home of a terminally ill patient: "General legal and ethical standards offer no safe alternatives to immediate CPR. Current prehospital technology does not provide definitive means of determining death, and at any rate, the final determination rests with the physician. Thus, if we are to avoid the ethical taboo of failing to treat viable patients, we must resuscitate unless we can document the presence of reliable postmortem signs such as rigor mortis in warm patients, dependent lividity, decomposition, or undeniable lethal trauma (decapitation for example)."[4]

While CPR is dramatically effective in certain selected instances, it usually fails in the long run.

Case No. 1

An intern approached me in the hall outside the Medical Intensive Care Unit (MICU). He was obviously distressed and wanted to share his feelings about a patient. The patient was a thirty-five-year-old woman who had developed progressive liver failure and ascites following an ilial bypass one year earlier for the treatment of obesity; at the time of surgery, she weighed 260 pounds. Her liver disease had led secondarily to severe portal hypertension and esophageal varices. The patient developed a severe gastrointestinal bleed, encephalopathy, and renal failure. At MICU admission, the patient weighed 100 pounds and her enormous, pregnant-appearing abdomen provided a grotesque contrast to her emaciated frame and elf-like face. She was being treated with repeated blood transfusions, parenteral hyperalimentation, hemodialysis, vasopressors, and repeated paracenteses and thoracenteses to remove the fluid accumulating in her abdominal and pleural spaces. The intern was afraid of a full resuscitation attempt in the event of cardiac arrest. "When we grab hold of her to turn her," he said, "the skin comes off in big pieces down to the mid-dermis. When you move her you can feel her tiny, brittle ribs moving in and out of their joints at the costochondral junction. My God! If we perform CPR on this poor woman, we will literally break her into pieces."

When success is measured in terms of the patient's surviving hospitalization, studies of CPR in hospital populations demonstrate a 5-20 percent success rate.[3,5] In some selected patient populations (for example, metastatic cancer or multiple organ failure), the success rate approaches zero.[5]

Finally, CPR is viewed by many as a particularly invasive procedure which robs people of their last shred of dignity before they die.

GUIDELINES FOR DNR ORDERS

In an attempt to resolve some of the problems and controversies surrounding DNR orders, various authors and groups have suggested guidelines for their implementation.[3,6-8] One advantage of formal guidelines is that they enable hospitals to evaluate existing policies and change them as necessary. These proposed guidelines share several themes:

1. DNR orders should be documented in the written medical record.
2. DNR orders should specify the exact nature of the treatment to be withheld.
3. Patients, when they are able, and families should participate in DNR decisions. Their involvement and wishes should be documented in the medical record.
4. Decisions to withhold CPR should be discussed with other staff, including nurses.
5. DNR status should be reviewed on a regular basis.
6. DNR is not equivalent to medical or psychological abandonment of patients.

Examination of each of these suggestions will provide a greater understanding of the underlying problems.

Documentation and Specification of DNR Orders

The general term "resuscitate" implies only an attempt to revive or bring back to life. Consequently, many patients, including health professionals, interpret a DNR order as a decision to let a patient die without any medical intervention, rather than a more narrow resolve to withhold CPR alone. Adding to this potential confusion is the common use of terms such as "slow-code," "partial code," and "chemical" or "pharmacologic code"—all designed, presumably, to allow intervention of a magnitude somewhere between a full-court press and medical abandonment. Unfortunately, the use of such vague terminology and the failure to specify the exact nature of the treatment to be withheld, often lead to confusion, misunderstanding, inconsistency, or worse.

Failure to document DNR decisions in the medical record, including both the order sheet and patient notes, only compounds the problem. As a result, nurses, house officers, or cross-covering physicians are often forced to make life and death decisions without clear direction or leadership.

In 1984, the *New York Times* reported that a grand jury in Queens, New York "had uncovered shocking procedural abuses" at La Guardia, a 302-bed nonprofit community hospital.[9] Apparently, the hospital had devised a policy for issuing orders not to resuscitate without consulting family members and without recording them on a patient's medical chart.

> Instead . . . dot-sized purple decals were stuck to the patient's nursing record cards as a signal to the medical and nursing staffs that CPR should not be initiated if the patient arrested. When a patient died . . . the nursing cards were routinely discarded, leaving no records of the order not to resuscitate. 'We found that this purple dot system virtually eliminated professional accountability, invited clerical error and discouraged physicians from obtaining informed consent from the patient or his family,' the grand jury said. 'We do not accept the proposition that doubts about the legality of the no-code decisions justified making them in secret.'
>
> Nurses also complained that the decals could be stuck to the wrong card as in the case of one patient who had two purple dots on her card for which no physician in the hospital would take responsibility. Moreover, the grand jury said that the surgeon, 'the original proponent of the color-coding system', tried to shift the blame to nurses when he

testified that oral orders by physicians not to call an emergency code 'were nothing more than suggestions, if you will, to the nurse who is perfectly at liberty to call the code if she desires to call the code.' However, the grand jury said that doctors at La Guardia did not allow nurses to give an aspirin to a patient without a physician's permission.[9]

The situation at La Guardia hospital represents an extreme of apparent deception and deliberate avoidance of responsibility. However, problems of documentation and specification can arise even when people are well-meaning and attempt to be open, as the following case illustrates:

Case No. 2

Mr. A. was an extremely proud, bright, successful, 63-year-old professional man. He had been referred to me three years earlier because of depression following diagnosis and treatment of a highly-malignant esophageal tumor. His depression was due, in part, to the debilitating effects of his surgery and radiation treatment. He felt helpless and defective, and had been unable to return to his productive, confident former self.

Psychotherapy enabled him to work through and overcome many of these troubling feelings. He returned to work and was as productive and energetic as ever. Although he had survived four years without a recurrence of the malignancy, he was always realistic about his poor prognosis and grateful for the 'extra time' gained through treatment.

When he began to experience abdominal pain and weight loss, Mr. A. was convinced that the malignancy had returned. However, an outpatient work-up revealed only a duodenal ulcer, which was managed medically by his internist. Over the next two months the patient continued to deteriorate, but his physicians could find no direct evidence that the cancer had returned. He was finally admitted to the hospital, where an exploratory laparotomy revealed multiple metastases to virtually all of his abdominal organs. When his surgeon told him the bad news in the recovery room, the patient requested that he be allowed to die as quickly and comfortably as possible. The surgeon agreed that 'no heroic measures' would be undertaken to prolong the patient's life. The patients refused his internist's suggestion that an oncologist be consulted to consider the possibility of palliative chemotherapy. "I'm not interested," he said. "Let's face it—this is it."

Following surgery, he became markedly weaker and began having difficulty breathing. He met with his lawyer and went over the final details of his will. He met with various family members and friends individually to say his good-byes. His tremendous dignity and sense of control were evident and impressive to everyone.

When I went to visit him, he was sitting slumped forward in a chair struggling to breathe. In the course of our brief conversation, he mentioned that the surgeon has agreed that 'no heroic measures' were to be taken. Overcoming some of my own discomfort, I sought to clarify this issue by asking whether that included cardiopulmonary resuscitation. The patient was confused. "What exactly does that mean?" he asked. When I explained, he strongly rejected the idea of CPR, but was unsure about its inclusion as a 'heroic measure.' I offered to check his medical record and talk with his surgeon.

The physician's progress notes mentioned nothing about the level of treatment to be given or withheld should the patient suffer an arrest. There was no mention of withholding 'heroic treatment.' The physician's orders only contained the instruction, "In the event of a cardiac or respiratory arrest, please page the surgical house officer." As I was reading through the record, I noticed a nurse standing behind me. She volunteered the information that she and the other nurses were quite uncomfortable with the way the order was written. If the patient arrested, she would feel obligated to perform a full resuscitation until the surgical house officer arrived, an action which she considered contrary to the wishes of both the surgeon and patient. She was grateful when I offered to call the surgeon to clarify the issue.

The surgeon was also grateful for my call. He had not fully considered the consequences of his written orders, and agreed that the entire situation should be explained in the progress notes. He came to the floor, talked further with the patient, and then documented that conversation in the chart, along with a specific order to withhold CPR in the event of an arrest. The patient died quickly and peacefully the next day.

Recent studies reported in the medical literature emphasize the need for improved documentation and specification of DNR orders. Uhlmann et al. studied 56 patients who had received "no-code" orders.[10] Forty-three percent of these patients' charts "contained no documentation of treatment limitation plans beyond the no-code order." The specific interventions to be withheld varied from patient to patient, and when "cross-covering" physicians were questioned about their interpretations of specific no-code orders, both "the intention and interpretation of the orders was characterized by variability, and the interpretation of the orders was characterized by uncertainty as well." Uhlmann and his colleagues suggested that, "This potential for misinterpretation of a no-code order increases with the number of physicians, nurses, and other personnel who may become responsible for patient care when the primary physician is not available, a common situation in large teaching hospitals and in urgent care situations."[10]

Evans and Brody studied DNR orders at three teaching hospitals.[11] They found that when a DNR decision was made, a wide range of medical care was administered. While there may have been "legitimate reasons for the widespread variation," Evans and Brody conclude that "house officers and nurses are often confused about what sort of care is to be provided for patients who are not to be coded."[11]

In a study of 71 DNR patients in a Medical Intensive Care Unit, Youngner et al. found that these patients, even *after* being designated DNR, continued to receive more intense levels of treatment than a control group of seriously ill patients.[12] Active medical interventions that were continued after DNR orders included the use of ventilators, vasopressors, antiarrhythmics, intravenous antibiotics, and Swan-Ganz catheters. All of the interventions started before DNR designation were continued in at least 76 percent of the patients. Each intervention was continued for at least 71 percent of the patient's post-DNR stay in the MICU. Furthermore, the study showed that ventilation was not withdrawn in 89 percent of the patients undergoing ventilation when they were declared DNR; with the exception of ventilation, there were incidences in which each intervention had been initiated after DNR designation. Three emergency diagnostic procedures (bronchoscopy, sigmoidoscopy, and abdominal ultrasound) were performed on DNR patients. However, specific treatment instructions beyond the DNR order, as well as the overall treatment goals, were rarely documented, thus raising concerns about the consistency and clarity of treatment planning.

There are a number of factors that influence this apparently widespread failure to adequately document and specify decisions to limit treatment. First, physicians may not realize the importance of such measures. The explosion of medical technology may have simply outpaced the development of adequate procedures and processes for understanding and governing its use. Second, physicians, especially those in critical care settings, are incredibly busy and stressed by their enormous responsibilities. Attention to the written medical record may seem expendable in such circumstances. Third, physicians often fear the legal consequences of documenting DNR decisions. The threat of malpractice or even criminal prosecution is the most likely explanation for the aforementioned behavior at La Guardia hospital.

Psychological factors often play a major role in documentation failure. The decision to withhold life-sustaining treatment is almost inevitably a difficult one—a fact that often eludes those who have never had to exercise this awesome responsibility. Verbal orders and vague terms, such as "partial code," may help attenuate physicians' discomfort; spelling things out on paper may heighten it.

The failure to adequately document and specifically define DNR and other nontreatment decisions may actually reflect the absence of an overall treatment goal. Is the goal to maintain life at any cost, or merely to provide comfort so death may come as quickly and mercifully as possible? Because the answer generally lies somewhere in between these two extremes, different and often competing values may influence the application of specific interventions.

Finally, one must not not minimize the influence of medical uncertainty that clouds most critical care decisions. Medical judgments are usually based on probability; one is only able to speak authoritatively about the time of death when it is very near. Thus, the "overall picture" may be neglected or even ignored as new, often conflicting data appear. Decision makers may choose to focus on individual organ systems and biological functions, where understanding and control seem more palpable.

There are, however, very good reasons for documenting DNR orders and making them as specific as possible. Documentation establishes clear responsibility for the DNR decision, including its rationale and the process used in its formulation. Such accountability can only enhance the decision-making process and staff morale. A written record of who made the decision and its rationale increases communication, discussion, and review of DNR decisions—as opposed to the suspicion, uncertainty, doubt, and anger that accompany vague and anonymous DNR decisions. Furthermore, improved confidence and communication can only enhance treatment consistency.

Documentation of the decision-making process itself helps to protect the right of patients and families to participate, an issue which will be examined in the next section. Finally, although the legal status of DNR orders has not been unequivocally resolved, especially with regard to incompetent patients, a President's Commission[3] and a number of state courts[13-18] have approved the withholding of life-sustaining treatment under certain circumstances. Therefore, it would seem most prudent to document both the DNR decision and its rationale.

Several approaches have been suggested to the problem of inadequate documentation and specificity of DNR orders. Uhlmann et al. propose "use of a no-code order form which includes a checklist of interventions with significant ramifications, such as invasiveness or discomfort, for which urgent decisions may be required. . . . Space should also be supplied for specifying any other interventions which are to be withheld."[10] Some groups have suggested graded categories of care for critically ill patients.[19-21]

Patient and Family Involvement in DNR Decisions

Patient autonomy—that is, the right of patients to make decisions about their own medical treatment, has received much attention over the last ten years. Theoretically, at least, there is now little debate about this issue. A review of the studies to date, however, shows a surprising lack of patient and family involvement in decisions about whether or not to institute CPR. On the whole, the record seems worse with regard to the decision to give CPR, although patients and families are all too frequently left out of DNR decisions as well.

Bedell and Delbanco studied 154 patients who were resuscitated at a university teaching hospital.[22] Before the arrest, only 19 percent of these patients had discussed CPR with either their private physician or house officer; only 33 percent of the families were consulted. While 151 (96%) of the 157 physicians involved in the care of the study patients "believed that patients should at least sometimes participate in decisions about resuscitation," only 15 (10%) actually talked with these patients before the arrest; 32 (21%) discussed resuscitation with the family. The authors also interviewed the 24 competent patients who survived CPR, to compare their actual attitudes about resuscitation with their physicians' opinions about their attitudes. Eight of the 24 "stated unequivocally that they had not desired cardiopulmonary resuscitation and did not wish to be resuscitated in the future." Yet, only one of the 16 physicians caring for these eight patients believed that the patients had not desired CPR. Bedell and Delbanco raise the question, "Would it be worthwhile to address these issues routinely with all patients when they are admitted to the hospital?" They suggest that such a practice might improve communication because, "Many patients may know what they want and welcome the chance to make their own contribution to this difficult debate."[22]

Evans and Brody studied DNR orders in three teaching hospitals and found that:

> the goal of promoting patient self-determination regarding resuscitation is not really being implemented in resuscitation decisions. For the vast majority of patients who were to be resuscitated that decision was made without either patient or family input.[11]

Although patient and family participation was still far from ideal, they found it was more likely to occur in decisions to withhold CPR —that is, DNR. This phenomenon can probably be explained by the fact that physicians, as well as patients and families, assume that life-saving treatment is expected and desired in most instances. However, as the Bedell/Delbanco study so convincingly demonstrated, this is not always the case. In addition to there being a significant number of patients who rejected the notion of CPR, their physicians failed to appreciate their wishes in this regard.[22]

Why do physicians regularly fail to involve patients and families in decisions to institute or withhold CPR? Reasons similar to those that account for failure to document nontreatment decisions may provide a partial explanation—that is, lack of awareness or time pressures. Of course, some patients may be judged incompetent to participate in medical decisions due to coma or other serious central nervous system impairment. Furthermore, the severe emotional stress (that is, anxiety, pain, depression) and mechanical realities (intubation) of critical care may render meaningful communication with patients difficult if not impossible.[23,24]

More decisive, however, is the traditional paternalistic attitude of physicians, who frequently feel more comfortable acting in their patients' "best interests" than in actively involving them as partners in the decision-making process. Central to this view is the concept of *therapeutic privilege*, according to which physicians justify withholding important information from patients on the grounds that is might overly upset them, rob them of hope, or jeopardize their recovery.[25] It is significant that a landmark article recognizing the competent patient's right to refuse CPR prominently endorsed the notion of therapeutic privilege. Rabkin et al., in a 1976 issue of the *New England Journal of Medicine*, wrote:

> It is recognized that it may be inappropriate to introduce the subject of withholding cardiopulmonary resuscitation efforts to certain competent patients when, in the physician's judgment, the patient will probably be unable to cope with it *psychologically* [emphasis added]. In such event, Orders Not to Resuscitate may not be directed because of the absence of an informed choice.[8]

It is apparent that the notion of therapeutic privilege has a tremendous potential for abuse. Physicians may use it to promote their own values or notions about what constitutes an acceptable quality of life, which may be quite different from those of the patient. Physicians can also use it to protect themselves, rather than their patients, from painful discussions about poor prognosis and death. In fact, patients usually sense when things are going badly, have considered treatment options, and are grateful when a trusted physician is willing to discuss these matters openly. Almost ten years after the appearance of Rabkin's article,[8] the notion of therapeutic privilege, while still a potent force, is increasingly being challenged. In 1984, a group of nationally prominent physicians addressed the issue of therapeutic privilege in an article entitled, "The Physician's Responsibility Toward Hopelessly Ill Patients."

> Although some physicians and families avoid frank discussions with patients, in our view, practically all patients, even disturbed ones, are better off knowing the truth. A decision not to tell the patient the truth because of fear of his or her emotional or psychological inability to handle such information is rarely if ever justified, and in such a case the burden of proof rests on the person who believes that the patient cannot cope with frank discussion. The anxiety of dealing with the unknown can be far more upsetting than the grief of dealing with a known, albeit tragic, truth. A failure to transmit to the patient knowledge of terminal illness can create barriers in communication, and the patient is effectively placed in isolation at a time when emotional sharing is most needed.[26]

It may also be unfair to put other health professionals responsible for the patient's care in a position of performing an invasive procedure such as CPR without knowing the desires of the patient or family.

Despite all arguments in its favor, it is rarely easy to discuss the issues of death and treatment limitation with a patient or family. No time seems like the right time. When patients are relatively healthy, we do not want to upset them needlessly; when they are terribly sick, they seem upset enough as it is. There is no easy answer to this question of timing. In general, it is easier if discussions about these issues have been part of the ongoing physician/patient relationship, instead of being precipitated for the first time by a crisis. If there is an understanding between the patient, family, and physician about the way in which a patient wants to live and die, there may be less need to negotiate specific details in the midst of a medical catastrophe. More and more patients are aware of, and have opinions about, these issues. Increasingly, these opinions are being formalized in documents called "living wills," now recognized by law in many states.[3]

It may be most practical and efficient to target certain groups (for example, people with chronic progressive disease) for the most specific, thoughtful discussions about treatment limitation. One innovative approach was used at the Mather Home. All residents (a geriatric population) were informed on admission about the possibility of cardiac arrest and the poor chances for successful CPR, and then asked to state their preferences in writing.[27] Only 11 (7%) of the 163 residents opted for CPR; 77 (47%) said they did not want it performed.

It is interesting that 64 (39%) said they would like their physician to decide about CPR at the time of the arrest.

It is not always possible to anticipate every eventuality, even if one has carefully evaluated the medical situation, talked with the patient ahead of time, and documented the plan of action in the chart. As the following case illustrates, sudden and unexpected medical problems may confuse efforts to pursue the agreed-upon goals of treatment.

Case No. 3

A 93-year-old woman was admitted to a medical division with pulmonary edema, bronchospasm, and wheezing. She had a diagnosis of 'end-stage' congestive heart failure, but was leading a relatively independent and satisfying existence outside of the hospital. She had made it clear on numerous occasions that she would never want to become helpless and dependent on others. When she came into the hospital for relief of her symptoms, her medical resident discussed the possibility of a cardiopulmonary arrest. Although she insisted that she did not want CPR, including intubation, she willingly agreed to the medical treatments which might well restore her, at least temporarily, to her pre-hospitalization life-style. A deeply religious person, she said, "The Lord will either take me or let me go."

The resident, mindful of her wishes, wrote a DNR order and a note in the chart stating, "The patient does not wish CPR, including intubation." Four days later, the patient had a serious hypotensive episode and was transferred to the Intensive Care Unit. The physician's note in chart read, "Since the patient is functional, she is a Unit candidate, but not a code or a candidate for intubation." Her blood pressure was stabilized and she was returned to the medical division.

Three days later, upon returning to the division from a routine echocardiogram, the patient was noted by her nurse to have garbled, incoherent speech. The change in speech was followed by lip smacking and fine tremors which spread to the left leg, right arm, and right leg. After fifteen minutes of seizure activity, the patient became flaccid and stopped breathing. Artificial respirations were initiated via bagging and 100% oxygen. Seizure activity resumed in an irregular twitching pattern. Bagging was continued and anti-seizure medications were administered, to no avail. The physicians could not determine the etiology of the seizures, which they believed might be entirely reversible.

After two hours of bagging, the patient was transferred to the Intensive Care Unit, where she was intubated by anesthesiology. The physician's note read, "It was decided to intubate the patient because she may have had a reversible cause of her seizures, thus making non-aggressive management inappropriate." The patient died later that day.

Many difficult questions are raised by this case. Were the patient's rights violated by the intubation? Would it have been better not to intubate the patient, even if she stood a good chance of sustaining significant brain damage during the seizures and surviving in a permanent vegetative state? Did the DNR order actually compromise her medical situation by discouraging immediate and effective intubation when she stopped breathing? In the resident's initial conversation with the patient, should he have given a detailed description of all the possible medical eventualities, including seizures of unknown etiology? Could he have been expected to foresee this eventually? The answers to these question are not obvious.

Would formal procedures, policies, or checklists be helpful in avoiding this type of unfortunate occurrence? I don't think so. Although we must strive to develop the best possible procedures for dealing with these issues, the subtleties of diagnosis, illness progression, and human communication sometimes defy anticipation and planning.

Discussion and Input from Involved Health Professionals

Health care is rarely delivered in a vacuum. It is becoming increasingly common for patients to be cared for by a number of health professionals working together, each with a particular area of competence and sense of professional responsibility. Although this is particularly true of acute wards or critical care units of tertiary hospitals, it is not uncommon in smaller community hospitals. In addition to a primary physician, critically ill patients may be cared for by a number of consultant medical specialists, house officers, nurses, social workers, physical therapists, and so on. These health professionals must function together as a team in order to deliver optimum care to their patients.

In this context, there are a number of very practical reasons that make it essential that any decision for or against CPR be discussed with key team members, whose input should be welcomed. First, such communication is necessary to maintain morale. Most decisions to initiate or withhold life-sustaining interventions are complicated and painful. Since all possible options may have unfortunate or even tragic consequences, everyone involved may have significant ambivalence about whatever course of action is taken. The primary physician, who is ultimately responsible for a DNR decision, is likely to cope with his or her ambivalence by minimizing the attractiveness of the option not chosen. Nurses, on the other hand, rarely have to make final decisions themselves. The nature of their work (for example, close contact with patients and families for eight-to-12-hour shifts, often "one on one"), however, forces them into intimacy with the pain and tragedy. As a result, the option(s) not taken may seem more attractive, and the nurse may feel angry or resentful. This somewhat inevitable situation is unnecessarily exacerbated by excluding the nurse from the decision-making process. Furthermore, as Barbara Daly points out in Chapter 6, critical care nurses increasingly see themselves as professionals, with unique skills and special responsibilities as advocates for patients and families.

Bernard Lo, in an excellent discussion of the issue, considers several reasons why involving nurses can only enhance the decision-making process.[16] He points out, "Because nurses have close contact with patients and families, they may be required to answer questions, deal with family reactions, and explain decisions." This position is untenable if they do not understand the reasons for the physician's decision, or "especially when notes in the medical record are not clear and comprehensive."[16] Nurses often have a greater awareness of patient and family emotional responses, giving them an invaluable perspective that may be different from the physician's. He encourages physicians to

> elicit the nurses' concerns, feelings, and perceptions. . . . Individual discussions or staff meetings may help nurses and other staff understand the medical situation . . . and to discuss emotions, beliefs, and values that may underlie disagreements. If the nurses understand the physician's reasoning and the decision-making process has been careful, nurses will usually agree with the decision, or at least accept it. . . .
>
> Attending physicians may be unwise to insist on decisions in the face of persistent, thoughtful disagreement. Such disagreements should be considered a warning to reconsider the decision. . . . Discussions with staff may in fact help the physician improve decision making. Nurses and social workers may provide information about the patient and family or raise new considerations and viewpoints.[16]

Finally, excluding other professional staff from the decision-making process may affect more than morale and the quality of decisions. When involved professionals feel that they have no way to influence the process or even to be heard, they are more likely to go outside of usual channels and seek redress through the legal system.[15,16]

DNR Status Should Be Reviewed on a Regular Basis

The reasoning behind this guideline is straightforward. The basis for any DNR decision may change in accordance with changes in patient and family wishes and/or the medical situation. Furthermore, new medical or psychosocial information may come to light. DNR decisions should be reviewed at least daily, and more frequently when warranted.

DNR Is Not Synonymous with Abandonment

When patients are considered "hopeless," there is always the danger that health professionals will lose interest and abandon them. Most of us can remember the time when patients dying in hospitals were regularly avoided and ignored by the professional staff because they were regarded as medical "failures." In addition, a broader cultural discomfort with death made health care professionals feel impotent and uneasy around dying patients. While these problems have not been entirely resolved, the work of Avery Weisman, Elizabeth Kubler-Ross, and others, as well as the development of the hospice movement, have taught us that death and dying are problems that can indeed be studied, understood, and approached actively and constructively.

In this context, health professionals must not view a DNR order as a cue or excuse for neglecting the physical and emotional needs of patients and their families. Relief of pain, maintenance of cleanliness, and ongoing human interaction are essential to minimize suffering and maximize a sense of human dignity. In fact, this may be the time when physicians and nurses are needed most, because the emotional and spiritual needs of patients and families are the greatest.

It is also important to realize that a DNR order need not indicate that the patient is medically hopeless. As the President's Commission stated,

> Any DNR policy should ensure that the order not to resuscitate has no implications for any other treatment decisions. Patients with DNR orders on their charts may still be quite appropriate candidates for all other vigorous care, including intensive care.[3]

At first glance, it might seem inconsistent to treat DNR patients with "vigorous care," and especially "intensive care." If the decision has been made to let a person die in the event of an arrest, why would you want to treat him or her with dialysis, intravenous antibiotics, or mechanical ventilation? Why would you expend the valuable resource of an intensive care unit bed for a patient whom you are unwilling to resuscitate? An examination of these questions is an excellent way to better understand the entire decision-making process and how it might be improved.

First, DNR is an order made in advance—in other words, *if* the patient suffers a cardiopulmonary arrest, he or she will not be resuscitated. DNR orders are sometimes written for patients who are quite viable, as long as they do not arrest. In some instances, their medical conditions are potentially reversible; however, an arrest would signal an irreversible deterioration which would result in death or unacceptable quality of life (such as severe brain damage and irreversible coma). Other patients may have reversible conditions but with characteristics —that is, severe osteoporosis or bleeding disorders—that preclude their surviving the rigors of a full resuscitative effort. In the study by Youngner et al., nine of the 71 MICU patients designated DNR survived the hospitalization, and three of these were alive three months later.[1 2] In summary, aggressive care short of CPR may be entirely justified on medical grounds.

In actuality, CPR is but one of a myriad of possible interventions that may save or merely prolong life in any given instance. Although CPR is more dramatic and has powerful symbolic meaning, a decision to withhold vasopressors, antibiotics, or even nutrition may have the same implications—under the right circumstances—that is, represent a means of allowing death to come more quickly. The problem is that different and often competing *nonmedical* values may influence the application of individual interventions, thus making the overall pattern of treatment/nontreatment seem confused or inconsistent. We are more comfortable and familiar with this concept in noncritical care medical settings, where patient behavior rarely reflects a totally consistent pattern of choosing to either maximize longevity or allow death to come as quickly as possible. For example, a man with hypertension might choose to smoke cigarettes because he "likes them" and refuse to take antihypertensive medication because it makes him impotent, but avoid eating red meat and welcome an admission to a cardiac monitoring unit when he develops severe chest pain. He might refuse bypass surgery because he "fears the knife," but accept a pacemaker and drug therapy for treatment of heart disease.

One might conceptualize the progression from health to disease and, finally, death as a journey down a funnel. Beginning at the widest part, one encounters an almost countless variety of disease processes, injuries, and physiologic disruptions, which are caused by a comparable variety of etiologic agents. As one journeys down this metaphorical funnel toward death, the slope becomes steeper and the disease process begins to affect more and more of the organism's vital functions. As the funnel narrows, we find a gradually diminishing number of possible conditions, any and all of which will lead to a relatively limited pathophysiologic "common pathway" of death. In other words, whether one has lung cancer due to cigarette smoking, end-stage renal disease from chronic hypertension, multiple sclerosis, or *E. coli* sepsis, the final stages before death will inevitably involve the failure of one or more vital body systems. The last point in the funnel, the very final "common pathway" to death, is cardiopulmonary arrest. (The possibility of brain death is excluded from this formulation.)

While a number of nonmedical values may compete with the goal of maximizing longevity when one is high up in the funnel, decisions contrary to that goal are usually reversible, and have statistical and remote, rather than concrete and immediate, effects on the length of life. When one nears the bottom of the funnel, the consequences of nontreatment are immediate and irreversible.

Even in critical care settings, however, nonmedical values are extremely influential and introduce a tremendous complexity to treatment planning. For example, moral distinctions, discussed by Mayo and Bennett in Chapter 2, influence the application of different interventions. Foremost among these is the unwillingness to *withdraw* life-sustaining treatments once they have been initiated.

Patients, families, and even health professionals may refuse a particular life-sustaining treatment because of personal preference—for example, it may seem too invasive, frightening, or repulsive—while accepting another. Thus, a patient might agree to artificial feeding through a nasogastric tube, but refuse a gastrostomy. It is not unusual for patients to refuse CPR for the same reason—that is, it is too invasive and "undignified." Mayo and Bennett refer to this kind of reasoning as the "burdens of treatment." Such burdens may be spiritual in nature, as in the case of the Jehovah's Witness who refuses life-saving blood products, but accepts other, more invasive, interventions. Certain treatments may be rejected because patients, families, and even physicians have had "bad experiences" with them in the past.

Even when a decision has been made to let death come as swiftly as possible, life-sustaining treatment is sometimes continued in order to keep the patient comfortable. So, for example, antibiotics might be used to treat a painful urinary tract infection, or mucous secretions might be suctioned from the trachea—more to avoid unnecessary suffering than to prolong the patient's life.

Another nonmedical value that affects treatment decisions is a perceived need to contain costs. Rationing of expensive critical care interventions is an obvious and increasingly discussed mechanism for containing health costs. Unlike health professionals and loving relatives, persons concerned with financial issues (hospital administrators, third party payers, and government bureaucrats) are far removed from the bedside. Decisions based on financial concerns may often conflict with both traditional physician concerns about protecting patients' best interests, and the more recently legitimized rights of patients to control their own medical decisions.

CONCLUSION

The efforts by hospitals and health professionals to establish guidelines for DNR orders are a good beginning. We must be careful, however, to keep DNR from becoming a red herring that gives a dramatic but oversimplified picture of critical care, while discouraging a closer and more rigorous examination of the other, more common, treatment/nontreatment decisions.

Because of the growing complexity of, and public concern over, nontreatment decisions, we must make greater efforts to understand and evaluate the complicated processes and values that influence them. Only then can we, as a nation, begin to formulate fair and prudent policies. This will be no easy task in a pluralistic society that is becoming increasingly conscious of medical expenditures. If we fail to address these issues now, treatment decisions at the end of life will become increasingly arbitrary, idiosyncratic, inconsistent, confused, and, ultimately, unjust.

REFERENCES

1. Cummins RO, Eisenberg MS: Prehospital cardiopulmonary resuscitation. Is it effective? *JAMA* 1985, *253*:2408-2412.
2. Sanders AB, Meislin HW, Ewy GA: The physiology of cardiopulmonary resuscitation. An update. *JAMA* 1984, *252*:3283-3286.
3. President's Commission for the Study of Ethical Problems in Medicine and Biomedical and Behavioral Research: *Deciding to Forego Life-Sustaining Treatment*. Washington, D.C., U.S. Government Printing Office, 1983.

4. Marshall L: Resuscitating the terminally ill. *JEMS* April, 1985, 24-28.
5. Bedell SE, Delbanco TL, Cook EF, Epstein FH: Survival after cardiopulmonary resuscitation in the hospital. *N Engl J Med* 1983, *309*:569-576.
6. Miles SH, Cranford R, Schultz AL: The do-not-resuscitate order in a teaching hospital. *Ann Intern Med* 1982, *96*:660-664.
7. Lee MA, Cassel CK: The ethical and legal framework for the decision not to resuscitate. *West J Med* 1984, *140*:117-122.
8. Rabkin MT, Gillerman G, Rice NR: Orders not to resuscitate. *N Engl J Med* 1976, *295*:364-366.
9. Sullivan R: Queens hospital accused of denial of care. New York *Times*, March 24, 1984, *133*:17.
10. Uhlmann RF, Cassel CK, McDonald WJ: Some treatment-withholding implications of no-code orders in an academic hospital. *Crit Care Med* 1984, *12*: 879-881.
11. Evans AL, Brody BA: The do-not-resuscitate order in teaching hospitals. *JAMA* 1985, *253*:2236-2239.
12. Youngner SJ, Lewandowski W, McClish DK, et al.: 'Do not resuscitate' orders. Incidence and implications in a medical intensive care unit. *JAMA* 1985, *253*:54-57.
13. Suber DG, Tabor WJ: Withholding of life-sustaining treatment from the terminally ill, incompetent patient: Who decides? Part I. *JAMA* 1982, *248*: 2250-2251.
14. Suber DG, Tabor WJ: Withholding of life-sustaining treatment from the terminally ill, incompetent patient: Who decides? Part II. *JAMA* 1982, *248*: 2431-2432.
15. Breo DL, Lefton D, Rust ME: MDs face unprecedented murder charge. *Am Med News* September, 1983, 1-34.
16. Lo B: The death of Clarence Herbert: Withdrawing care is not murder. *Ann Intern Med* 1984, *101*:248-251.
17. Annas GJ: When procedures limit rights: From Quinlan to Conroy. *Hastings Center Report* 1985, *15*:24-26.
18. Swick T: After Conroy: 'When is enough enough?' *Am Coll Physicians Observer* July/August, 1985, 14-15.
19. Grenvik A, Powner DJ, Snyder JV, et al.: Cessation of therapy in terminal illness and brain death. *Crit Care Med* 1978, *6*:284.
20. Tagge GF, Adler D, Bryan-Brown CW, et al.: Relationship of therapy to prognosis in critically ill patients. *Crit Care Med* 1974, *2*:61.
21. Critical Care Committee of the Massachusetts General Hospital: Optimum care for hopelessly ill patients. *N Engl J Med* 1976, *295*:362.
22. Bedell SE, Delbanco TL: Choices about cardiopulmonary resuscitation in the hospital. When do physicians talk with patients? *N Engl J Med* 1984, *310*:1089-1093.
23. Jackson DL, Youngner S: Patient autonomy and "death with dignity": Some clinical caveats. *N Engl J Med* 1979, *301*:404-408.

24. Youngner SJ: Patient autonomy, informed consent, and the reality of critical care. In: Orlowski JP, Kanoti GA (eds): *Critical Care Clinics of North America: Ethical Moments in Critical Care Medicine* 1986 2:41-51.
25. Katz J: *The Silent World of Doctor and Patient.* New York, The Free Press, 1984.
26. Wanzer SH, Adelstein SJ, Cranford RE, et al.: The physician's responsibility toward hopelessly ill patients. *N Engl J Med* 1984, *310*:955-959.
27. Wagner A: Cardiopulmonary resuscitation in the aged: A prospective survey. *N Engl J Med* 1984, *310*:1129-1130.

2 The Role of Burden/Benefit Analysis in the Orchestration of Death in the ICU

David Mayo and Marilyn Bennett

Death poses one of the most significant problems of human existence. Life is a precondition of virtually anything else a person might want; yet we know that death comes to us all eventually.

As biological events, disease and death are subject to control and manipulation by medical intervention. However, medicine can only hope to delay death, not eliminate it; time is on death's side in the long run. In fact, it is only in this century that the prolongation of life has become a primary goal of medicine, along with the relief of suffering. Previously, medicine could often promise little more than comfort. Before 1900, most people died from communicable diseases. The patient who received aggressive treatment was either restored to "good health" or not helped at all. Besides the minimization of suffering and disease, the Hippocratic writings mention the physician's duty to refrain from interfering with those who are succumbing to their diseases. Medicine held no hope for persons rendered critically ill by the breakdown of major body systems, and the medical resources available for combatting death were so limited that physicians rarely faced painful choices about when to use them.

This medical acceptance of some illnesses as fatal occurred within a larger teleological worldview, within which death could be seen as a fitting and natural event that was not under human control. Death was regarded as a release from worldly troubles or as the first step in the transition to an afterlife. Comfort could be found in the idea of of death occurring within a planned universe, in which creatures lived and died according to their destinies. The notion of a "natural death" was an attempt to rob death of its sting by construing it as an event for which no one could be held responsible.

Remnants of this view can still be found in the distinction between natural and unnatural deaths—that is, those resulting from accidents or violence, in our contemporary medico-legal taxonomy. This terminology notwithstanding, however, modern medicine now assumes a less passive stance on death. Although medical technology has given the physician new power to sustain life, it is accompanied by the responsibility for deciding when it is to be used. Those who place the preservation of life above all other values contend that disease must always be treated aggressively. Increasingly, however, the imperative always to treat aggressively is coming to be viewed as indefensible. Critics condemn the needless, painful, and costly prolongation of the dying process for critically ill patients. The only advantage of this practice is that it provides a simple black-and-white response to a reality that contains many shades of grey, thus sparing physicians from having to make morally difficult choices. It is easy to sympathize with those who want to resist the slippery slope upon which determinations have to be made about the prolongation of life. However, few health care professionals working in intensive care environments believe that aggressive treatment is always morally appropriate.

Decisions on Death in Intensive Care Settings

For patients receiving modern medical care, death is often not the result of inexorable processes that defy all treatment efforts; instead, death occurs because of human decisions to forego medical intervention at some point. According to the President's Commission for the Study of Ethical Problems in Medicine and Biomedical and Behavioral Research, "For almost any life-threatening condition, some intervention can now delay the moment of death."[1] We can no longer derive comfort from the view that death is "natural." "Very little is 'natural' about our present day existence, and least natural of all is the prolonged period of dying that is suffered by so many incurable patients solicitously kept alive to be killed by their disease," writes Barrington.[2] And Lasagna remarks, "In this age of surgical derring-do and widespread use of drugs, almost no disease can be said any longer to have a 'natural history.' "[3]

Decisions to withhold life-prolonging therapies are sometimes construed as strictly factual judgments about a patient's unsalvageability." This is often an illusion, however. If a treatment can delay the moment of death, however slightly, then a responsible decision about whether to provide such treatment must be based on the assignment of values to the overall costs of the treatment and the possible benefits in terms of additional days or even hours of life.

In many cases, admission to an Intensive Care Unit (ICU) is the result of a preliminary decision about the appropriateness of aggressive treatment. Presumably, ICU care is intended to bring patients through crises to more stable conditions of health. However, since admission errors do occur and even carefully screened patients may get worse, physicians may have to consider withholding or withdrawing intensive efforts after the patient is in the ICU. It is somewhat ironic that such decisions, which are clearly moral and involve highly personal and individual values, are made by strangers who work in an environment that allows little time for reflection. Indeed, some decisions must be made after an emergency has arisen—for example, a cardiac arrest. Some have argued that physicians are trained to evaluate data and make decisions in such a way that value judgments are disguised as technical ones.[4] In fact, a physician evaluating a situation from the clinical perspective may not even realize the significance of a decision, much less the contribution of values to the process. It is impossible, however, to make a nonarbitrary decision that is value-free.

Patient Autonomy

While the physician's bias is (and should be) toward the preservation of life, the actual treatment decision is, in principle, the patient's responsibility. The principle of informed consent, which underlies treatment decisions, requires that after the competent patient has been provided with all relevant medical information, he or she has the right either to authorize *or* refuse any proposed treatment. Although the moral and legal right to forego life-sustaining treatment does theoretically belong to the competent patient, we will address a number of situations in which the implementation of this principle is anything but straightforward. Even when the competent patient makes a treatment decision, the physician bears the ultimate moral and legal responsibility for what is done. Nurses and other medical personnel are primarily responsive to the physician's orders, rather than to the patient's wishes. Moreover, it is the physician who must provide the patient with information, judge whether the patient is competent, and implement the patient's wishes. Thus, the principle of informed consent notwithstanding, it is the physician who ultimately orchestrates the decisions and activities that determine the timing of the patient's death.

Two Kinds of Reasons for Withholding Life-Sustaining Therapies

Although there may be a number of factors influencing competent decisions to forego life-sustaining therapies, we will primarily be concerned with two general categories of reasons. A patient who still values life might opt to forego treatment because of its associated *burdens and benefits*—for example, invasiveness, painfulness, disfigurement, psychological costs, and expected gains in length and quality of life. The terminal cancer patient who is not eager to die but opts to forego radical chemotherapy treatments that might marginally prolong his or her life has made a decision on the basis of "burden of treatment" considerations. On the other hand, a patient who views his or her very existence as undesirable might opt to forego even a minimally burdensome treatment—as an example, a patient who declines antibiotic treatment in the event of an infection. Such a patient is avoiding the burden of further life, not the burden of treatment. Such factors will hereafter be referred to as "burden of life" considerations.

The underlying principle we will argue for here is simple—that is, a rational decision to undertake life-sustaining therapies should depend only upon whether the patient stands to benefit from the therapies. The central issue is whether, given the patient's values, the potential benefits outweigh the burdens associated with the therapy. Although most of us agree in general about what is burdensome and what is beneficial, these assessments may differ in particular cases. Differences may be due to such factors as willingness and ability to tolerate pain, reasons for living, or different religious views or beliefs about death. For example, a Jehovah's Witness may decide that the burden of receiving blood products outweighs the benefits of surviving a medical crisis and prolonging life significantly. Adhering to the principle of informed consent optimizes the possibility of using the patient's own values as a guide for treatment.

Of course, abundant uncertainty surrounds any medical decision. Unless the patient is faced with an immediately life-threatening condition, it is impossible to predict the future precisely. Specifically, neither the effectiveness nor the burdensomeness of possible interventions is completely predictable. In the ICU setting, these problems are intensified. Patients may have to consider foregoing expensive, traumatic, and perhaps fatal treatment that offers only the hope of salvaging an already compromised life condition.

Two Kinds of Complications

Any number of factors may operate to complicate the ICU physician's attempt to respect patient autonomy regarding potential life-prolonging therapies. These factors can be divided into two categories: those having to do with the physician's determination of the patient's competence to make such a decision, and those having to do with influences that may affect the competent patient. We will consider each of these in turn.

1. *Assessment of Patient Competence.* A person who is critically ill is unlikely to display the characteristics usually associated with cool rationality. His pain, anxiety, depression, and/or sedation may lead the physician to question the patient's competence to make any important treatment decisions on his own behalf. Further, technical factors such as intubation or extreme weakness may prevent even a competent person from being able to communicate clearly. For these reasons, the physician has the ultimate moral and legal responsibility for determining that the decision to forego life-prolonging treatment represents the considered choice of a competent individual.

Detailed examination of problems associated with the assessment of competence is beyond the scope of this work. In general, the problem of assessing competence becomes critical only when there is some divergence of opinion about a particular treatment; if physician, family, and patient all agree on the desirability of a particular treatment, it is unlikely that the issue of competence will even be raised. Where no consensus is reached, a psychiatric consult can be helpful and is certainly prudent. Should an incompetent patient refuse treatment that is clearly appropriate, a court order may be sought.

One way of dealing with the general problem of competence in critically ill patients is for persons to specify their treatment wishes before reaching a stage of terminal or critical incapacity. The living will is a document that can be used to communicate such decisions to the family, physician, lawyer, or clergy. In some states, "right to die" legislation has been passed which gives living wills legal force. Even this approach is not free of problems, however, for it is impossible to anticipate the specifics of a medical crisis. The physician must still determine whether the patient has reached the condition he had in mind when he specified his wishes.

2. *Influences on the Competent Patient.* Even if the patient is alert, understands his situation, and can communicate his wishes clearly, the physician must still give careful attention to the views and role of family members. They naturally have a strong interest in the patient's situation, and are apt to influence his decision in a time of crisis. The physician may suspect that the patient's expressed wish is the result of family coercion, as well as concern for family members. He must also realize that complying with a patient's decision to forego treatment may provoke legal action by angry and resentful relatives, who may later claim that the patient's treatment refusal did not reflect a competent decision.

Family members are not the only ones whose values may influence the patient's decision. Because the physician occupies a position of special responsibility, authority, and privilege, he usually has the greatest influence on patient and family decisions. If the physician is not sensitive to the need to respect patient autonomy, his own values will probably determine the course of treatment. The patient's decision about whether to authorize treatment must be based primarily on information provided by the physician. As a matter of practical necessity, physicians will always fall short of the theoretical ideal of fully informing the patient, and their choices about what information to provide may be biased in favor of treatment.

In some cases, the patient does not volunteer opinions, nor is he questioned, on these matters. Family members who are only aware that the patient is critically ill urge the physician to "do everything he can" to pull the patient through the crisis. As long as there is a reasonable chance that the patient may recover, it may seem unnecessary to raise questions with the family or patient about abandoning aggressive treatment.

A combination of these factors frequently accounts for the physician's being the first to consider the possibility of withholding therapy. Often the physician's bias in favor of doing everything possible for the patient prevails until it appears that recovery is very unlikely. At this point, both the substance and the tone of communications with the patient and family change and the orchestration of death begins. The physician and other caregivers begin to prepare everyone involved for the realization that available therapies no longer promise significant improvement. Differing perceptions and attitudes among family members must be addressed and, if possible, resolved. A psychiatrist may be helpful at this point in determining what the patient has understood and where he stands. The social worker may help the patient and family to understand and accept the bleaker prognosis, and arrive at a consensus on what option to pursue. Nurses, of course, play central roles in every stage of these delicate tasks of informing, assessing comprehension, and hearing the patient's decision.

The Decision Itself: The Moral Reasoning

Thus far we have been focusing primarily on the setting in which decisions to forego life-prolonging therapies take place, and the different roles, values, and expectations which the various participants may bring to such decisions. We have tried to emphasize both the importance of patient autonomy and the fact that respect for this autonomy does not override the physician's ultimate responsibility for both making and implementing the decision to forego life-prolonging therapy, which leads to the patient's death. We must now examine some of the reasons behind decisions to terminate treatment.

We argued above that responsible decisions to terminate treatment are similar to most other decisions in that they ultimately involve a burden/benefit analysis. We normally place such a high value on human life that it seems repugnant to speak of assigning a value to its prolongation. Unless one is to pursue aggressive treatment in every case without regard for any of its associated burdens, the prolongation of life must be evaluated. If such an assignment of value is not shared by the patient, this strategy violates individual autonomy.

There are two results of burden/benefit analysis which would warrant the withholding of life-sustaining treatments: the burden of treatment might be so great as to outweigh the benefit of prolonging life; or, life itself might be seen as a burden which would be magnified by even a minimally burdensome life-prolonging treatment.

A variety of factors conspire to cloud thinking and inhibit rational decision making in these contexts. The patient or family may be plagued by guilt and denial, which may preclude their acknowledging responsibility for making the decision. Those involved may welcome any misconstrual of the situation that disguises the magnitude of the decision that has to be made. As a result, a number of considerations often creep into the decision-making process that tend to be irrelevant, are sometimes obfuscatory, and are usually counterproductive to a rational outcome. These considerations are expressed as various distinctions—that is, between "ordinary" and "extraordinary" means or therapies; the intended consequences of a therapy and those which are merely foreseen; withdrawing a life-prolonging therapy which has already been initiated and withholding such a therapy in the first place; actively killing a critically ill patient and passively allowing such a patient to die. While none of these distinctions speaks in any straightforward way to the burdens or benefits of life-prolonging therapies, each is sometimes held to be morally significant. We will examine each of these distinctions in turn.

Ordinary versus Extraordinary Therapies

The decision to withhold life-sustaining treatment is sometimes based on the claim that the treatment at issue would constitute "heroic" or "extraordinary" means. There are two completely different interpretations of those terms in this context. "Extraordinary" sometimes means "very unusual." Some treatments are, therefore, extraordinary in that they are highly unusual, exotic, or still experimental. Alternatively, a treatment may be extraordinary in that it is exceptionally burdensome in the broadest sense—that is, very painful or unpleasant, risky, expensive, demanding of time and/or labor, or otherwise difficult to provide.

The setting in which medical care is being provided may, of course, determine what is extraordinary in either of these senses. In the ICU of a teaching hospital, the use of exceedingly complex and costly equipment is routine; in a bush hospital, use of an IV catheter might be extraordinary in both senses. No procedure is inherently extraordinary; this will always depend upon the context.

Can the mere fact that a life-prolonging treatment is extraordinary in either of these senses ever provide sufficient justification for withholding it? Surely the fact that the procedure is unusual, highly exotic, or still experimental could not do so by itself. The appropriateness of any treatment, routine or otherwise, depends only on whether its benefits outweigh its burdens in the particular situation. It would be inappropriate to withhold a potentially beneficial therapy merely because it was unusual.

Historically, the emphasis has been primarily, but not exclusively, on the second interpretation of extraordinary—that is, burdensome. McCartney[5] provides an excellent historical discussion of this distinction. It was introduced in the late sixteenth century, when the Catholic church first indicated that the prolongation of life by means of extraordinarily burdensome surgical procedures (those which were extraordinarily risky, painful, or disfiguring) was not morally obligatory. Pope Pius XII's 1957 pronouncement also indicated there was no obligation to prolong life if it required treatments that were extraordinarily burdensome.

But how burdensome is "too burdensome?" We have already seen that it is appropriate to withhold a treatment only if the burden it imposes outweighs its benefits. If calling a treatment "extraordinary" only means "more burdensome than beneficial in this particular case," then the fact that it is extraordinary is not what justifies its being withheld; in this context, the use of the term "extraordinary" adds nothing to the analysis that cannot be said more clearly by speaking directly of burdens and benefits. In fact, there seem to be two dangers in using the term "extraordinary" to refer to a treatment as probably being more burdensome than beneficial in some particular situation. The first is that it may mislead people into thinking that the treatment should be withheld simply because it is so exotic. The second is that it tends to obscure the extent to which a treatment must be burdensome before it ought to be withheld. The fact that it is extraordinarily burdensome only justifies its being withheld if the treatment does not also promise an extraordinary benefit. The burdens of amputation, toxic chemotherapy, or dialysis are obviously very great. But such therapies are often appropriate precisely because they also provide great benefits. Thus, at best, referring to such treatment as "extraordinary" adds nothing to what can be said more precisely by speaking of burdens and benefits; at worst, it suggests either that a treatment may be withheld simply because it is exotic, or that a treatment may be withheld simply because it is very burdensome. Since neither of these facts alone constitutes a good reason for withholding any therapy, we suggest that use of the term "extraordinary" is counterproductive. Optimal medical diagnosis requires the honest acknowledgment of even those medical facts which are unpleasant and the avoidance of irrelevancies. Similarly, optimal moral reasoning about the value of preserving a life requires that the relevant value judgments be faced squarely, and not obscured in ways that invite confusion of moral and technical judgments.

Foreseen versus Intended Consequences

It is sometimes proposed that it is not permissible to withhold a life-sustaining treatment (or administer a potentially lethal dose of a narcotic) if the patient's death is intended; such actions may be permissible if the death is merely a foreseeable consequence of what is intended—that is, the relief or minimization of suffering. This distinction is also suspect, however. It is true that our moral evaluations of harmful actions sometimes depend upon an agent's intentions, and certainly our evaluations of *agents* depend upon them. We are inclined, for instance, to tolerate the unintended harmful effects of insecticides on crops if their use is necessary to maximize the crop yield, but would certainly condemn anyone who introduced poisons into the environment simply for the purpose of causing harm. (Similarly, we would probably condemn a sadistic dentist who intentionally and gleefully inflicted pain in the course of doing excellent dental work, even if he inflicted no more pain than any other dentist.)

Some people, however, have mistakenly inferred that a person is responsible only for what he directly intends, so long as the intended good consequences of his action outweigh the foreseen, but unintended, harm. Thus, a physician who intends to keep a suffering patient free from pain is not held morally responsible if the patient dies because a burdensome treatment was withheld, or because an analgesic caused respiratory depression. In fact, this argument is sometimes used to show that such a physician has not killed his patient. It is, of course, absurd to suggest that people can only be said to have *done* what they *did intentionally*. If this were the case, drunken drivers could not be said to cause car accidents, and persons who engage in irresponsible sex could not be considered accountable for the unintended pregnancies that sometimes result.

We suggest that this use of the distinction between what is intended and what is foreseen is not legitimate. First, it is often impossible to distinguish between the foreseen and intended consequences of an action. For example, does the abortionist who crushes the fetus' skull *intend* its death, or merely *foresee* it as an undesirable consequence of reducing the size of its head? Second and more important, agents are generally responsible for all of the reasonably foreseeable consequences of their actions, even if they clearly do not intend them. Acknowledgment of this principle is implied by our expectation that an agent will weigh all of the costs associated with some action which he or she believes will achieve some good. The person who spends family funds wisely is still responsible for the diminution of the account balance.

This does not mean that all actions having harmful consequences are blameworthy. A harmful action may be acceptable if its performance will fulfill an obligation, or if the harm is seen as a worthwhile means of achieving a benefit. This point is illustrated by the use of any burdensome therapy to benefit a consenting patient. Thus, although a dentist is responsible for the pain he inflicts, his actions are acceptable because the anticipated benefits outweigh the pain. (This conclusion assumes, of course, that the agent is not violating any duties in performing this action—for example, administering a potentially beneficial treatment to a competent patient without consent.)

The use of this distinction is particularly insidious because it typically serves only to obscure the proper focus of nontreatment decisions—namely, whether the intended or merely foreseen burden of treatment is likely to outweigh the benefits. If this issue is not faced squarely, rational nontreatment decisions will remain elusive.

Withholding versus Withdrawing

The distinction between withholding a life-sustaining therapy in the first place and withdrawing such a therapy once it has been initiated is widely believed to be morally significant. Many medical personnel are quite comfortable with the idea of withholding a therapy to which a patient has not given consent, but are reluctant to withdraw a life-sustaining therapy that is already in place—even if the patient decides that he or she wants it withdrawn. We wish to argue that this, too, is a mistake. Since the factors underlying the intuitive belief in the moral significance of this distinction are somewhat subtler and more complex than those in the first two cases, our criticisms must be correspondingly more elaborate. We offer three criticisms:

The first criticism is that the distinction itself is vague, and cannot always be made with certainty. Never starting a patient on a ventilator, renal dialysis, or antibiotics constitutes withholding treatment; removing a patient from a ventilator exemplifies withdrawing treatment. But what if a series of individual treatments (for example, renal dialysis, injections of insulin, antibiotics) is discontinued, or a pacemaker battery or IV drip is not replaced? In answer to these questions, it has been suggested that if some action is required, lack of compliance could be construed as "withdrawing"; if no action is required, one is "withholding" treatment. It is certainly true that one may psychologically *feel* more responsibility for doing something that requires physical action. Nevertheless, this explanation cannot bear the moral weight ascribed to it by those who endorse this distinction. Otherwise, the many cases involving patients on ventilators (which physicians are reluctant to disconnect even though life on the ventilator has become unacceptably burdensome for the patient) could easily be resolved by replacing their power switches with 24-hour "timer" switches, which would require daily resetting in order to continue treatment. Since treatment would be stopped without any physical action, not resetting the machine could be construed as withholding treatment. But surely it is absurd to suggest the resolution of any moral problem through "technological" means. Physicians who refrained from resetting such "timer" switches would surely be just as responsible for the lack of ventilator function as those who turn off more conventional ventilators. Although consideration of this hypothetical solution shows that the presence or absence of physical action does not make the moral difference, it is difficult to understand how the distinction between "withholding" and "withdrawing" can be understood more precisely.

The second criticism is that physicians are generally willing to withhold or withdraw therapies that they believe are not or will not be beneficial; it is not clear why the case should be different with non-beneficial *life-sustaining* therapies. The initiation or continuation of *any* treatment should depend upon whether its potential benefits outweigh its associated burdens, a principle which is violated by the continuation of some life-sustaining therapies. One possible rationale for exempting life-sustaining therapies from this criterion of usefulness is that if they are withdrawn the patient will die. However, death is often an acceptable—perhaps even desirable—consequence of withholding treatment. Why, then, should it become so problematic in the case of treatment withdrawal? If the treatment is clearly nonbeneficial and merely prolongs a burdensome life, the fact that the person will die without it should become a reason *for*, not *against* its withdrawal. The physician who persists in such a treatment clearly violates the injunction to do no harm, regardless of whether the treatment is life-sustaining.

The third criticism is that other patients may be harmed by the physician's attachment of moral significance to the distinction between withholding and withdrawing treatment. Sometimes an uncertain, but potentially life-saving, treatment (for example, use of a ventilator) which might get a patient past a crisis is not undertaken because the physician believes that the therapy will have to be continued as long as it is sustaining the patient's life—even if the underlying condition does not improve. The perceived risk of ending up with a patient who is ventilator-dependent, will never recover, and who will find life on a ventilator burdensome may prompt the decision to withhold the potentially life-saving treatment in the first place. Sometimes physicians make this determination. In other cases, patients refuse a potentially life-saving therapy rather than risk the possibility of spending the final weeks of their life on a ventilator. It is difficult to imagine a stronger criticism of any alleged "moral principle" than to show that its implementation sometimes foreseeably leads patients to refuse potentially beneficial treatments.

Given these criticisms, one might ask why anyone would think the distinction between withholding and withdrawing treatment had a moral significance in the first place. It might be because of the psychological association with "action" vs. "inaction." Soldiers commonly believe that it is less psychologically traumatic to destroy entire villages from an altitude of 30,000 feet by pressing a button, than to have to kill one enemy woman or child face-to-face. We have already seen, however, that the distinction between withholding and withdrawing therapy cannot be clearly defined in terms of the presence or absence of any physical action.

Another possible explanation is that this intuitive belief derives from a failure to distinguish between the physician's two different levels of commitment. When a physician takes on a case, he or she becomes committed to offering the patient continued medical care, and incurs an obligation not to abandon the patient. In another sense, by initiating a *course* of treatment, rather than a single attempt, a physician becomes committed to the entire effort. (In this second sense, anyone undertaking any course of action commits him- or herself to that course of action.) The former "commitment" is clearly moral—that is, one incurs an ongoing moral obligation to provide the patient with needed medical care. The latter, however, is something quite different. By "committing oneself" to a course of treatment, the physician assumes the moral obligation to persevere with the treatment even if it has proven to be ineffective or counterproductive. By their very nature, some projects require sustained effort if they are to succeed (for example, losing weight, saving money, completing college, treating an infection with antibiotics). By and large, it is this fact that is being acknowledged when people speak of "being committed to a course of action." Simply making a commitment neither precludes the possibility nor absolves one from the responsibility of abandoning a project at any stage. Only extraordinarily perverse logic could lead someone to conclude that a physician's commitment to a patient entailed a commitment to continue a course of treatment that was clearly harmful.

More generally, anyone who embarks upon any course of action behaves irrationally if he or she perseveres after it becomes clear that the course of action has become counterproductive. A person who does so when acting as another person's agent is behaving both irrationally and immorally. This seems to be the case when a physician insists upon continuing life-sustaining therapy when it is no longer in the patient's best interest.

Finally, it might be suggested that the intuition gains its force from the fact that the withdrawal of life-prolonging therapy seems to involve killing the patient, while withholding only involves letting the patient die; killing someone is morally worse than merely letting someone die. Let us examine the role of this latter distinction in termination-of-treatment decisions.

Killing versus Letting Die

The common intuition that there is an important distinction between killing and letting die seems to apply whether the death at issue is bad, as most deaths are, or good, as death would be for a patient whose life had become a burden. Intuitively, it seems that it is virtually never right to kill someone except in self-defense. However, most people will readily agree that, under certain circumstances, it may be morally permissible to let someone die—for example, in cases of the sort we have been discussing or when someone cannot be rescued without great danger to the potential rescuers. Although most physicians would never consider administering poison in order to kill a terminally ill patient, they would readily consider refraining from resuscitation attempts if there was no hope of substantial recovery. Thus, it seems that killing and letting die can not be morally equivalent. We must consider two serious criticisms of this deep-rooted intuition.

While the terms "killing" and "letting die" are *sometimes* used in a purely descriptive way, that is often not the case, especially in medical contexts. When they are not used descriptively, they can obscure moral assumptions. Let us first consider situations in which the terms are being used descriptively. In general, if someone performs an action which causes a person's death, we say that he killed the person; if someone refrains from acting to prevent a death, we say that he allowed the person to die. Thus, for instance, an assailant killed his victim when he shot him, but a patient who refused to be put on a ventilator was allowed to die of respiratory failure.

When critically ill patients die, however, it is frequently difficult to know which of these characterizations is a more accurate description. In these cases, a death may be characterized as "killing" or "letting die" only *after* it has been assessed morally; while the term that is used will simply *reflect* that evaluation, it will simultaneously appear to *justify* it. The moral assessment is apt to be more dependent upon the particular responsibilities of the persons involved than on whether they "performed an action" or "refrained from acting." If, for instance, a physician on duty in an emergency room stood by idly while an accident victim bled to death, we would consider him blameworthy and might even go so far as to say that his negligence killed the patient. Consider a patient who dies because the ventilator is withdrawn. If a hired assassin crept into the hospital and decided to bring about the intended death of his victim by disconnecting the ventilator, we would certainly say that the assassin had killed the patient and was guilty of homicide. If, on the other hand, a physician had removed the ventilator at the request of his competent patient, we would say that the patient's death had been allowed, though not caused, by the physician. Which is it when "surgical misadventure" results in a patient's death? If we suspected the surgeon of greed and carelessness, we might well say that he had killed the patient; if we view the situation as an unavoidable accident for which the surgeon could not have been expected to prepare, we may simply say that the patient died from complications of his disease. In these cases, then, the choice between "killing" and "letting die" is not merely a matter of description; it involves a normative element. The normative force of these two terms conveys the moral evaluation that has already been reached about the death.

Naturally, this evaluative use of one of these terms is more likely to occur in cases that are ambiguous or unclear from the beginning. But many cases that involve the withholding or withdrawing of life-prolonging therapy are also ambiguous. Indeed, our tendency to use these terms to reflect our prior moral assessments of particular cases is so great that even the administration of lethal doses of narcotics is seldom interpreted as an example of a physician killing a patient; rather, such cases are routinely interpreted in ways that obscure the fact that the patient has been killed. In summary, then, we must be wary of attempts to condemn or justify particular treatment/non-treatment options on the grounds that the proposed course of action would either amount to killing or merely letting the patient die. This terminology is more apt to conceal than to elucidate the real basis for the moral judgment that is being made.

The second criticism of the killing/letting die distinction acknowledges the possibility of there being a distinction, but denies that it has any intrinsic moral significance. This criticism has been advanced by a number of philosophers, most prominently in an important article by James Rachels.[6] Rachels claims that incidental features of various cases mislead us into believing there is an inherent moral difference between killing and letting die. In most actual cases of killing, the agent acts from malevolent motives and does serious harm to his victim. Rachels suggests it is these common, but logically incidental, features of most killings that make them morally wrong. When we hear of cases in which someone is allowed to die, on the other hand, these features are usually not present. We are most apt to hear about benevolent caregivers who attempt to help a suffering patient by refraining from action that would only prolong his or her misery.

Rachels asks us to consider various pairs of cases in which these incidental differences are minimized, to see whether our intuitive reaction changes. For example, he uses two cases which include the features that make most killing wrong. The first case involves a greedy uncle who drowns his nephew in the bath in order to gain an inheritance. In the second case, the uncle approaches the child in the bathtub with the intention of drowning him. When he discovers, to his delight, that the boy has slipped in the tub and is drowning accidentally, he stands by until the child is dead. Surely, argues Rachels, the two cases contain equal amounts of moral evil; the uncle's action in the first is no worse than his inaction in the second. He also offers two cases which lack these morally objectionable features. In the first case, a terminally ill patient's caregivers allow him to die slowly by withholding treatment for pneumonia. The caregivers in the second case administer a lethal injection to a similarly suffering patient in order to put him out of his misery. The motive in each case is to minimize the patient's suffering. But this motive is served even better in the second case, where the patient is actively relieved of the burden of a painful life in such a way that his total suffering is reduced even further. Rachels believes that in this case killing may actually be preferable to allowing someone to die. Since this seems perfectly obvious in the case of suffering animals, why should it be so hard to grasp in the case of humans suffering terminal illness? The simple answer, "We value life," cannot be correct, for that consideration would apply equally against killing and letting die.

Finally, Rachels points out that what amounts to inaction under some circumstances may constitute action under other conditions. Rachels notes that the AMA opposes "the intentional termination of the life of one human being by another."[6] He argues, however, that physicians are simply deluding themselves if they believe that by respecting the killing/letting die distinction they absolve themselves of the charge of intentional termination of life. Just as I may intentionally insult a person by refusing to shake his hand, a physician may intentionally terminate a suffering patient's life by withholding a life-prolonging therapy. Consider, for instance, an advanced and miserable Alzheimer's patient who has contracted an infection; a decision not to administer antibiotics amounts to a decision to terminate the patient's life intentionally. Since the desirability of the patient's death is the motivating factor in the decision, treatment is withheld *in order that* the patient will die sooner than he would if treated.

How sound is Rachels' criticism of the primitive intuition that killing is intrinsically worse than letting die? Rachels' arguments certainly do suggest that part of the reason we view killing as worse is based on features of the situations that are accidental to the killing/letting die distinction. But has Rachels shown that, in the context of critically ill patients, the distinction is never of any moral significance? We must tease apart a number of subtle issues that are intertwined here. First, it must be noted that Rachels has *not* shown that in *all* situations in which it would be right to let a patient die, it would also be right to kill that patient. At most, this will be so only when the reason for letting the patient die is that life itself has become a burden. In cases where treatment is withheld because the *treatment* is too burdensome—for instance, the cancer patient who would like to extend his or her life, but not at the expense of painful chemotherapy treatments, it would be absurd to suggest that since withholding treatment is justified, so is killing the patient. Thus, at best, Rachels' argument only holds in cases involving the patient's intended death. The cancer patient does not want or intend to die, even though he or she wants and intends to avoid the burden of painful chemotherapy. In light of this qualification, then, is his argument persuasive?

It is our view that neither the primitive intuition nor Rachels' view is completely correct. We suggest that both views are too simple in that both overlook the potential significance of special moral relationships among the persons involved. It is a mistake to think that the moral evaluation of actions or omissions that lead to a person's death depends only upon whether they are actions or omissions and the agent's motives. It is also essential to consider whether the parties have any special moral relationships which entail particular rights and duties.

Let us consider two cases involving parties with *no* special moral relationships. One person, through indifference, fails to aid another, whose life he could save at little or no cost to himself. His action is deplorable, but not as bad as that of a driver who indifferently kills a pedestrian he could have avoided hitting. Both cases involve the evil of a regrettable and easily avoidable death; the second involves the additional evil of interfering adversely in the welfare of another person in a way that violates that person's rights. Thus, when strangers are involved, the primitive intuition seems correct and Rachels is wrong; killing a stranger is worse than letting one die.

But physicians and their patients are engaged in a special moral relationship. The physician is the patient's agent and is responsible for his or her welfare. Here Rachels' argument may appear to have more substance, especially when death constitutes a harm to the patient. If any person (a physician or parent) who is responsible for another's welfare stands by while that person is harmed by influences such as disease (or slippery bathtubs) that could easily be counteracted, such inaction is probably just a morally reprehensible as active killing.

Does the special moral relationship between physician and patient reinforce Rachels' argument that there is no difference between a physician's killing a patient and letting him or her die when the patient's death is a beneficial release from a burdensome life? Several philosophers believe that Rachels' claim rests on a misconstrual of the duties that form the basis of the doctor/patient relationship. Specifically, Bonnie Steinbock argues that Rachels is mistaken in stating that physicians withhold treatments and allow patients to die because they are motivated by either a duty or a benevolent impulse to see that the patient is relieved of a burdensome life. She claims that such a duty or impulse has no place in the ethics of the physician/patient relationship. Rather, physicians who withhold life-prolonging therapies are, or should be, motivated either by the desire to spare the patient the burden of painful treatment (compare the chemotherapy case), or by a duty to respect the patient's right to refuse treatment. She argues that the right to informed consent gives the competent patient the right to refuse treatment, hence obliging the caregiver to withhold it; it does *not* give the patient the right to demand from his caregivers whatever might be to his benefit, including assistance in intentionally hastening his own death. Steinbock claims that physicians are not bound by any principles that require them to kill patients upon request. Such actions, she argues, would be totally contrary to the spirit of medicine, and should not be permitted under any circumstances.

In her critique of Rachels, Steinbock contends that physicians should never act or refrain from acting with the intention of hastening a patient's death. Her view is remarkable for two reasons. First, Steinbock has no quarrel with Rachels on one central point; she seems to accept Rachels' claim that there would be little moral distinction between what she calls passive and active euthanasia—that is, between a physician killing a patient while intending his or her death, and a physician withholding or withdrawing treatment while intending a patient's death. She grants that these might be morally equivalent, but then insists that *both* are wrong because they are incompatible with the moral principles that define the physician's role and the 1973 AMA code, which forbids "the intentional termination of the life of one human being by another."[7]

Her argument with Rachels, then, focuses on whether physicians *ever* intend the deaths of their patients—regardless of whether treatment is withheld or withdrawn, or lethal doses of painkillers are administered. Her contention is that they do not. In order to maintain this view in the face of decisions by physicians to withhold antibiotics from advanced Alzheimer's patients, withdraw ventilators from patients in respiratory failure, and administer lethal doses of painkillers, Steinbock must rely very heavily on the "intended/foreseen" distinction.

The second remarkable feature of Steinbock's view, then, is her insistence that in each of these cases the death is merely foreseen and not intended. We noted earlier that this distinction is problematic. Although physicians may find it comforting to imagine that they never intentionally hasten the deaths of their patients, we doubt that this belief can often survive honest and critical scrutiny. Patients who refuse therapy or request painkillers in doses that may be lethal are often not the only ones who view their lives as burdensome; their families and physicians may share their belief that their deaths will be a desirable release from suffering. Under these circumstances, Steinbock's suggestion that such physicians do not intend the deaths which they are hastening seems ill-advised. An abortionist might similarly argue that he or she is not intentionally killing the fetus, but merely foresees its death as an inevitable consequence of suctioning it from the uterus. The political assassin might plausibly argue that he or she didn't intend to kill the president when he/she shot him, even though he or she did see his death as an inevitable consequence of removing him from office by putting a bullet through his heart. Also, one wonders what the physician in such cases does intend, if it is not the patient's death. According to Steinbock, the physician's intention is either to honor the patient's refusal of treatment, or to spare the patient the burden of the painful therapy that might prolong life. With the first possibility, Steinbock suggests that the physician, passive and duty-bound to honor the patient's wishes, stands back and lets the patient (or suitable proxy) decide whether his or her life is to be prolonged. With the second possibility, Steinbock suggests that it *is* appropriate for the physician to be concerned with the minimization of suffering, and to participate in the burden-benefit analysis which determines whether the patient's life is worth prolonging, given the burden of treatment. It seems odd, however, to suggest that physicians participate in the process of assessing costs and benefits so selectively.

In all of this, Steinbock is driven to forced and implausible interpretations of decisions and intentions and their justifications. In order to insulate the physician from anything that can be construed as intending the patient's death, Steinbock recognizes, for instance, that in some cases *patients* (or suitable proxies) may refuse treatment because they decide that they are better off dead. Given this fact, isn't it obvious that physicians may share this view with their patients—especially since they may well have a more accurate understanding than either the patient or the family of how bleak the patient's prognosis really is? And in such cases, isn't it undeniable that part of a physician's intention—for instance, in withholding an antibiotic from an advanced Alzheimer's patient—is to hasten the patient's death? This realization may be painful for the physician, for it forces him or her to acknowledge the taking of a particular stand on the straightforward moral dilemma concerning the conflicting imperatives to preserve life and minimize useless suffering. Once he or she has decided that the minimization of suffering has priority in a particular case, Rachels' central argument again becomes persuasive—that is, this goal can be realized even more quickly by killing the patient than by merely withholding life-prolonging therapy.

The Slippery Slope Argument

This final argument on these issues is sometimes cited in defense of the prohibition on mercy killing, which Rachels is attacking. It also has application as part of a more comprehensive concern about termination-of-treatment decisions. The central premise is that the practice of medicine involves and requires a fundamental bias in favor of the preservation of life. Thus, even if Rachels is right about killing being the most compassionate and beneficial thing to do in certain individual cases, physicians should continue to respect the distinction (and, by parity of reasoning, the other distinctions we have criticized above), in order to prevent a general erosion of the respect for life which is essential to the practice of medicine. Steinbock alludes to, but does not develop, this argument in her critique of Rachels, and it recurs in one form or another throughout the literature. James Childress, for instance, writes, "Because the distinction between killing and letting die is inextricably tied up with our understanding of medical care, we cannot remove it without tearing the whole fabric. For the community or the medical profession to authorize physicians actively to kill patients would so alter the moral ethos of medicine as to necessitate a new basis of trust. Trust is the expectation that others will respect moral limits. . . . Trust in the context of medical care involves the expectation that medical practitioners will work for our health and life, will provide 'personal care,' and will do us no harm."[8]

The claim that allowing mercy killing in some cases would lead to a general erosion of the respect for life is based on the belief that there is no clear way to distinguish between the cases in which mercy killing would be defensible and those in which it would not. According to the argument, we find a continuum of cases. Near the top of the "slippery slope," one finds the patient who is alert and clearly competent, terminally ill, and suffering intolerable and uncontrollable physical pain; because life has become burdensome, the patient wants to be released from his suffering. At the bottom of the "slope," there are helpless and dependent persons who may be incompetent, suffering nonterminal conditions that may involve only emotional distress, or who may even be fairly content, but whose continued existence inconveniences others (Downs syndrome newborns are perhaps cases in point). Rachels would presumably have physicians kill patients near the top of the slope; allowing such an action is a step onto a slope so slippery as to involve the risk of precipitating or "sliding into" the morally unacceptable killing of others further down the slope.

The slope is doubly slippery. First, the very terms used to describe the above continuum of acceptable to unacceptable killings are characterized by imprecision. How competent is "competent?" How terminal is "terminal?" While a patient in multiple system failure is obviously terminal, what of the newly diagnosed AIDS patient or the multiple sclerosis patient? How much pain is "intolerable?" Considerable difficulties are encountered in defining competence and prognosis, with respect to both terminality and pain management; the determination of the quality of life of incompetent persons is even more difficult. Thus, even the most cautious and best-intended physician, who views all four of these conditions as necessary for actively killing a patient, will find these tests difficult to apply.

The other reason for the slope's being slippery is that each of these conditions can be challenged as being necessary for mercy killing. In fact, each of the four *has* been challenged by compassionate, well-intentioned thinkers. First, the condition of competence is not met by anencephalic neonates or comatose patients who have never voiced any opinions about the circumstances under which they would not want to be kept alive. If mercy killing can be beneficial to competent patients, why should it be denied as an option to proxies making decisions on behalf of similar patients who happen to be incompetent? (Mightn't this even constitute systematic discrimination against the handicapped?)

Secondly, although the condition of terminality is not met in any straightforward sense by persons with diabetes or emphysema, their right to refuse treatment guarantees their right to end their own lives intentionally. If we take this to be a right to mercy killing in the case of the terminally ill, why should we not extend it to patients who, although not yet near death, request suicide assistance?

Thirdly, the condition of *physical* pain seems arbitrary. It has been suggested that some persons who endure chronic emotional pain or anguish as the result of advanced dementia should be as eligible for mercy as those who have the good fortune to be suffering physically instead of mentally.

Fourth and last, while it may seem difficult at first to imagine that someone would justify mercy killing on the basis of a person's burdensomeness to others, this is often a reason for withdrawing ventilators from severely brain-damaged patients. It is difficult to construe such termination of treatment as beneficial to the patients, since it is doubtful whether the patients still embody a perspective from which anything could be either a benefit or a harm. While attention is given to any previously expressed wishes in such cases, it would be naive to suppose that none of the motivation for terminating treatment derived from concern for the family and others for whom scarce medical resources promise greater benefits.

Thus, each of these four conditions seems in some way relevant to distinguishing between morally justifiable and morally offensive killing. On closer scrutiny, however, it becomes clear that none provides a sure toehold for the well-intentioned physician who is lured onto the "slippery slope" by arguments such as Rachels', but who wants to guard against transforming medicine from a life-affirming institution into one in which there is not only little respect for life, but which freely dispenses death as well.

A natural extension of this argument applies to our previous criticisms of the other distinctions, since our attacks on each of them may be construed as contributions to the slipperiness of the slope. Physicians observing the distinction between ordinary and extraordinary therapies reflect medicine's life-respecting ethos by insisting upon treatment for patients suffering life-threatening conditions for which nonexotic treatments (for example, antibiotics) are available. Physicians relying heavily on the distinction between foreseen and intended consequences will reflect that ethos by administering lethal doses of morphine only to patients who are in serious pain. Physicians observing the distinction between withholding and withdrawing treatment will do so by refusing to withdraw life-prolonging therapy from those presently receiving it. Physicians who are persuaded by our arguments about the moral irrelevance of each of these distinctions for termination-of-treatment decisions will be much more inclined to opt for death than physicians who believe all of these distinctions are morally significant. Thus, according to the argument, in order to preserve the life-respecting ethos of medicine, physicians must continue to respect these distinctions and ignore as irrelevant (or perhaps denounce as subversive) the exhortations of medical ethicists to the contrary.

A final dimension of the slippery slope argument shifts the focus from the respect-for-life bias of medicine *as it guides physicians* to the *public perception* of that bias. According to this line of reasoning, public trust is obviously necessary if medicine is to be effective, since physicians generally treat only those persons who trust them enough to seek medical attention. But if the public begins to perceive physicians as dispensers of both death and life, this confidence in medicine will be eroded and health care will obviously suffer as a result. Childress construes patient trust in medical practitioners as the belief that they will "work for our health and life."[8] David Louisell develops this theme: "Euthanasia would threaten the patient-physician relationship: confidence might give way to suspicion . . . Can the physician, historical battler for life, become an affirmative agent of death without jeopardizing the trust of his dependents?"[9] Patients who already view hospitals as places where people die, *in spite of* what can be done, will come to realize they are also places where people are sometimes killed intentionally. The cost of this shift in perception in terms of the public trust is thus an additional consideration against liberalizing physicians' views and termination-of-treatment decisions.

Two fundamental strategies have been adopted by theorists responding to this slope argument. The bolder of the two embraces a position which the proponents of the argument see as unacceptably far "down the slope." Mary Rose Barrington acknowledges that her argument for mercy killing entails a radical revision in the way we think about death.[2] She grants, for instance, that her vision includes the possibility of people viewing doctors as dispensers of death. She insists, however, that such a possibility, far from eroding trust, would provide comfort and reassurance to anyone concerned about possibly being subjected involuntarily to the pain and indignity of a protracted death in an intensive care setting. (There is no evidence that the hospice movement has tarnished public trust in medicine, in spite of the fact that its underlying ethos renounces the goals of restoring health and prolonging life, and substitutes the more modest and attainable goals of comfort and "supportive care.") Barrington even accepts the possibility that those who are both elderly and infirm might some day feel obligated to step aside voluntarily and gracefully, rather than insisting upon the use of every possible intervention to eke out a few more days of life, however marginal, at costs, however staggering— especially in the face of competing demands for limited medical resources. Barrington would presumably see this as indicative of a need for the infirm and critically ill to speculate about whether it was their duty to step aside, instead of clinging to life until every conceivable resource for its prolongation has proven futile.

A different response to the slope argument is offered by Daniel Maguire.[10] He also grants the slipperiness of the slope, but argues that morality in an open society depends upon learning to negotiate slippery slopes responsibly, rather than simply avoiding them. Maguire dismisses the view that morality requires adherence to unequivocal rules as indicative of a "taboo" mentality, which is inadequate because it fails to recognize the complexity of our moral world, in which we must often choose between conflicting values or principles. For Maguire, there are no straightforward rules that delineate the moral white from the moral black. Rather, one must be able to face the greys found in moral reality, in which simple solutions do not exist.

Maguire's claim echoes the beliefs of learning theorists J. Piaget, R.S. Peters, and L. Kohlberg. All of these theorists maintain that the moral development of children involves various stages, including an early one in which moral rules are construed as "given," absolute, and unalterable. Peters writes, "[Children] finally pass to the level of autonomy when they appreciate that rules are alterable, that they can be criticized and should be accepted on a basis of reciprocity and fairness. The emergence of rational reflections about rules . . . is the main feature of the final level of moral development."[1]

The complexity of our moral life is a direct consequence of the fact that it embraces more than one principle or value, thus making conflict inevitable. One way to deal with such conflicts is to declare in advance that one value or principle will always take priority. This was essentially the strategy of those who dealt with the conflicting values of preserving life, minimizing suffering, and respecting patient autonomy, by insisting that all patients must always be treated aggressively. Physicians who adopted this strategy steadfastly refused to step onto the slippery slope. As we noted at the outset, however, most critical care providers find this position untenable precisely because it fails to acknowledge the conflict between values such as minimizing suffering and respecting patient autonomy.

Significantly, one steps onto the slope at the point that one acknowledges respect for competing values. Thus, those who are quite comfortable with withholding or withdrawing life-prolonging therapy for reasons of compassion or autonomy are already *on* the slope. Although those who are persuaded by Rachels' arguments may hold a position further down the slope than those who are not, it is simply a mistake to believe that his arguments must be resisted because they lure one *onto* the slope. It is crucial to realize, moreover, that those who would avoid this slope by always opting for aggressive treatment are, in fact, defining their position on competing slopes; competing values manifest themselves as "intersecting slopes." The fact that we also value respect for patient autonomy, for instance, gives rise to the "slope of medical paternalism"—that is, the range of possible views on when it is appropriate to disregard a patient's wishes. He who avoids stepping onto the "termination-of-treatment" slope by adhering to a policy of always treating aggressively, will do so without regard for the autonomy of the patient who cries "no more," thereby defining his position as rather unacceptably far down on the slope of paternalism. This, then, is the force of Maguire's claim that our moral world is too rich and complex to be handled adequately by a "taboo" mentality.

Maguire's rebuttal to the slope argument gains additional force from consideration of its role throughout history. Most major human advances in science, religion, or social order have occurred in spite of "slope" arguments akin to the one considered above. "If we permit research and experimentation in the areas of dissection of human cadavers/organ transplantation/genetic engineering/human reproduction, we open the door to a whole range of complicated moral considerations, which may be mishandled in a way that will lead to morally abhorrent practices." "If we allow people to develop methods of birth control which will tend to disassociate sex and reproduction, we invite moral decay and the destruction of the family." The same sort of argument has been made in closed societies against the questioning of established authorities. "While it's true that the authorities are sometimes mistaken, they serve the people well generally, and if dissenting opinions are allowed to be heard, there will be no place to draw a clear moral line between dissent and anarchy." From this argument some have concluded that people must not be allowed to stray onto the slippery slopes of free speech or religion or political dissent.

A final criticism points out that slope arguments can backfire. Berger and Berger, who favor a more conservative stand on abortion than that represented by *Wade* v. *Roe*, claim that the extreme "pro-life" faction has actually used the "slope" argument in a way that has been counterproductive to their own goals.[12] By insisting that no abortion is to be tolerated because all abortion is murder, "pro-lifers" are, in effect, claiming that abortion following rape or abortion to save the life of the mother is *as wrong as* abortion for convenience. But that, unfortunately, is logically equivalent to saying that abortion for convenience is *no worse than* abortion in these other circumstances. Having argued that there are no moral differences, they have actually enhanced popular belief in the slipperiness of the slope; this has, in turn, prompted some persons, who were initially sympathetic to abortion only following rape or to save the life of the mother, to believe that abortions under any other circumstances are equally acceptable.

We suggest that the slope argument is not merely faulty, but dangerous, if it leads us to believe we can avoid coming to grips with the moral complexities of situations in which the timing of death is the result of human decisions. We have suggested that some of the distinctions that currently figure in termination-of-treatment decisions do not serve us well; the principles that should guide such decisions are the same as those which prevail elsewhere—that is, respect for patient autonomy and the burden/benefit analysis which normally guides all other treatment decisions. These are the principles that can provide the surest moral footing on the slope. The simplicity of this framework should not belie the complexity that must be faced head-on when it is applied in actual critical care situations. We have tried to acknowledge some of the special problems associated with responsible decision making in this area, including those of patient competence, communication with patient and family, and, not least of all, legal ramifications.

Physicians must, of course, heed the legal reality of the situations in which termination-of-treatment decisions must be made and implemented. Unfortunately, the legal reality is sometimes even murkier than the moral one. In this connection, however, physicians should not view the courts as hopelessly conservative on these issues. Moreover, they should be aware of their own potential to influence those legal realities, for better or worse. We suggest that facing the moral issues as squarely as possible helps to ensure the best decisions in individual cases, and also optimizes the chances of clearer and saner legal precedents in the future. This observation is not naive and utopian. On January 7, 1985, the New Jersey Supreme Court authorized the withdrawal of feeding tubes from an 84-year-old incompetent patient who "had no cognitive abilities" and was terminally but not critically ill. Emphasizing the importance of previously expressed wishes, the court stated, "The right we are seeking to effectuate is a very personal right to control one's own life." In so doing, the court clearly rejected the distinctions between ordinary and extraordinary care, withholding and withdrawing treatment, and—explicitly—"the distinction that some have made between actively hastening death by terminating treatment and passively allowing a person to die of a disease."[13] The spirit of the Court's decision echoes the findings of the President's Commission for the Study of Ethical Problems in Medicine and Biomedical and Behavioral Research report on *Deciding to Forego Life-Sustaining Treatment*. This may prove to be a landmark decision.

CONCLUSIONS

We have argued that a number of distinctions traditionally considered morally significant in fact obscure the real basis on which rational decisions about prolonging life are (and ought to be) made—namely, an analysis of burdens and benefits to be expected from any treatment option. Respect for patient autonomy requires that such analysis be made from the patient's perspective and, if he or she is competent, with his or her active participation. Since both assessment of competence and decision making in the absence of full competence fall largely to the physician, it is the physician who must orchestrate and implement treatment decisions. Such decisions are painful and complex enough without introducing irrelevancies.

REFERENCES

1. President's Commission for the Study of Ethical Problems in Medicine and Biomedical and Behavioral Research: *Deciding to Forego Life-Sustaining Treatment*. Washington, D.C.: U.S. Government Printing Office, 1983.
2. Barrington MR: Apologia for suicide. In Gorovitz S, et al. (eds.): *Moral Problems in Medicine*. Englewood Cliffs, N.J.: Prentice-Hall, 1983, pp. 472-476.
3. Lasagna L: The prognosis of death. In Brim Jr OG, et al. (eds): *The Dying Patient*. New York: Russell Sage Foundation, 1970, p. 68.
4. Carlton W: *"In Our Professional Opinion . . .": The Primacy of Clinical Judgment over Moral Choice*. South Bend, Indiana: University of Notre Dame Press, 1978.
5. McCartney JJ: The development of the doctrine of ordinary and extraordinary means of preserving life in Catholic moral theology before the Karen Quinlan case. *Linacre Quarterly* 1980, *47*:215.
6. Rachels J: Active and passive euthanasia. *N Engl J Med* 1975, *292*:78-80.
7. Steinbock B: The intentional termination of life. In Gorovitz S, et al. (eds.) *Moral Problems in Medicine*. Englewood Cliffs, N.J.: Prentice-Hall, 1983, pp. 290-295.
8. Childress JF: To kill or let die. In Bandman EL, Bandman B (eds.): *Bioethics and Human Rights*. Boston, Mass.: Little, Brown and Company, 1978.
9. Louisell DW: Euthanasia and Biathanasia. *Linacre Quarterly* 1973, *40*:234.
10. Maguire D: *Death by Choice*. Garden City, N.Y.: Doubleday, 1974, pp. 131-140.
11. Peters RS: In Dearden RF (ed.): *Education and the Development of Reason*. London: Routledge and Kegan Paul, 1972, p. 130.
12. Berger PF, Berger CA: Death on Demand. *Commonweal* 1975, *102*:585-589.
13. Sullivan R: 'Right to die' rule in terminal cases widened in Jersey. New York *Times* January 18, 1985. *134*:1,10.

3 Ethical Decisions in Neonatal Intensive Care

Mary B. Mahowald

It is sometimes remarked that medical and ethical problems involving infants are so unique that an understanding of adults, or even older children, is inadequate in addressing them. While acknowledging the unique aspects of newborn care, I believe there are also important similarities between newborns and many other patients in intensive care units. Two common features are the inability of patients to make decisions for themselves, and an unknown outcome for their critical illnesses. Since these features are especially applicable to newborns, consideration of ethical decisions in neonatal intensive care units may facilitate an understanding of their broader application.

Unfortunately, both the media and the federal government have recently focused on a few controversial cases regarding handicapped infants,[1-4] possibly to the neglect of ethical issues involving other patients and the larger social/ethical problems of long-term care for disabled individuals.[1] This chapter includes a brief account of the historical, cultural, and medical contexts in which neonatal dilemmas arise, and a description of alternative approaches to their resolution. I also discuss principles applicable to cases in which nontreatment of extremely ill, handicapped, and low birthweight infants may be morally justified. Although these conditions are commonly addressed separately, in practice they often occur in the same patient. Accordingly, the infant should be treated as an individual, just as older patients are to be treated as individuals. In both cases, the patient's identity represents a unique embodiment of limitations, abilities, and possibilities.

HISTORICAL AND CURRENT CONTEXTS

Facilities and technologies for neonatal intensive care are a relatively recent phenomenon, still comparatively unavailable or inaccessible to the populations of less-developed nations. The first treatment center for care of newborns in the United States was established early in this century, when infant deaths were primarily associated with infection or malnutrition.[5] At that time, rudimentary incubators provided necessary warmth for premature newborns, and oxygen supplementation was introduced to combat respiratory difficulties due to immature lung development. Progress in survival was not devoid of setbacks, however. For example, by 1954 it was recognized that the high oxygen concentrations which had saved some premature newborns had also caused blindness. Subsequent curtailment of this treatment was accompanied by a corresponding rise in infant mortality.[5] Similarly, diethylstilbestrol (DES) was shown effective in bringing problematic pregnancies to term, but the drug was later implicated in carcinogenic and reproductive problems of the offspring.[6]

Further advances produced sophisticated techniques for prenatal diagnosis and treatment, monitoring neonatal heart rate, blood gases, and chemistries, and microsurgical procedures for newborn anomalies. Neonatology became a major pediatric specialty, spawning a huge and ongoing research effort with impressive clinical results.[7] Two techniques introduced during the 1960s enabled successful treatment of infants weighing less than 1500 grams: constant distended airway pressure, a method by which oxygen requirements could be constantly monitored; hyperalimentation, a method of providing nutrition to those who could not tolerate other types of feeding.[8] By 1970, the mortality rate from hyaline membrane disease, a common problem of premature newborns, had dropped from 60 percent to 20 percent of those affected. By 1978, the survival rate for very early and very small babies had improved to the point where those weighing less than 1000 grams warranted treatment.[8] During the 1980s, fetal viability has advanced earlier into pregnancy, resulting in smaller and younger survivors of premature birth and even late abortions. Currently, an increasing number of newborns weighing between 500 and 750 grams are treated, survive, and fare well. The majority of very low birthweight babies (less than 1.5 kg) who survive sustain no serious impairment to motor or mental functions. For example, 65 percent of the 781 infants weighing less than 1500 grams who were admitted to the neonatal intensive care unit at Rainbow Babies and Childrens Hospital in Cleveland between 1975 and 1978 survived; 80 percent of these have had normal neurodevelopmental outcomes.[9] These data are consistent with studies of other neonatal intensive care units throughout the country.

Despite such impressive developments, not everyone agrees that all critically ill newborns should be provided with life-saving or life-prolonging treatment. A sizable number of these infants suffer both curable problems and incurable serious disabilities, such as Down's syndrome, spina bifida, and other genetic anomalies. Some health care practitioners, ethicists, attorneys, and government officials maintain that parental refusal of life-saving treatment for such defective newborns should be respected, while others argue that physicians ought to make these decisions on their own. Some deny the need to make a decision, reasoning that all lives should be prolonged wherever possible. Others stipulate certain conditions under which cessation of treatment is justified, basing the stipulation on "the interests of the infant," a phrase with diverse and conflicting interpretations. Still others invoke the interests of society as a criterion for nontreatment —that is, the cost (in terms of benefits as well as harms) to both families and taxpayers who are responsible for subsequent care of disabled citizens.[10] In our pluralistic society, such a range of positions is perhaps not unexpected. In the broader contexts of history and culture there have also been conflicting views. Infanticide is a long-standing practice with which nontreatment decisions may be compared.

Anthropologists tell us that infanticide has been practiced throughout history in many cultures, including those of the Western world.[10,11] At times, the practice was deemed acceptable because it was undertaken indirectly, rather than directly. In other words, infants were not killed outright, but were left to die—often because they were defective, and sometimes because they were female or illegitimate. Since abandonment of an infant inevitably leads to death, there does not appear to be much of a conceptual distinction between killing and letting a newborn die. Just as euthanasia is morally problematic, regardless of its definition as active or passive, so is infanticide, whether defined as direct or indirect.[12] Refusing to institute life-saving treatment, such as intubation, in a newborn may thus be construed as indirect infanticide. The refusal to provide intravenous nutrition to an infant who is incapable of normal digestion may be construed similarly.[13] The difficulty of maintaining a sharp distinction between direct and indirect termination of life-saving treatment has led Robert Weir to argue that it is sometimes morally justified to terminate an infant's life directly and actively.[10]

Several factors in contemporary American society conspire to exacerbate moral problems regarding infants. One is the emphasis on patient autonomy, which is generally referred to in legal terminology as "informed consent." While this concept is obviously inapplicable to newborns, it is sometimes applied to parents who make decisions on behalf of their children. In fact, the distinction between informed consent and proxy, or substitute, consent is often overlooked, and parents are falsely assumed to provide the former, rather than the latter.[14] Legal and moral grounds for requiring informed consent of competent patients are clearly stronger than those for substitute consent. Nonetheless, parental rights regarding their children are often perceived as primary, requiring practitioners to respect their decisions, even when these involve the refusal of life-prolonging treatment.[15]

In the past, a variety of treatment options were unavailable to many infants, regardless of whether or not they were handicapped. Reversible life-threatening medical problems, which have a greater incidence among permanently impaired newborns, are now routinely repaired through surgery. The development of antibiotic therapy, feeding techniques, and fluid exchange procedures has greatly increased the actual number of handicapped children who survive to adulthood. Moreover, while greater numbers of severely premature infants now survive to live normal lives, some pay for their survival with iatrogenically induced permanent disabilities. There is thus an inevitable connection between very low birthweight babies and handicapped infants.[9]

Two conflicting social phenomena make neonatal ethical dilemmas even more prevalent and complicated. One is the "premium baby" mentality which has resulted from the trend toward reduced family size, as well as the availability of contraceptive measures and abortion. The choice of allowing severely handicapped infants to die is clearly consistent with this mentality. In contrast, the "right to life" ideology and movement affirm the primacy of fetal interests over those of other individuals. Not surprisingly, "right to life" activists have recently joined the government and organizations representing the disabled in arguing that infants should not be denied treatment on the basis of handicap.[16]

Government embroilment in cases concerning treatment of handicapped infants was sparked by a 1982 case in Bloomington, Indiana. A newborn male child was noted to have both Down's syndrome and a surgically correctable blockage of his digestive tract. Only the latter condition was life-threatening. When the child's parents refused consent for surgery, hospital authorities sought and obtained court sanction for their decision at county and state levels. An attempt to overturn the lower court rulings through recourse to the U.S. Supreme Court became moot when the child died at six days of age.[17,18] By that time, the case had been well publicized, provoking widespread criticism.

Within a week of Baby Doe's death, the government notified all federally supported institutions caring for infants that funds would be denied if they discriminated against the handicapped, as had allegedly occurred in the Bloomington case.[17] In March of 1983, the Department of Health and Human Services issued a ruling which required all such institutions to post signs citing both the government statute prohibiting discrimination against the handicapped and a phone number to use in reporting suspected violations of the statute.[19] This ruling was overturned one month later by U.S. District Judge Gerhard A. Gesell, who described it as conceived in "haste and inexperience," and "based on inadequate consideration of the regulation's consequences.[20] In February, 1984, the government published another formulation of the ruling. While it retained the mechanisms of posted notices and anonymous phone access, it added a recommendation that hospitals form their own review committees to deal with difficult ethical decisions about neonates.[1]

Litigation relevant to another Baby Doe, born in 1983 in Port Washington, New York, tested the government's right of access to medical records of handicapped infants.[21] That right is, of course, crucial to the government's ability to investigate specific cases. Since repeated appeals denied governmental access to the records, "Baby Doe" regulations became virtually ineffective. Nonetheless, in 1984 Congress passed an amendment to federal child abuse legislation prohibiting "withholding of medically indicated treatment from disabled infants with life-threatening conditions," unless such treatment is "virtually futile" in prolonging a child's life, or ineffective "in ameliorating or correcting all of the infant's life-threatening conditions."[22,23] The American Medical Association opposed this measure as mandating therapy that may entail "inhumane" prolongation of an infant's life.[24]

The continuing controversy over "Baby Doe" legislation raises doubts as to whether the matter will ever be definitively settled from a legal standpoint. However, by provoking practitioners, families of

newborns, and the general public into carefully scrutinizing both procedural and substantive grounds for ethical decisions in the nursery,
the controversy has served a useful purpose. Two broad questions encompass the range of issues associated with such complex cases: Who
decides, and according to what criteria?

Who Should Decide?

"Informed consent" is often seen as a sine qua non of justification
for medical interventions from moral or legal perspectives.[15,25,26]
Competent adults may legally decline even life-saving therapy by removing themselves from hospital treatment programs against medical
advice. Exceptions have been based on the patient's responsibilities
to others, or the claim that hospital personnel are not obligated to
violate their own professional standards or commitments.[27] Since
newborns are incapable of providing informed consent, their parents
usually act as proxy or surrogate decision makers in their behalf. The
legal right of parents to act as proxies may be overruled, however, if
their decision opposes their child's best interests. For example, if a
Jehovah's Witness parent declines a blood transfusion essential to the
life of his or her child, hospital authorities will obtain a court order
allowing them to intervene in the child's behalf. Thus, the parents'
right to decide about their infant's treatment is legally less binding
than their right to decide on their own treatments.

This distinction between informed and proxy consent is also significant from a moral point of view. It suggests that a priority of decision makers be observed, based on the degree to which each decision
maker is related to the infant. Typically, the child's parents would
hold first place. However, the child's caretakers are also related to
the child through their professional commitment, as well as the personal and contractual relationships that they maintain with the infant
and family.

Despite the legal and moral requirement of informed or proxy
consent, a long-standing model of the physician-patient relationship
assigns the role of principal decision maker for medical dilemmas to
the physician.[28,29] The justification for this priority is sometimes
comparable to the argument presented by the cardinal in Dostoevsky's
story of the Grand Inquisitor in *The Brothers Karamazov*.[30] By assuming control of people's lives, the cardinal claimed that his church had
gradually removed the burden of freedom which Christ had brought
to the world. Similarly, the physician or the health care team may

accept sole responsibility for difficult decisions in order to spare families the anguish and unnecessary guilt that often occur in such situations. Despite its plausibility and appeal, this line of reasoning has several crucial flaws. One is the failure to acknowledge that a sense of guilt may be experienced regardless of how a decision is made. In light of this fact, it is more helpful to focus on the moral justification for a decision to prolong *or* discontinue treatment—that is, the intent to do what is best for the patient. Both families and practitioners may need explicit reassurance that relinquishing the hold on another's life is sometimes the most loving and caring alternative available.

Another flaw in arguments favoring decisions made solely by physicians (or parents) is the fact that responsibility for decision making is inevitably shared by all of the autonomous participants in a dilemma. Even if an attending physician writes an order or parents indicate their wishes, others may choose to implement, ignore, or challenge those decisions. At times, a practitioner does not consider his or her actions to be a matter of choice; rather, the person is simply following the order of the attending physician or supervisor. At other times, a practitioner may subtly, perhaps even inadvertently, interpret an "order" in a manner that compromises its intent. For example, in a situation where a physician has instructed staff to resuscitate a critically ill patient if necessary, a nurse or resident who disagrees with that decision may respond with deliberate slowness to a signal that the patient has suffered cardiac arrest.

In many cases regarding neonates, there is neither ambiguity nor controversy about what constitutes morally appropriate behavior. For example, the vast majority of pediatricians and pediatric surgeons agree that an anencephalic newborn who is also afflicted with intestinal atresia should not have corrective surgery for the latter condition.[31] The invasiveness of surgery cannot be justified on the basis of benefit to the patient, because the infant is already afflicted with an incurable, terminal condition. In cases where agreement has been reached about moral aspects of treatment or nontreatment decisions, it is probably neither necessary nor helpful to extend the decision-base beyond the delivery room or nursery. In fact, involving others in the decision process increases the possibility of violating confidentiality or family privacy.

Moreover, treatment deferral sometimes entails a real risk of harming the patient. Possibly the most common example of such a situation involves intubation of very small (for example, less than 750 grams) or very premature (for example, less than 24 weeks' gestation) newborns. Without intubation, the infant cannot survive. At such times, it would seem that whoever is competent to provide the treatment is justified in making the decision on the patient's behalf. Subsequently, however, and in most chronic cases, there is time for discussion and broader input, which ought to be obtained in cases where ambiguity and/or disagreement continue. Since most decisions to terminate life-saving treatment are irrevocable, treatment should continue until some resolution of the conflict is achieved.

Why should there be broader input? Mainly because neither health care practitioners nor parents have any special moral expertise, and the possibility of arriving at well-reasoned moral decisions is increased by the collaborative efforts of reasonable people. Another advantage of such an approach is that those who maintain some distance from the situation can provide a more objective perspective, which may complement and supplement the views of those whose involvement in the situation may preclude a totally rational analysis. Extending the decision-base in unclear or controversial cases may also be reassuring to those closest to the patient because it represents one more attempt at responsible resolution of a difficult dilemma.

A decision-base may be extended beyond the physician and/or parents through consultation with other clinicians, the entire health care team, a hospital-based review committee, or through recourse to the courts. In the interests of maintaining confidentiality and family privacy, it is preferable to use the least public forum in which ambiguity or disagreement may be resolved. The widespread endorsement of the team concept's effectiveness in providing basic health care suggests that it might also be effective in dealing with medical/moral problems.[32] Hospital-based review committees are a newer phenomenon whose efficacy deserves to be tested.[33]

Recourse to the courts is a particularly troublesome means of extending the decision-base for ethical dilemmas. The legal system introduces an adversarial dimension into a set of relationships that should ideally be based on trust, openness, and consensus. Litigation threatens, and sometimes severs, those relationships, thwarting the therapeutic purpose of the practitioner-patient alliance. Nonetheless, there are times when legal recourse may be the only way of resolving ambiguity and disagreement—for example, blood transfusions for children of Jehovah's Witnesses. But court decisions are not necessarily morally correct. In the case of Bloomington's "Baby Doe," for example, there is widespread agreement that the court's concurrence with the parents' decision to decline treatment was morally unjustified.[34]

Recent government attempts to impose investigative procedures on federally funded facilities which care for newborns seem to be intrusions on the right of privacy and the confidentiality of the physician-patient relationship, and may even be harmful to the patients affected. After investigating many anonymous reports of suspected neglect of handicapped infants, the Department of Health and Human Services concluded that appropriate medical, legal, and moral decisions had been made in the vast majority of cases. In cases at Vanderbilt University in Nashville and Strong Memorial Hospital in Rochester, however, it was reported that the governmental investigation obstructed care of both the infants who had allegedly been neglected and other patients. The time required for personnel to respond to the queries of investigators could only be purchased at the price of time spent in caring for patients.[3 5]

In January, 1984, under the aegis of the Rehabilitation Act of 1973, the Department of Health and Human Services published its last attempt to regulate decision making in the nursery. In addition to reaffirming the requirement that notices citing the law prohibiting discrimination against the handicapped and a "hot line number" for reporting cases of suspected violation be posted in hospital nurseries, the government strongly encouraged the formation of hospital ethics review committees.[1] It was recommended that these committees include both public members and health care professionals. In general, the government's encouragement of the committee review mechanism supported the recommendation of the President's Commission for the Study of Ethical Problems in Medicine and Biomedical and Behavioral Research.[3 6] The American Academy of Pediatrics also recommended the formation of local review committees, and suggested appropriate procedures and principles.[3 7] However, the Commission had proposed the local review mechanism as an alternative to federal investigative procedures, arguing that the latter was unlikely to promote the best interests of infants, and might actually impede the achievement of that purpose.

During the past few years, the continuing legal controversy surrounding "Baby Doe" cases has evoked fairly widespread interest in the use of hospital review committees to address difficult cases. The extent of this interest and the influence of committees on practice remain to be seen. Regardless of how decisions are made, however, we must also deal with the substantive issues that are inseparable from the process. In other words, we must inevitably address the criteria for ethical decisions regarding neonates.

According to What Criteria?

Three values or principles have generally been considered applicable to ethical issues in health care: beneficence, autonomy, and justice.[38] Beneficence entails reiteration of the Hippocratic tradition—that is, "to help, or at least to do no harm."[39] If the interests of the patient are paramount, this principle is obviously most pertinent to newborns. From an ethical perspective, however, obligations to do good, avoid harm, and respect the autonomy of others clearly extend beyond the physician-patient relationship. Accordingly, the physical and psychological benefits and harms that accrue to any of those affected by decisions regarding neonates are morally (if not professionally or legally) relevant. The principle of justice balances harms and benefits by equitably distributing them among all those affected by specific decisions. In that light, an exclusive focus on the patient's interests, the attending physician's responsibility, or parental rights is an inadequate response to the moral complexity of neonatal decisions. Other members of the health care team and the patient's family are also affected.

In applying the principle of justice to critical care decisions, it is crucial to assess the proportionate impact on the patient, family, practitioners, and others in society. Life is obviously essential to the preservation of other human values. For any patient, therefore, loss of life is clearly more important than the distribution of health care costs among others. The patient's welfare and preferences take precedence over the welfare and preferences of other separate individuals precisely because he or she is most affected by the decision. Similarly, the welfare and preferences of a family take precedence over those of health care practitioners because harms and benefits to the family are generally more intense, direct, and longer lasting. In particular cases, proportionate impact may shift in its application to these groups. Consider, for example, the emotional and economic costs to the family of maintaining a patient who is irreversibly comatose. Consider the patient whose treatment imposes such great health risks that it is more costly to caretakers than to the family (for example, blood exchanges for a dying hepatitis patient). Or consider the fact that individual and government funds might do more good if they were used to fund prenatal programs that might prevent premature birth, rather than using them to overcome some of the more difficult medical problems which accompany premature birth.

It is obviously not relevant to consider the autonomy of newborns themselves. Moreover, unless treatment or nontreatment imposes greater harms or benefits on others than it does on the infant patient, the principle of justice is not crucial to ethical decisions regarding neonates. Thus, it appears that beneficence towards the infant is the primary value or principle to be considered. Recently, this principle has been characterized as "the interests of infants."[10,40,41] I wish to argue that sometimes an infant's best interests may be served by allowing him or her to die. Further, prolonging an infant's life may promote the interests of others more than those of the infant. Finally, certain handicapping conditions or quality-of-life factors are relevant to the determination of when an infant's "right to die" should be respected.

Prolonging Life in Others' Interests

If life is considered a great good, it may credibly be maintained that loss of life is always negative for the patient, and can only possibly be justified on the basis of others' interests. In certain cases, however, it may be the interests of others which are primarily served through the prolongation of an infant's life. Prolonging patients' lives obviously increases the possibility for gaining new knowledge through experimental therapies, which would benefit clinician-researchers and future patients. More subtle rewards for health care practitioners include the feeling of accomplishment achieved by taking some action, rather than just letting go. Whether or not such attitudes are justified, many people are less likely to feel guilty about acting to prolong life than they are about refraining from those actions. As one neonatologist put it, "It is easier for me to live with the consequences of something I've done than it is to worry about something I have not done which might have given better results."[42]

For those who define the very purpose of medicine as the prolongation of life, even the death of a patient whose life was fraught with suffering evokes a sense of professional failure. Moreover, regardless of the degree of illness, the affective ties that are likely to be formed between caretakers and neonates sometimes obfuscate recognition of the patient's best interests. For example, a nurse commented on an infant whose life had been prolonged for two years with little expectation of survival or relief from suffering, "We have been doing this for ourselves, rather than for him."[43] Initially, there had been a slim, but real, prospect of recovery for this infant. During the ensuing weeks and months, however, the staff had clearly become more attached to their patient, even as his prospects dwindled with each unsuccessful therapeutic procedure. The nurse had recognized the alignment of the staff's own interests with the prolongation of this infant's life. His death was more difficult for them to accept than the deaths of other patients.

At times, prolonging the lives of infants may be in the best legal interests of professionals and parents. Although malpractice suits may be filed for prolonging life, they are more likely to occur when treatment has been withdrawn. Even in such cases, however, the probability of success is very slim, as long as "letting a patient die" (passive euthanasia) is distinguished from active euthanasia.[12] It is also possible to further political interests by prolonging the lives of handicapped infants. The statements and actions of the Reagan administration in this area have enhanced its popularity in some quarters. Finally, the economic interests of others are often strengthened through prolongation of infants' lives. At a time when unfilled beds in many hospitals are causing economic crises, prolonging lives provides an opportunity to cut financial losses. The same economic principle can also be used as justification for terminating lives—for example, where prepayment plans based on diagnostic categories do not cover the costs of treating a particular patient.

Prolonging Life in Infants' Interests

While motives for prolonging life are sometimes mixed, it may still be maintained that the prolongation is always in the infants' interests. This position is justified only if life is assumed to have an absolute value, apart from any consideration of quality or social or familial costs. That assumption has often been associated with an essentially religious perspective, such as that of the Roman Catholic church in its teaching on abortion.[44] It may also be associated with the tenet of orthodox Judaism that human life must be preserved no matter what its quality.[45] Yet these same religious traditions also offer different views. For example, Roman Catholic theology employs a distinction between ordinary and extraordinary treatment, claiming that extraordinary means are never required in order to save or maintain a person's life.[36,44,45] Jewish law labels the death of a preterm infant as a "miscarriage." According to Jakobovits, "unless a full-term pregnancy can be proven beyond doubt (for example, by the parents' separation for nine complete months) . . . the killer of such a child is not liable to capital punishment, nor are the normal mourning regulations to be observed upon its death."[46] Protestant ethicist Joseph Fletcher maintains that religion as such does not predict decisions regarding termination of treatment.[46] While Fletcher himself believes that Christian love (*agape*) endorses the taking of life in order to minimize human suffering, he acknowledges disagreement among theists. Regardless of religious affiliation, the meaning of divine omniscience and omnipotence preclude the possibility of human beings either prolonging or shortening life; thus, the assumption that we can interfere with the divine plan may be considered blasphemous. If faith in an afterlife is affirmed, death may sometimes be judged preferable to life on earth.

Several nonreligious factors also support an assertion of the absolute value of an infant's life. One such factor is "the uncertainty principle," which applies more to infancy than to other periods of extrauterine human existence. Despite the wondrous advances of neonatology in recent years and the impressive results of programs for facilitating maximum development of handicapped children, it is still impossible to accurately predict the subjective or objective future experiences of a particular newborn. Most clinicians can cite cases involving major and minor "miracles"—that is, cases with happy outcomes that were totally unexpected in light of the available facts and technology. For example, an infant in our pediatric intensive care unit had heart defects that had always proven fatal in other infants of similar weight and age. The original plan was to help her grow, thereby increasing her chances of surviving corrective surgery; this proved impossible because of repeated cardiac and respiratory arrests. The surgery was finally performed despite the odds, because it seemed that the child would surely die otherwise. Her subsequent recovery changed the mortality rate that became applicable to others.

Another relevant feature concerning newborns or children in general is the obvious contrast between them and adults with regard to how long they have already lived and their anticipated life span. Those who have as yet scarcely lived are usually considered to have a stronger "right to life," which partly explains why the deaths of children seem more tragic than those of the elderly. In some respects, new life signifies the fullness of hope, which is dashed by death.[47] With neonates, however, there has obviously been less time and opportunity to build the complex network of affective ties and relationships that are established with older people.

If the interests of the infant are to be considered primary, I do not believe there is adequate justification for the preservation of every newborn's life. Nonetheless, the features that are peculiar to an infant's situation do argue persuasively for a conservative approach to irreversible decisions to withhold or withdraw life-prolonging treatment. By "conservative" approach, I mean one that seeks to prolong life if there is some real, although improbable, chance that its continuation is in the infant's best interests. Where there is high probability that this is not the case, then the same principle argues against prolonging life. To the extent that prolongation imposes unacceptable suffering upon the child, a decision not to prolong life may be morally mandatory. For infants, children, and adults, the right to die is included in the right to live.[48] To deny this right to children is to practice what Richard McCormick has called a "racism of the adult world."[49]

An Infant's Right to Die

While the priority of the infant's interests suggests that decisions to prolong life will be made much more frequently than decisions to the contrary, that principle also suggests the relevance of "quality of life" considerations. Three types of cases may be discussed in this regard. In the first and simplest, therapy is futile because the underlying condition is fatal. No matter what is done, survival beyond a few days or weeks is neither expected nor desired. Anencephaly, a condition in which the infant's brain has failed to develop, is a commonly accepted example of this situation. Even those who claim that "quality of life" factors are irrelevant agree that the life of an anencephalic infant need not be prolonged through medical technology. Treatment may be withheld in such cases because death is clearly inevitable and imminent.[31]

The second type of case in which "quality of life" is a factor is one in which repeated, intrusive, painful interventions would prolong the infant's life indefinitely, but would probably entail no satisfaction for the infant, and might deepen and prolong the anguish experienced by the child's parents. In such a situation, efforts to preserve life are likely to cause the infant to endure a preponderance of negative experiences with no realistic expectation of improvement. The multiple diagnostic and therapeutic procedures necessary to prolong the child's life only cause additional suffering and hospitalization. Such interventions cannot be considered manifestations of the principle of beneficence, by which harms are justified on the basis of expected benefits.

An example of this second type of case is an infant with the chromosomal abnormality trisomy 13, which entails profound mental retardation and frequent seizures for the 18 percent who survive beyond the first year of life.[50] Such infants often face the immediate life-threatening problem of severe heart defects. Correction of these and concomitant problems requires multiple surgeries, medical and orthopedic interventions, and permanent hospitalization. While the prolongation of life in such cases might serve the interests of parents and clinicians, it is doubtful that it is in the patient's best interests. Prolonging life will simply cause the infant too much suffering. While it might be argued that such a clinical judgment is fallible, we are still obligated to weigh the anticipated harms of treatment against the corresponding benefits to the patient. Decisions made for newborns cannot justifiably ignore the fact that the costs of prolonging life may be greater than a person should be required to pay.

The most problematic "quality of life" case involves life-sustaining therapy that is neither painful nor curative. Moreover, the infant probably derives no qualitative satisfaction from the life thus prolonged. Consider, for instance, a newborn who has had a Grade IV cranial hemorrhage (bleeding into the cerebral tissues), who experiences persistent, uncontrollable seizures, and can only be fed intravenously because bowel function has been permanently impaired. Clinically, the child appears to have suffered irreversible loss of cognitive function or capacity for social interchange. While the child might conceivably survive for years, it is doubtful that survival is in the infant's or anyone else's best interests. Unless biological life is an end in itself, rather than a necessary condition for the actualization of human experience and potential, its maintenance in these circumstances may actually constitute exploitation of the child—that is, using him or her to suit the purposes of others.

Even when family members, practitioners, and the courts agree that prolongation of life is not in an infant's best interests, the cessation of certain treatments still involves controversy. Cardiopulmonary resuscitation or mechanical ventilation are usually regarded as dispensable in such cases. Blood transfusions, dialysis, and certain surgical procedures (for example, tracheotomy) are perceived by some as essential to patient comfort, and by others as unnecessary and unjustified interventions. More controversial still is the question of whether such patients should be fed, either intravenously or orally. The government has indicated that nutrition and hydration should always be provided as part of routine patient care.[1] Others argue that intravenous feeding of a dying patient constitutes an unjustifiably invasive procedure.[13] In the case of Bloomington's "Baby Doe," the obstetrician suggested to the parents that a refusal of surgery be coupled with a request not to feed the baby, so as not to prolong his dying.

The view that infants have a right to die is obviously based on a conception of life that is not merely quantitative. Life is considered a continuing physiological function of a human organism that has a crucial, but relative, value. In fact, this position implies that quality of life factors are essential to any full affirmation of the value of human life. However, choosing which factors are relevant and how they are to be applied remains complicated and problematic.

With competent and conscious patients, the determination of the relevance of quality of life considerations is facilitated by two features which are not applicable to the newborn situation: patient autonomy and patient history. If the patient's wishes are known, their observance provides a clear justification for nontreatment decisions. Even with adults, however, loss of consciousness often precludes patient consent. In such cases, the decision is usually based on: 1. proxy consent (substitute judgment) based on patient history—that is, the proxy's understanding of the patient's desires; 2. invocation of a "reasonable person" standard—in other words, what any competent, conscious person would reasonably choose in similar circumstances. Although infants may hardly be described as "reasonable persons," the standard is applicable.[51] For example, a reasonable person would decline surgery that could have no benefits and might actually prolong a predominantly painful existence; this same criterion could be used to justify a similar decision involving an infant. This criterion could also be applied to each of the three types of cases mentioned above. In certain situations, it is reasonable to decide not to prolong life beyond its natural limits—that is, where therapy is futile, where it would prolong a life of predominant anguish, or where it would prolong the life of a patient who is neurologically incapable of enjoying the benefits of living. To reject the applicability of this standard of reasonableness to infants or children suggests complicity in what we have already described as racism of the adult world.

Applying the Priority Principle

Certain distinctions are often important in attempting to observe the priority of infant's interests. For example, natural law theology has long invoked the distinction between "ordinary" and "extraordinary" treatment, claiming that the former is obligatory while the latter is not.[36,44] "Ordinary" and "extraordinary" treatment are terms that are relative to the treatment's usefulness for a particular patient, as opposed to the burden it imposes on the patient or others. In spite of persistent disagreement as to which outcomes are useful or burdensome, the courts have invoked this distinction in cases where treatment was judged futile or of doubtful benefit to the patient. Patients and families themselves sometimes use this distinction when they request that "no heroic measures" be pursued in their behalf.

The distinction between optimal and maximal care is also applicable to difficult cases.[52] Maximal care involves the prolongation of life, regardless of the cost to the patient; optimal care involves the prolongation of life only to the extent that it is in the patient's interests. Treatment that serves the interests of others—for example, family members, health care practitioners, or medical students—may be defended as constituting maximal care. Such care may, however, simultaneously impede the provision of optimal care. The obligation to provide optimal care implies that treatment may not be continued or refused on the basis of others' interests. In fact, a refusal to provide maximal care is mandatory if the care is not in the patient's best interests.

Other clinical interpretations that have served as guides in handling problematic cases include a distinction between "coercing" and "helping" someone to live, and between "doing to" and "doing for" a patient.[53] "Coercing" or "doing to" constitute unjustifiable intrusions, while "helping" or "doing for" are justifiable because they are oriented toward the patient's own interests. While these distinctions may never be made with absolute certainty, there are surely some cases in which it is highly probable that survival will entail prolonged and unmitigated misery for a particular infant, child, or adult. An example, of "coercing" someone to live might involve starting dialysis on a patient with terminal cancer who has suffered kidney failure. Performing corrective cardiac surgery on a newborn who has a fatal genetic disease is another illustration. In such cases, the right to die seems an undeniable component of the patient's right to live.

The distinction between "defensive" and "patient-centered" medicine is also helpful. It is unfortunate that the practice of *defensive medicine*—that is, medicine aimed at avoiding legal entanglements, is increasingly responsible for the prolongation of life when persuasive evidence indicates that this is not in the patient's best interests. According to a recent article by James Strain, president of the American Academy of Pediatrics, today's pediatricians disagree with those interviewed for a 1977 national survey, which disclosed that the majority would accede to parental refusal of life-saving treatment for an infant with a severe birth defect.[54] Strain believes that a new survey would indicate a "major shift" in physicians' attitudes. For example, most would not accept parental refusal of life-saving surgery for a newborn with Down's syndrome. Strain bases his expectations on the following factors: early intervention; the Education for All Handicapped Children Act; deinstitutionalization of care for the handicapped; recognition of the fact that a handicapped child can have a positive effect on a family; awareness that parents do not always act in their children's interests. While these factors have undoubtedly had some effects on physicians, a shift in practice does not necessarily reflect a change in attitude. My own impression is that the changes in practice that have occurred have been largely precipitated by a factor not mentioned by Strain—that is, a desire to avoid the legal entanglements that may ensue from decisions to forego treatment—a "defensive medicine" mentality. Empirical studies could be useful in determining where attitudes and practice coincide and what factors besides individual moral views influence the practice of medicine. David Todres, a pediatrician who conducted one of the earlier influential surveys, recently embarked on a follow-up study that may enlighten us in this regard.[55]

Another important distinction in problematic cases is that between answers and decisions. While there are objectively correct answers to some questions about which procedures are clinically or morally indicated, we are never absolutely certain that we have those answers. As decision makers, then, we remain fallible, rather than omniscient. In order to minimize the gap between the answers we seek and the decisions we make, rational analysis and input from knowledgeable others are particularly important. Moreover, initial decisions to prolong life may need to be reconsidered because a patient's condition has gravely and permanently deteriorated. The deterioration can result from the natural course of the disease, or from the treatment itself. For example, extremely premature or very low birthweight babies who are kept alive through intubation immediately after birth may fail to develop independent respiratory function and suffer further internal malfunction, such as renal failure and cerebral hemorrhage. The increasing numbers of such cases in our neonatal intensive care units demonstrate that the distinction between very ill and handicapped infants is not clear. Although certain illnesses can be cured, the "cure" itself may induce permanent and profound defects.[56]

Similarly, decisions not to prolong life need to be continually reassessed in light of the infant's progress or regress. Because clinical judgments are fallible, certain patients may both qualitatively and quantitatively outlive a decision not to provide them with life-saving treatment. In such cases, the decision to terminate or withhold treatment needs to be reversed. Aggressive treatment must then be instituted, and continued as long as there is reason to believe that such actions are in the infant's best interests. Reversals of ethical and/or clinical decisions should not be considered as evidence that the original judgments were wrong or right in the context of what was known at the time. Such results can influence subsequent decisions by adding to existing knowledge about certain conditions.

Possible Relevance of "Quality of Life" Factors

While the phrase "quality of life" is often used with reference to criteria for foregoing or discontinuing treatment, the term seems to have different meanings for those who endorse and those who reject its relevance. For example, organizations representing the disabled have argued that "quality of life considerations are subjective evaluations which disregard the fact that infants' interests may be different from those of families or health professionals."[1] Although government regulations have eschewed the relevance of quality of life considerations, the current legal exceptions to treatment requirements (for example, irreversible coma, futile or inhumane treatment) may be construed as being dependent upon quality of life criteria.[57] In contrast, the American Medical Association specifically asserts that "quality of life is a factor to be considered in determining what is best for the individual."[58] This suggests that physicians are both morally and professionally responsible for taking such factors into account.

Quality of life considerations may apply to any patient, regardless of disability. However, since the term is subject to diverse and controversial interpretations, it should probably not be used with regard to complicated cases. An emphasis on the infant's own interests is more conducive to agreement on the parts of all concerned. Concern for the totality of the infant's interests can be expanded to encompass similar decisions—such as the possibility of nontreatment in cases where medical interventions would be noncurative and painful. The first two types of cases cited above illustrate this possibility—that is, support of the child's right to die and the responsibility of practitioners to respect that right. There may still be disagreement about the third class of cases, in which treatment is not invasive but the infant has no capacity for social interaction. In such cases, an argument based on the treatment's consequences for parents and society may be more persuasive than one based exclusively on the infant's interests. Even when treatment is painless, its imposition on infants may be viewed as an affront to their dignity as human beings; as such, it requires stronger justification. For example, the indignity of having multiple tubes inserted into one's body to maintain basic functions of nutrition and elimination is defensible only in terms of expected benefits to the patient. The fact that the patient is unaware of the indignity is not sufficient justification for their use.

CONCLUSIONS

Three crucial principles or values are applicable to any ethical dilemma regarding newborns: beneficence, autonomy, and justice. Although the precise application of these principles must be determined for each specific case, all three are indispensable ingredients of a morally justified decision. I have argued that beneficence toward the infant has priority over beneficence toward others, as well as over autonomy and justice. However, that priority does not obviate responsibility to practice beneficence toward others, and to respect the autonomy of all those affected by the decision. Justice demands that an effort be made to balance conflicting interests in applying these principles.

With regard to each infant, beneficence entails concern for both immediate and long-range needs; these are often inseparable from consideration of the family and social supports upon which the child depends. In certain tragic circumstances, this principle entails recognition of the fact that caring extends beyond curing, and affirmation of the right to die as part of an individual's right to live.

In addition to substantive principles or values, the procedural question of who makes decisions has also been considered. I have basically maintained that diverse decision makers all have roles to play—that is, parents, physicians, health care team, hospital ethics committees, and the courts, in that order. The same order is appropriate in decisions about other patients, except that a competent patient's preferences should surely be honored before those of other participants in the decision process. Actually, patients in intensive care units are often incompetent, unconscious, or both, as a result of the severity of their illness and the effects of treatment. The principles and procedures discussed are thus applicable across the entire spectrum of the patient population.

Accordingly, much of what I have written here is relevant to ethical quandaries involving other patients. Information included elsewhere in this volume may also be enlightening with regard to infants —at least to those of us who regard infants as persons. Surely, the fundamental human rights which we insist upon having for ourselves ought not to be denied to our children.

REFERENCES

1. Nondiscrimination on the basis of handicaps; procedures and guidelines relating to health care for handicapped infants. *Federal Register* Jan. 12, 1984, *49*:1622-1654.
2. Big Brother Doe. *Wall Street Journal* Oct. 31, 1983, p. 20.
3. Baby Jane's big brothers. *New York Times* Nov. 4, 1983, p. 28.
4. Mahowald M, Paulson J: The Baby Does: Two different situations. *Plain Dealer* Dec. 31, 1983, p. 9-A.
5. Tooley WH, Phibbs RH: Neonatal intensive care: The state of the art. In Jonsen AR, Garland MJ (eds.): *Ethics of Newborn Intensive Care*. San Francisco, Calif.: Health Policy Program, University of California, 1976, pp. 11-15.
6. Tilley BC: Assessment of Risks from DES. In Holmes H, Hoskins B, Gross M (eds.): *The Custom-Made Child?* Clifton, N.J.: Humana Press, 1981, pp. 29-38.
7. Klaus MH, Fanaroff AA: *Care of the High-Risk Neonate*. Philadelphia, Pa.: W.B. Saunders, 1973, p. xi.
8. Stahlman MT: Newborn Intensive Care: Success or failure. *J Pediatrics* 1984, *105*:162-167.
9. Hack M, Rivers A, Fanaroff A: The very low birth weight infant: The broader spectrum of morbidity during infancy and early childhood. *J Develop Behav Pediatrics* 1983, *4*:243-249.
10. Weir R: *Selective Non-Treatment of Handicapped Infants*. New York: Oxford University Press, 1984.
11. Williamson L: Infanticide: An anthropological analysis. In Kohl M (Ed.): *Infanticide and the Value of Life*. Buffalo, N.Y.: Prometheus Books, 1978, pp. 61-75.

12. Rachels J: Active and passive euthanasia. *N Engl J Med* 1975, *292*:78-80.
13. Paris JJ, Fletcher AB: Infant Doe regulations and the absolute requirement to use nourishment and fluids for the dying infant. *Law. Med Hlth Care* 1983, *11*:210-213.
14. Shaw A: Dilemmas of "informed consent" in children. *N Engl J Med* 1973, *289*:885-890.
15. President's Commission for the Study of Ethical Problems in Medicine and Biomedical and Behavioral Research: *Making Health Care Decisions*, Vol. 3. Appendices: Studies on the foundations of informed consent. Washington, D.C.: U.S. Government Printing Office, 1982, pp. 175-245.
16. Ehrhardt HE: Abortion and euthanasia: Common problems—the termination of developing and expiring life. *Human Life Rev* 1975, *1*:12-31.
17. *The Herald-Telephone*, Bloomington, Indiana, April 23 and May 1-3, 1982.
18. *The Criterion*, Indianapolis, Indiana, April 23, 1982.
19. *Federal Register*, March 7, 1983, *48*:9630-9632.
20. Culliton BJ: "Baby Doe" regs thrown out by court. *Sci* 1983, *220*:479-480.
21. Holden C: Government intercedes in "Baby Jane Doe." *Sci* 1983, *220*:908.
22. Ahern ML: Senate passes amendment to child abuse act regarding treatment for disabled infants. *Hlth Law Vigil* 1984, *7*:2.
23. Cooper JA: *President's Weekly Activities Report* #84-38, Association of Medical Colleges, Oct. 25, 1984.
24. *Handicapped Americans Report*, July 12, 1984, pp. 7-8.
25. Jonsen A, Siegler M, Winslade W: *Clinical Ethics*. New York: Macmillan, 1982, pp. 67-71.
26. Ramsey P: *The Patient as Person*. New Haven, Conn.: Yale University Press, 1970, pp. 1-11.
27. Dickens BM: Legally informed consent. In Davis J, Hoffmaster B, Shorten S (Eds.): *Contemporary Issues in Biomedical Ethics*. Clifton, N.J.: Humana Press, Inc., 1978, pp. 199-204.
28. Thomasma D: Beyond medical paternalism and patient autonomy: A model of physician-patient relationship. *Ann Int Med* 1983, *98*:243-248.
29. Szasz TS, Hollander MH: The basic models of the doctor-patient relationship. *AMA Arch Int Med* 1956, *97*:585-592.
30. Dostoyevsky F: The grand inquisitor. In Dostoyevsky F: *The Brothers Karamazov*. New York: Random House—Modern Library, 1950, pp. 255-274.
31. Shaw A, Randolph J, Manard B: Ethical issues in pediatric surgery: A national survey of pediatricians and pediatric surgeons. *Pediatrics* 1977, *60*: 590.
32. Rosini L, Howell M, Todres D, Dorman J: Group meetings in a pediatric intensive care unit. *Pediatrics* 1974, *53*:371-374.
33. McCormick RA: Ethics committees: Promise or peril? *Law Med Hlth Care* 1984, 150-155.

34. Fleischman AR, Murray TH: Ethics committees for infants Doe? *Hastings Ctr Rep* 1983, *13*:6.
35. Strain J: The American Academy of Pediatrics comments on the "Baby Doe II" regulations. *N Engl J Med* 1983, *309*:443-444.
36. President's Commission for the Study of Ethical Problems in Medicine and Biomedical and Behavioral Research: *Deciding to Forego Life-Sustaining Treatment*. Washington, D.C.: U.S. Government Printing Office, 1983.
37. American Academy of Pediatrics: *Guidelines for Infant Bioethics Committees*. Evanston, Ill.: American Academy of Pediatrics, 1984.
38. Beauchamp TL: *Contemporary Issues in Bioethics*, 2d ed. Belmont, Calif.: Wadsworth Publishing Company, 1982, pp. 26-32.
39. Reiser S, Dyck A, Curran W (Eds.): *Ethics in Medicine*. Cambridge, Mass.: MIT Press, 1977, pp. 5-9.
40. Arras JD: Toward an ethic of ambiguity. *Hastings Ctr Rep* 1984, 14:25-33.
41. Strong C: The neonatologist's duty to patient and parents. *Hastings Ctr Rep* 1984, *14*:10-16.
42. Hoggman JE: Withholding treatment from seriously ill newborns: A neonatologist's view. In Doudera AE, Peters JD (Eds.): *Legal and Ethical Aspects of Treating Critically and Terminally Ill Patients*. Ann Arbor, Mich.: AUPHA Press, 1982, p. 243.
43. Miller B, at health care team conference, Pediatric Intensive Care Unit, Rainbow Babies and Childrens Hospital, Cleveland, Ohio, Sept. 27, 1983.
44. Ashley BM, O'Rourke KD: *Health Care Ethics, A Theological Analysis*, 2d ed. St. Louis, Missouri: Catholic Health Association of the United States, 1982, pp. 227-239.
45. McCormick R: To save or let die. *JAMA* 1974, *229*:174-175.
46. Jakobovits I: Jewish views on infanticide. In Kohl M (Ed.): *Infanticide and the Value of Life*. Buffalo, N.Y.: Prometheus Books, 1978, pp. 23-31.
47. Benfield DG, Leib SA, Vollman JH: The grief response of parents to neonatal death and parent participation in deciding care. *Pediatrics* 1978, *62*: 171-177.
48. Jonas H: The right to die. *Hastings Ctr Rep* 1978, *8*:36.
49. McCormick R: Experimental subjects—Who should they be? *JAMA* 1976, *235*:2197.
50. Smith DW: *Recognizable Patterns of Human Malformation*, 2d ed. Philadelphia, Pa.: W.B. Saunders Company, 1976, pp. 14-15.
51. Beauchamp TL, Chidress JF: *Principles of Biomedical Ethics*, 2d ed. New York: Oxford University Press, 1983, pp. 75-76.
52. Smith DH: On letting some babies die. *Hastings Ctr Studies* 1974, *2*:41.
53. Donald Schussler (on distinction between "coercing" and "helping" to live), senior resident; Jeffrey Blumer (on distinction between "doing to" and "doing for"), Director, Pediatric Intensive Care Unit, Rainbow Babies and Childrens Hospital, Cleveland, Ohio, 1983-1984.

54. Strain J: The decision to forego life-sustaining treatment for seriously ill newborns. *Pediatrics* 1983, *72*:572.
55. Conversation with the author, Boston, June 15, 1984.
56. Strong C: The tiniest newborns. *Hastings Ctr Rep* 1983, *13*:14-19.
57. Child abuse and neglect prevention and treatment program. *Federal Register* April 15, 1985, *50*:14878-14892.
58. Judicial Council of AMA: Principles of medical ethics. In Judicial Council of AMA: *Current Opinions of the Judicial Council of the American Medical Association–1984*. Chicago: American Medical Association, 1984, 2.14 p. 10.

4 Resource Limits and Allocation in Critical Care

Claudia J. Coulton

How much intensive care is necessary or justified? What kind of care should be available, and where and to whom should it be provided? How should society control the supply and use of intensive care? The widespread growth of intensive care, coupled with the heightened concern about health care costs, has focused attention on these and other related questions. The fact that these questions are being asked reflects a recognition of the competition between intensive care and other developing health care technologies for societal resources and other valued goods and services. Thus, the supply of intensive care is not unlimited. When such a valued resource is constrained, questions of how it should be distributed inevitably arise. Moreover, recent changes in the financing and delivery of health care are changing the historical influences on the development and provision of intensive care. This chapter will review the growth and current distribution of intensive care resources, as well as the possible causes and consequences of these patterns. Issues related to the allocation of societal resources to intensive care versus other health and welfare programs (that is, macroallocation) and the allocation of existing intensive care resources among patients (that is, microallocation) will also be discussed.

PATTERNS OF INTENSIVE CARE

Intensive care has grown rapidly during the last two decades. Stimulated by the development of life-saving and monitoring techniques requiring specialized personnel and equipment, intensive care units (ICUs) developed in a relatively uncontrolled fashion. Their spread was facilitated by the predominance of cost-reimbursement as a means of financing hospital care and the lack of hospital internal constraints on creating intensive care units. The approximately 80,000 intensive care beds currently available in U.S. hospitals are estimated to account for more than 15 percent of hospital charges. Almost 95 percent of acute care hospitals reportedly have intensive care beds.

The widespread availability of intensive care beds has made this type of care the current standard practice in many instances. Many patients who are at high risk for experiencing a complication requiring prompt treatment are now admitted to intensive care for monitoring.[1] Intensive care is now considered routine following many complicated surgeries, and it is quickly becoming the norm for treating acute exacerbations of chronic and terminal conditions. Since intensive care beds have been increasingly available in many facilities, the criteria for admission have been lowered. Thus, the growing number of beds has influenced clinical decision making toward the use of intensive care whenever it may be helpful.[2]

Concern about this growing use has led us to research on the types of patients receiving intensive care and the degree to which they are benefitting. Knaus et al. found that there were two types of patients who did not seem to derive much benefit from treatment in an intensive care unit.[3] Patients admitted for routine monitoring (20%), who were at such low risk that their ICU admissions could have been deferred, constituted one group. A second group included those admitted for cardiovascular and respiratory support, even though death was imminent.

It is unclear whether patients who are expected to die soon actually use large amounts of intensive care resources to little avail. Knaus et al. found that patients with written Do Not Resuscitate (DNR) orders used 13 percent of ICU resources before, and 3 percent after, the order was written.[3] A somewhat different picture emerges from another study. Youngner et al. found that ICU patients who were ultimately declared DNR were the highest consumers of resources, both before and after the orders were written.[4]

Since the elderly constitute a large percentage of those treated in intensive care, questions have been raised about their utilization patterns and clinical decisions made regarding their care. Although elderly patients do not stay in intensive care longer than younger patients, they do require more interventions and have a lower survival rate (for example, there is 44% mortality for those over 65 years old, as opposed to 21.8% for those aged 55-64). Elderly patients are generally admitted to intensive care for exacerbations of chronic conditions, rather than acute illness.[5] The fact that charges for younger nonsurvivors in one study were higher than those for elderly nonsurvivors suggests that the most aggressive treatment may be reserved for younger patients.[5] Decisions to limit use of intensive care may also be inferred from the finding that the 5.2 percent of ICU patients who entered from nursing homes did not differ greatly from the population over 65 in nursing homes.[6] Given the chronically ill nature and high mortality of the nursing home population, one would expect nursing home transfers to account for a higher percentage of ICU admissions, if most of the seriously ill or dying patients in this group were admitted. It is likely that hospital and nursing home clinicians make decisions to not treat all patients aggressively.

The degree to which the high costs of intensive care produce positive outcomes is important in determining the justification for intensive care. Studies have demonstrated the effectiveness of intensive care for respiratory failure[7] and other selected groups of critically ill patients. For example, Wagner et al. found that study patients classified as being the most severely ill consumed large amounts of resources in intensive care units, but received treatments that could not have been given on the wards.[1] The two-month mortality rate for these patients was 54 percent.

It is disconcerting, however, to discover that the costs of intensive care are often highest for those with the worst outcomes.[8] Knaus found that the most severely ill patients constituted only 4 percent of the ICU admissions, but consumed 8 percent of the resources; most of them (92%) died within six months of hospitalization.[3] Another study found that the most critically ill and costly patients had a one-year death rate of 73 percent.[9] When the same study was performed eight years earlier, this group had a similar death rate, suggesting that improved technology had not affected the outcome.[10] Parno et al. found that hospital charges were highest for those patients who died in the hospital after spending time in the ICU.[11] In fact, there seems to be a U-shaped relationship between intensive care costs and the probability of death. Using a severity of illness measure on 613 consecutive admissions to the ICU, Scheffler et al. identified three groups of patients.[12] Forty-five percent of the admissions used 19 percent of the total resources consumed, with the probability of death decreasing as resource consumption increased; their diagnoses were mainly acute, including ketoacidosis, cardiac arrest, and reversible shock. Another 46 percent of the patients were in a group in which the probability of death did not vary with resource consumption; this group consumed 57 percent of the resources. The other 9 percent of the patients consumed 24 percent of the resources, and the probability of death rose markedly with increased resource consumption.

Prognostic uncertainty also seems to contribute to high ICU costs. Detsky et al. published a study which divided patients into survivors and nonsurvivors.[13] The entire group of nonsurvivors cost more than survivors. Of the nonsurvivors, those with a good prognosis cost more than those with a clearly poor prognosis. These study findings suggest that clinicians are more likely to treat aggressively when a prognosis is uncertain, but there is some hope.

The above studies reflect many of the current concerns about the high cost of intensive care relative to outcomes. Yet, the adequate assessment of the cost effectiveness of intensive care involves methodological problems. Studies that uncover the high costs of intensive care for particular groups of patients are based on charges for an episode of care—usually a hospital or ICU admission. There are several flaws in this approach. First, charges do not necessarily reflect resource consumption, especially in terms of nursing care. Patients receiving both intensive and routine care consume widely varying amounts of nursing time. In fact, ICU patients who receive routine monitoring may consume less personnel time than ward patients, a fact which is not reflected in the room charges. Routine monitoring patients cost less than their bed charges in intensive care, while sicker patients can cost much more than their charges.[1] Traditional step-down methods of cost calculation do not take these differences in resource consumption into account. The flaw in this approach is that most studies use a hospital stay as the unit of analysis, rather than a patient's total consumption of health care in a given period. Because patients in intensive care typically have more costly stays, people tend to assume that they are the most costly group of patients in the health care system. Yet, studies that focus on the patient over time as the unit of analysis have found that the ICU patients cost less per year than chronic patients who are repeatedly admitted for routine care.[14] Thus, while the per diem and per admission costs of intensive care patients are high and are rightly areas of concern, they should be viewed in the context of the total hospital costs, which may be more attributable to chronic, not critical, illness.

Despite the difficulties in assessing costs, there is still a question as to whether we devote more than the optimal amount of resources to intensive care. One useful approach to this issue might be a comparison of our intensive care expenditures with those in Great Britain, where medical practice and science are similar. The per capita cost of British hospital care, after adjustment for salary differences, is less than one half of the cost in the United States. The supply of health care is controlled through a nationally fixed budget; primary care physicians control access to specialists in hospitals. There are one-fifth to one-tenth as many intensive care beds relative to the population in Great Britain as there are in U.S. hospitals.[15] While British physicians generally report that they could use more intensive care beds, they believe this would pull resources from other needed programs. Despite these differences, life expectancy and general medical practice in the two countries are quite similar.

The preceding data suggest that the available technology and the related costs of intensive care are growing rapidly, and constitute a noteworthy portion of health care expenditures. Further, these expenditures may not always result in sufficient benefits. In order to understand the implications of this trend, one must be able to predict the future status of the population most at risk for receiving intensive care.

In the next few decades, rising life expectancy and a decline in mortality is expected to lead to higher morbidity, especially from the killer diseases. New advances in treatment will continue to lengthen the onset of the time between terminal phases of illness and death.[16] Thus, the need for care of the critically and terminally ill is expected to increase in the short run, placing growing demand on intensive care units. In the long run, however, primary prevention of these killer diseases is expected to improve. Prevention will also lead to lowered mortality from killer diseases and higher prevalence rates for the chronic non-killer diseases—which will probably require more chronic, rather than critical, care. Thus, in the more distant future, chronic care needs are apt to compete more directly for critical care resources.[17]

Macroallocation: Intensive Care versus Other Health Services

Issues based on technological developments, high costs, growing numbers of both critically and chronically ill patients, and limits on societal resources devoted to health care will increasingly focus attention on both societal and institutional allocation of health care resources. Previously, however, there have been few restraints on the percentage of total health care allocated to intensive care, and little willingness to confront the reality of resource limits. In fact, the resources devoted to intensive care have increased, while preventive and primary care programs have been constrained. One reason for intensive care's immunity may be the fact that life-saving medical services are consistent with a societal view of human life as priceless. While individuals may "ignore health hazards and avoid prompt treatment of illness suggesting that they often value other outcomes more than health, not to do everything near the point of death is difficult to accept and still maintain a humanitarian self-image."[18]

Another explanation for the discrepancy between the growth of intensive care and that of other types of programs is the distinction between identifiable and statistical lives. Preventive programs are usually designed and evaluated on the basis of epidemiological data and statistical evidence regarding the probabilities of illness under certain conditions. The thousands of children who will be impaired by inadequate prenatal diets and resulting low birthweight remain anonymous. On the other hand, the possibility of you or I or another critically ill person not receiving care that has even a remote chance of saving us brings us in direct symbolic contact with individuals and their mortality.[18-20]

The importance we attach to the symbolic value of life-saving care is evidenced by our choices regarding resource macroallocation to health programs.[21] Yankauer discusses this issue in relation to recent cutbacks in the women, infants, and children (WIC) program, a nutritional program for pregnant mothers and newborns.[22] While other countries provide these types of basis services to all their citizens, we seem compelled to justify their extension with tax dollars in terms of direct results in other areas—such as reduced infant mortality. Yet, twice as much money has been spent on making the benefits of an end-stage renal disease (ESRD) program universally available (that is, 1 billion on WIC as opposed to 2 billion on ESRD). Public and private insurance programs ensure the universal availability of coronary bypass operations. The existence of these services need not be justified by proving that they result in other benefits, such as greater employment or productivity. Our tendency not to question these infrequently used but very costly services is in direct opposition to our position on basic and less costly services.

The existence of these types of implicit macroallocation decisions is illustrated by Cook County Hospital, where 30 percent of the women delivering infants have had no prenatal care. Yet, continued governmental cuts of prenatal programs are accompanied by the mandate that all efforts be made to save seriously ill newborns and provide neonatal intensive care. The estimated cost of prenatal care is approximately $200 per child; intensive care fees range from $15,000 to $45,000 per child.[23]

The existence of a technological imperative in health care provides an additional explanation for the relatively unbridled growth of intensive care. A common viewpoint has been that if something can be done it should be done.[23] Further, the technological treatment innovations provided in intensive care have not been subjected to the same controls as other types of treatments and programs. The widespread use of new drugs and food additives must be preceded by extremely rigorous experimental evidence of efficiency and safety. Social welfare programs, such as day care and employment training, are severely cut if cost-effective results cannot be demonstrated. The diffusion of medical technological innovations, on the other hand, is only subject to indirect control, primarily through the lack of immediate reimbursement for procedures which are considered experimental. Initial reimbursement, however, is not based on uniform demands for proof of efficacy or benefit.

Public resistance to direct confrontation of the possibility of limited resources for life-saving treatment is reflected in opinion polls that oppose medical care rationing, even for those with little hope of recovery; 61 percent were opposed in one survey. Yet, restrictive public policy suggests an unwillingness to completely assume the costs for those who are medically indigent.[19] The difficulty in reconciling these inconsistent attitudes may partially account for the failure to openly consider the problems of resource allocation to critical care.

The experience with the end-stage renal disease program illustrates society's difficulty in making tough choices with regard to life-saving treatments. The federal government reacted to limited supplies of dialysis by making complete coverage for this disease a universal entitlement. While the enormous cost of this experience ($1.2 billion in 1980, with annual growth rate of 37% since inception) with an early life-saving technology suggests that this will not occur again, it does demonstrate how far our society will go to avoid the issue.[24]

Despite the lack of direct efforts to control the development and growth of intensive care, there are several mechanisms that have the potential to affect its supply. Certificate of need (CON) programs have attempted to control health care costs by restricting excessive or duplicative services. Although CON was a prerequisite for large capital expenditures in all states but Louisiana by 1980, it is difficult to detect any CON-related limitations on intensive care. In fact CON programs have apparently decreased the number of beds while increasing hospital assets per bed. Thus, there seem to have been general per diem increases in costs and intensity of care.[25] Only a few instances can be cited in which CON programs have controlled the growth of intensive care beds or other technology; such instances seem to result from the combination of a CON program and state rate-setting activities.[26]

Since the need for intensive care is directly proportional to technological development, controlling the growth of technology can indirectly slow the growth of intensive care. Technological development can be reduced by limiting research funds, and there is some evidence that this is occurring at the federal level. To the extent that intensive technologies are profitable, however, the private sector can be expected to invest in research and development efforts. Recent work on the artificial heart illustrates this type of private investment. Consideration is also being given to the use of a more thorough government review process as a means of controlling technology. Both new and existing technological innovations and procedures may be subjected to an effectiveness assessment prior to their adoption and reimbursement in the future.[27]

Recent changes in health care financing are influencing hospitals' incentives for supplying intensive care. Prospective payment based on diagnostic-related groups (DRGs) currently includes no differential for ICU care. Yet, the cost of care in an intensive care unit may well exceed the payment levels for medical DRGs that most commonly occur in intensive care.[28] Since patients receiving intensive care will produce financial losses for the hospital, the current payment system is likely to influence the supply of intensive care beds. Intensive care has flourished under a system in which the costs were more nearly reimbursable; in fact, cross-subsidization often resulted in payments that exceeded costs—for example, ancillary services. As funding continues to move in the direction of prospective payment, rather than cost reimbursement, hospital officials may decide that limiting the quantity of intensive care beds is preferable to attracting large numbers of critically ill patients and incurring financial loss.

The budgetary process in Great Britain effectively limits the availability of intensive care and other life-saving technologies—a practice that does not currently occur in the United States. This results in some clear patterns of resource allocation.[1 5] There are more restrictions on care for the elderly than there are for the young. Life-saving treatments have been curtailed less than those that improve quality of life—that is, elective admissions to hospitals are delayed. Treatments involving expensive equipment or new technology are also restricted. These limits are subtly manifested in physician behavior and practice patterns. Physicians, for example, do not recommend dialysis for older patients or those with other serious complications. Patients accept these recommendations with little question because they are consistent with standard medical practice. Although physicians justify decisions not to institute or to discontinue aggressive treatments as medically appropriate, they also seem cognizant of supply restrictions. Thus, the standards of medical practice have been adjusted to conform to the constraints imposed by limited resources.[1 5]

The rising level of debate and discussion suggests increasing recognition of the fact that health care resources are not unlimited;[2 9] doing more of one thing may mean having to do less of something else. Yet, difficult ethical and political concerns are involved in addressing these dilemmas of macroallocation. Many new questions of equity, fairness, and feasibility arise. Should a technology be available to all with equal need, or, are there some basic types of services that should be guaranteed for all, beyond which the individual would assume responsibility? Gutmann argued that "a principle of equal access to health care demands that every person who shares the same type and degree of health need must be given an equally effective chance of receiving appropriate treatment of equal quality so long as that treatment is available to anyone."[3 0] This suggests that while society is not obligated to provide any particular intensity of care, all persons with similar needs must have an equally effective chance of receiving any available high technology services, such as heart transplants. Such a principle places limits upon freedom of purchase, especially for the wealthiest members of our society.

Currently available methods of controlling expenditures on intensive care also pose ethical problems. Limitations which only apply to new technology and are enforced by payment restrictions could result in an inequity—in other words, there would be no restrictions on people needing older technologies, while those who could possibly benefit from new technologies would face limitations. For example, most people with kidney disease could be saved, but those with liver disease could not.

Using prospective payment to control intensity of care also poses dilemmas. Because the current method provides incentives for hospitals to treat the healthiest patients within each DRG, those who require costly treatments, such as intensive care, may be avoided. While holding down costs, this method would create a system in which those with the greatest need might actually receive the least care. This undesirable effect could be diminished by adjusting prospective payment to reflect severity of illness differences within DRGs. If patients with more serious illnesses, who are presumably in greater need of intensive care, are paid accordingly, they might take priority for ICU admission over those who are less ill.

While the thought of limiting the growth of intensive care raises immediate concerns about equity and restriction of liberty, the failure to limit intensive care in the face of scarce health care resources also produces ethical dilemmas. The fact that intensive care has been made widely available with little regard to age or health status suggests that our society has opted for extending life whenever possible. To the degree that this has restricted our ability to fund other types of programs, we may have reduced the possibility of maximizing the length and quality of life for all, while extending it for a few who become critically ill. Thus, the issue may really involve allocation for either preventive medicine or life-prolonging care. From one perspective, prevention may be a more effective means of raising the general level of health and quality of life. But it could lead to the neglect of needy persons who could directly benefit from the resources of intensive care. Resolving this issue requires weighing the goal of maximum cost-efficiency against the costly needs of a relatively small number of individuals.

Microallocation: Rationing Intensive Care Among Patients

It seems inevitable that the resources available for health care will be restricted. Within these limitations, it also seems likely that the supply of expensive technologies, such as intensive care, will be constrained. These facts raise the problem of how the available intensive care resources should be distributed. How much should go to which technologies and which patients? How will this rationing be implemented, and how will hospitals, physicians, and patients react?

Methods of allocating any scarce resource, such as intensive care, typically reflect one or more principles of distribution. The principles may be implicit or explicit; they may or may not be defensible from an ethical point of view or be practical to implement. Commonly cited justifications for distributing scarce societal resources to certain individuals include:

- the person's merit or past contributions;
- overcoming past wrongs done to the person (e.g., compensatory programs);
- severity of need;
- the amount of effort or other resources the person can exchange for services;
- an effort to distribute the resource equitably;
- an effort to produce the greatest good for society.

There is already some implicit rationing with regard to intensive care. Resource allocation at several levels determines whether a patient with a life-threatening condition receives intensive care. First, does the patient reach a hospital that offers intensive care? The geographic distribution of intensive care units and the patient's medical insurance status may determine the answer to this question. For example, there are currently fewer intensive care beds in rural areas, public hospitals, and hospitals that serve the poor.[31] Further, if the patient is either institutionalized or being cared for in the home, the providers' decisions about patient transfer may actually determine whether intensive care is received. Second, is the hospitalized patient admitted to an intensive care unit? The answer will be partially based on whether the patient's medical condition is judged serious enough to require intensive care and the possibility of benefit from intensive care. It will further be affected by the availability of an intensive care bed; if no bed is available, the decision will depend on whether this patient's need or potential to benefit is greater or lesser than those of other patients. It could also be affected by nonmedical considerations, such as patient and family preferences, judgments about the patient's social value, or the patient's financial situation.

Finally, what treatments are provided to the patient in the ICU? Although treatment decisions typically depend upon the patient's present medical condition, they are also influenced by prognosis, patient and family wishes, and staff reactions to caring for the patient. Treatment limitations may manifest themselves in the form of an explicit order, such as "do not resuscitate," or in a series of choices to not do everything possible.

At every point in this rationing process, several questions can be raised. First, are the decisions based on accurate facts and adequate analysis of the facts? Most problematic in this regard are attempts to estimate prognoses and predict the benefits to be gained from intensive care in general, as well as specific treatments. This aspect of decision making may be facilitated by protocols and indices which predict severity of illness, occurrence of complications, probability of mortality, and future functioning. Technological assessments and studies of treatment effectiveness will contribute to clinicians' ability to make these judgments accurately.

Second, are the decisions ethical? The ethical nature of these decisions is often viewed from the perspectives of the individual patient and clinician. When examined in this manner, the ethical concerns focus on protecting patient autonomy, fulfilling the clinician's obligation to do all that is best for the patient, and the clinician's duty to inform the patient about treatment options and their effects. However, because these decisions involve scarce resources, what is done for one patient will affect what can be done for other patients. Thus, the decisions must be examined simultaneously from the perspectives of patient groups and society as a whole. When this point of view is adopted, the major ethical consideration involves social justice, which asks whether patterns of treatment decisions are consistent with values such as fairness, equity, liberty, and maximum benefits for all.

Third, how can these decisions be made practically? What processes of clinical and patient decision making will facilitate both accurate factual analysis and ethical behaviors or outcomes?

Although rationing guidelines have seldom been made explicit, several implicit forms of health care rationing do exist. Using a method based on economics, a limited resource is given only to those who can pay. Thus, government financing, third party payor decisions, and the societal distribution of wealth actually determine who receives the service. Rationing based on economics occurs in intensive care when patients with little or no insurance are denied hospital admission, not scheduled for elective procedures, or die outside the hospital from conditions for which individuals with better insurance coverage would have been under medical supervision. The theory that the market is the most efficient allocator of resources has many supporters; it is often argued that this theory is not applicable to health care because limited knowledge or finances prevent many people from satisfying their desires through the marketplace.

A second method of implicit rationing is manifested in practical and administrative decisions.[32] For example, a person will not be moved from an intensive care bed because another patient is waiting (that is, first-come-first-served). Another illustration involves the provision of slightly less nursing time for each patient when the supply of nursing resources is short (that is, equal rationing).

A third rationing mechanism is based on nonmedical patient characteristics, some of which may reflect "social value." The limited supply of intensive care in rural areas serves to limit its availability to rural residents. There are also examples of rationing on the basis of race. The Indian Health Services, for instance, stopped funding dialysis, organ transplants, and other procedures in 1983, even though they are available to most other individuals.[20] The use of socioeconomic status as an implicit criterion for rationing medical care is exemplified by an examination of transfers from private to public hospitals. Ten percent of those transferred were found to be seriously jeopardized by the move; most of those transferred were young, uninsured, and minority patients.[33]

Rationing based on health status or need has seldom been made explicit, but is reflected in norms and practice patterns within institutions. Needs assessment can affect resource provision in two directions. Those with the most severe illnesses may be given the most resources because their needs are greatest; alternatively, they may be given fewer resources, because the benefit to them and society is judged to be minimal. For example, patients with DNR orders or terminally ill patients may receive fewer life-saving treatments or be denied admission to intensive care units. While not explicitly documented, decisions to forego specific life-sustaining treatment interventions (for example, dialysis, transfusions, antibiotics, hyperalimentation, and others) are sometimes made for patients whose condition is deemed hopeless.

In Great Britain, where resource limits have been acknowledged for some time, physicians implement rationing of care on the basis of health status. Certain expensive treatments are just not recommended for certain patients; for example, renal dialysis is considered inadvisable for older patients. The system makes denial of care seem routine and even optimal.[15]

Effective rationing on the basis of health status requires precise predictions of the benefits of particular treatments for particular patients. Recent investigations have focused on the degree to which various patients can be expected to benefit from intensive care. Attempts have been made to assess the risk of complications for patients who are often admitted to ICUs for monitoring. For example, a protocol developed to aid in acute chest pain diagnosis has substantially increased the efficiency of ICU admissions. The protocol reduced the number of false positive ICU admissions, while increasing the true negatives and maintaining the true positive rate.[3][4] The experience at Massachusetts General Hospital suggests the potential savings that may result from reduced monitoring admissions. When the number of intensive care beds was temporarily reduced, low-risk patients were not admitted to the ICU—with no negative results.[3][5]

Identifying patients who have an extremely poor chance of hospital survival regardless of care intensity is another means of resource rationing based on health status. Single factors or diagnostic categories have not been successful in identifying subgroups of patients with a high probability of death.[3][6] However, APACHE, a multi-attributable measure of severity of illness, has proven to be a good predictor of ICU mortality and resource consumption within selected diagnostic categories.[3] A much more controversial approach to rationing care would involve the assessment of future quality of life if the patient survives the ICU stay.

Another means of resource rationing is to limit treatment for patients already in the ICU. Little is known about how clinicians decide to institute or cease specific treatments. For example, some studies suggest that resource expenditures may be reduced when patients are declared DNR,[1] while others find no such limitation.[4] With the exception of cardiopulmonary resuscitation, where factors predicting nonsurvival have been identified,[3][7] few guidelines are available for specific procedures.

Terminal illness, an indicator of health status, makes patients ineligible for ICU admission in a few places, but this is not the norm. While patients have a right to refuse life-sustaining treatment, circumstances or the patient's own condition often preclude the effective exercise of this right. In the absence of a clear and cogent request not to do so, physicians often feel obligated to "do everything." Critics ask whether these cases result in an unreasonable amount of resource expenditures.[1,16] Some hospitals have used a classification of terminally ill patients to indicate the degree of treatment to be instituted when life is threatened. Levels range from those patients who are eligible for cardiopulmonary resuscitation and all other interventions to those who should receive only general nursing, hydration, nutrition, and comfort measures.[3][8] While the importance of patient and family involvement in decision making is stressed, the influence of the options presented by the physician is recognized.

Implicit or explicit rationing of intensive care entails clinical, ethical, and legal dilemmas. Clinicians often seem reluctant to use statistical predictors of health status to determine care, even if past experience predicts 100 percent mortality. The rationale is that while survival may be unprecedented, it may not be impossible. Studies also suggest that human decision makers are limited in their abilities to simultaneously process multiple criteria and their related probabilities.[39] Further, even when denial or termination of care is clinically, ethically, and legally justifiable, the emotional reactions of caregivers and family affect clinical decisions.

The individual clinician who must make rationing decisions is faced with a psychological and ethical struggle. The clinician's relationship with the patient involves ethical obligations; yet these duties to the individual patient invariably conflict with societal considerations. Because it results from resource scarcity, the concept of rationing must use society, as opposed to the individual, as the unit of analysis. Thus, guidelines for allocation of intensive care resources must be developed when one is not confronting an individual patient in need. Explicit criteria are essential to the promotion of practice patterns that are consistent with an ethical distribution of scarce resources.

The predominant ethical question applicable to general criteria for rationing intensive care, as opposed to bedside decision making about individual patients, is the degree to which the use of the criteria result in a just distribution of resources. A review of alternative conceptualizations of distributive justice is beyond the scope of this book.[40] However, two somewhat contrasting viewpoints are frequently offered in discussions of the ethical aspects of rationing. One focuses on a utilitarian or cost-benefit consideration, and the other focuses on equity.

From a utilitarian perspective, methods of rationing intensive care would be considered just if they resulted in the greatest total amount of benefit to all—that is, the greatest good for the greatest number.[41] In other words, treatment should be given to those critically ill individuals most likely to exhibit positive results—for example, survival, improved functioning, reduced morbidity, maximum life satisfaction, productivity, or any other outcomes judged to be desirable by both the individuals involved and society as a whole. At the same time, caring for these individuals should not interfere with the provision of care that produces more total benefits to society. Triage, as practiced in battlefield medicine, is an example of a rationing procedure that seems consistent with a utilitarian view. Patients who are critically injured but also most likely to recover following treatment are given priority over those whose injuries are less immediately dangerous or those with poor prognoses. Although the utilitarian conception of justice has received considerable attention and explication, its use in judging criteria for rationing intensive care is problematic.[42] Critics of utilitarianism, including John Rawls,[43] note that the concept is fraught with both practical and moral problems. The practical problem entails the quantification and aggregation of the total benefits that would accrue from the distribution of a resource in a certain way. The total benefits cannot be calculated by considering the gross numbers of people helped; consideration must also be given to what else could have been done with the resources. It is difficult to compare the benefits accruing to ten people who each receive 50 days of ICU care with those of 100 people who receive five days each. It is also difficult to judge how much a day of extended life for a patient may affect the total benefits to family and society. Simply stated, the greatest good for the greatest number principle lacks an operational method for determining the relative benefits of resources for different groups of people.

There are also moral problems within the utilitarian view. It has been argued that defining justice as that which produces the greatest good for the greatest number enables societal tolerance of the exploitation or suffering of a small minority—even, for example, an institution as abhorrent as slavery. The application of this principle to intensive care might dictate the nontreatment of a few very costly critically ill patients for whom death was imminent, even if the patients strongly desired a few more days of life. Such practice conflicts with the value placed on patient autonomy and rights. The utilitarian principle is typically applied within the context of other competing or higher order principles. In Mill's original work on utilitarianism, the accompanying principle was the concept of "maximum liberty for all."[41] In current discussions of intensive care, the goals of maximizing patient autonomy and preserving the physician's duty to act in ways that benefit the patient are essential. Rationing criteria that reflect utilitarian considerations would, therefore, need to be combined with methods for eliciting the patient's own judgments of benefits and affirming the duties of health care providers.

The egalitarian perspective for judging rationing mechanisms places priority on the value of equity—specifically, to what extent does the method of distributing resources treat individuals equitably?[30,43] Equitable treatment should not be confused with equal treatment. Equal treatment, such as that which is characteristic of a first-come-first-served or lottery approach, may also be just if peoples' needs and abilities to claim resources are equal. However, equal treatment will seldom be equitable with respect to intensive care because people differ markedly in their need for, and access to, intensive care. The egalitarian principle put forward by Rawls argues that people should generally be treated equally.[43] Unequal treatment is justified if it benefits the most needy or disadvantaged. In the case of intensive care, this suggests that people whose needs are similar be treated equally; when resources are scarce, those with the greatest needs are to be benefitted. Approaches to rationing which are consistent with a cost-benefit perspective but restrict access to a particular life-saving technology, such as the artificial heart, may be questioned on the basis of an equity principle (that is, all those with equal need do not receive hearts).

Need assessment constitutes the major practical difficulty in judging rationing mechanisms according to their contribution to equity. While progress has been made in measuring deviation from normal physiological status,[44] there are currently no methods for assessing the patient's subjective experience of being critically ill.[45] The patient's degree of suffering, discomfort, distress, and anxiety would certainly be an essential component of need under a system that allows unequal treatment when it benefits the most disadvantaged.

Several aspects of the egalitarian perspective present ethical difficulties. Those who have the greatest need are likely to be in an extremely deteriorated condition. Despite their consumption of vast amounts of resources, many of these individuals would die, leaving other less severely ill individuals without access to critical care. Further, this principle might impose inordinate demands upon all health care resources, thus restricting the supply of more basic types of primary and preventive care.[40]

Proponents of a libertarian view are likely to criticize both egalitarian and utilitarian allocation schemes for intensive care.[46] Allocation of valued resources on the basis of need or potential benefit would interfere with the unrestricted exchange of the marketplace, in which individuals freely exchange their holdings. Libertarians would argue that those individuals who place the greatest value on intensity of care in the event of their own critical illnesses could freely choose to insure themselves for such eventualities, thereby guaranteeing unlimited access. It would be argued that these individual choices should not be restricted by any rationing mechanisms.

While ethical and practical dilemmas make rationing intensive care difficult to contemplate, fear of malpractice litigation has probably been a more direct determinant of its unrestricted use in the United States. The U.S. tendency to believe that technology can solve most problems, and to respond to failure by seeking to pinpoint blame or liability, has been cited as a factor that would make open rationing extremely risky. The perceived threat of a lawsuit is often cited as a reason for patients being admitted to ICUs for monitoring. However, clearer monitoring and ICU admission criteria would be likely to set new standards of medical practice; this would lower concern about malpractice, which is typically defined as deviation from the norm. It is instructive to note that little malpractice litigation has resulted from the prevalent rationing in Great Britain.[15] One explanation for this phenomenon is the fact that British attorneys require payment for handling these cases regardless of the outcome; contingency fees are not allowed. Also, malpractice suits are typically based on the argument that the patient received care that deviated from standard medical practice. In Great Britain, where ICU care is not the standard for many conditions, failure to provide it is not judged as deviant. Therefore, this argument is not the basis for successful litigation.

CONCLUSIONS

It seems clear that unrestricted consumption of health care resources in critical illness conflicts with other health and welfare needs within society. Changes in payment mechanisms for hospital care and new developments in technology assessment and control suggest that we will soon experience limits on the availability of intensive care. This supply restriction can be attributed to the rising demands created by the population's aging and the increased life span of the chronically and terminally ill. These trends will inevitably lead to recognition of the need to ration intensive care.

In rationing intensive care, it will be necessary to create a balance between explicit criteria that guard against discrimination and promote distributive justice, and implicit judgments that allow some consideration of unique or subjective factors.[2] Reducing ICU admissions of patients who need only routine monitoring and are at low risk for complications seems to be a promising area for rationing criteria which are consistent with both egalitarian and utilitarian views of justice. Limiting care for patients who have little potential for survival or quality of life is another potential area for saving substantial resources.

Although restricting the development of new but expensive life-saving technologies also promises to reduce expenditures, this will be more controversial from an ethical point of view.

Decision makers in ICUs would be better able to deal with the problem of rationing if there were less uncertainty regarding prognosis and expected benefits of care. Studies of the natural history of intensive care illnesses, as well as studies that pinpoint clinical predictors for patients at high risk of complications, would help in this regard.[2]

The organizational structure of ICUs will also affect the ability to allocate resources fairly. The use of something other than a first-come-first-served or random approach requires a comparative view of needs, benefits, and demands across a population. Equitable rationing (that is, allocation) would require ICU directors who could consider all patients in decision making, rather than just their own.[2]

Public policy and the health benefits policies of employers and insurers will provide a context in which medical center rationing will take place. Policy changes, such as the recent use of DRGs for prospective payment, are often implemented with little consideration of their potential effect on the allocation of intensive care. Yet, these effects may be serious, and need to be analyzed in terms of their distributional consequences.[28,47]

Any mechanisms for allocating intensive care will work only insofar as they have widespread support. Thus, rationing criteria cannot produce situations that seem outrageous, upsetting, or unfair to clinicians, patients, or the public at large. The experience in Great Britain is an example of an evolved consensus, in which the practice patterns developed in response to limits are generally accepted; the extraordinary is neither desired nor considered reasonable by most people. Most Americans would have difficulty accepting the limited availability of intensive care. However, despite this lack of acceptance, the process of managing scarce intensive care resources seems to be underway in the United States, and will require research, scholarly analysis, and public debate. Clinicians, researchers, philosophers, social scientists, politicians, and consumers will all be involved in the evolving system of intensive care allocation.

REFERENCES

1. Wagner DP, Wineland TD, Knaus WA: The hidden costs of treating severely ill patients: Charges and resource consumption in an intensive care unit. *Hlth Care Financing Rev* 1983, 5:81-86.

2. Mulley AG: The allocation of resources for medical intensive care. In President's Commission for the Study of Ethical Problems in Medicine and Biomedical and Behavioral Research: *Securing Access to Health Care* (Vol. 3). Washington, D.C.: U.S. Government Printing Office, 1981, pp. 285-311.

3. Knaus WA, Draper EA, Wagner DP: The use of intensive care: New research initiatives and their implications for national health policy. *Milbank Mem Fund Qtrly* 1983, *61*:561-583.

4. Youngner S, Lewandowski W, McClish D, et al.: The incidence and implications of DNR orders in a medical intensive care unit. *JAMA* 1985, *253*:54-57.

5. Campion EW, Mulley AG, Goldstein RL, et al.: Medical intensive care for the elderly. *JAMA* 1981, *246*:2052-2056.

6. Goldstein RL, Campion EW, Mulley AG, Thibault GE: Nursing home patients admitted to a medical intensive care unit. *Med Care* 1984, *22*:854-862.

7. Knaus WA, Thibault GE: Intensive care units today. In McNeil BJ, Cravelha EG (eds.): *Critical Issues in Medical Technology*. Boston: Auburn House Publishing Company, 1982, pp. 193-215.

8. Seitovsky AA: The high cost of dying: What do the data show? *Milbank Mem Fund Qtrly* 1984, *62*:591-608.

9. Cullen DJ, Keene R, Waternaux C, et al.: Results, charges, and benefits of intensive care for critically ill patients: Update 1983. *Crit Care Med* 1984, *12*:102-106.

10. Cullen DJ, Ferrara LC, Gilbert J, et al.: Indicators of intensive care in critically ill patients. *Crit Care Med* 1977, *5*:173-179.

11. Parno JR, Teres D, Lemeshow S, Brown RB: Hospital charges and long-term survival of ICU versus non-ICU patients. *Crit Care Med* 1982, *10*:569-574.

12. Scheffler RM, Knaus WA, Wagner DP, Zimmerman JE: Severity of illness and the relationship between intensive care and survival. *Am J Pub Hlth* 1982, *72*:449-454.

13. Detsky AS, Stricker SC, Mulley AG, Thibault GE: Prognosis, survival, and the expenditure of hospital resources for patients in an intensive-care unit. *N Engl J Med* 1981, *305*:667-672.

14. Zook CJ, Moore FD: High-cost users of medical care. *N Engl J Med* 1980, *302*:996-1002.

15. Aaron HJ, Schwartz WB: *The painful prescription: Rationing hospital care.* Washington, D.C.: The Brookings Institute, 1984, pp. 1-160.

16. Bayer R, Callahan D, Fletcher J, et al.: The care of the terminally ill: Morality and economics. *N Engl J Med* 1983, *309*:1490-1494.

17. Verbrugge L: Longer life but worsening health? Trends in health and mortality of middle-aged and older persons. *Milbank Mem Fund Qtrly* 1984, *62*:475-519.

18. Blumstein JF: Rationing medical resources; A constitutional, legal, and policy analysis. *Texas Law Rev* 1981, *59*:1345-1399.

19. Friedman E: Rationing and the identified life. *Hospitals* 1984, 65-72.

20. Evans RW: Health care technology and the inevitability of resource allocation and rationing decisions, Parts 1 and 2. *JAMA* 1983, *249*:2047-2053, 2208-2219.
21. Jellinek PS: Yet another look at medical cost inflation. *N Engl J Med* 1982, *307*:496-497.
22. Yankauer A: Science and social policy. *Am J Pub Hlth* 1984, *74*:1148-1149.
23. Richards G: Technology costs and rationing issues. *Hospitals* 1984, *58*: 80-81.
24. Health Care Financing Administration: *Medicare Data Book, 1983*. Washington, D.C.: Supt. of Documents, 1984.
25. Salkever D, Bice T: *Hospital certificate-of-needs control*. Washington, D.C., American Enterprise Institue, 1979.
26. Brown LD: Common sense meets implementation: Certificate-of-need regulation in the states. *J Hlth Politics, Policy and Law* 1983, *8*:480-494.
27. Office of Technology Assessment: *Health Technology Case Study No. 28: ICUs Clinical Outcomes, Costs and Decision Making*. Washington, D.C.: U.S. Government Printing Office, 1981.
28. Coulton CJ, McClish D, Doremus H, et al.: Implications of DRG payments for medical intensive care. *Med Care* 1985, *23*:977-985.
29. Thurow LC: Medicine versus economics. *N Engl J Med* 1985, *313*:611-614.
30. Gutmann A: For and against equal access to health care. *Milbank Mem Fund Qtrly/Health and Society* 1981, *59*:542-560.
31. Russel LB: *Technology in Hospitals: Medical Advances and their Diffusion*. Washington, D.C.: The Brookings Institution, 1979.
32. Coulton CJ, Rosenberg M: Social justice and rationing social services. *Sociology and Social Welfare* 1981, *8*:15-21.
33. Himmelstein DU, Woolhandler S, Harnly M, et al.: Patient transfers: Medical practice as social triage. *Am J Pub Hlth* 1984, *74*:494-497.
34. Goldman L, Weinberg M, Weisberg M, et al.: A computer-derived protocol to aid in the diagnosis of emergency room patients with acute chest pain. *N Engl J Med* 1982, *307*:588-596.
35. Singer DE, Carr PL, Mulley AG, Thibault GE: Rationing intensive care—physician responses to a resource shortage. *N Engl J Med* 1983, *309*:1155-1160.
36. Chassin MR: Costs and outcomes of medical intensive care. *Med Care* 1982, *20*:165-178.
37. Bedell SE, Delbanco TL, Coon EF, et al.: Survival after cardiopulmonary resuscitation in the hospital. *N Engl J Med* 1983, *309*:569-576.
38. Wanzer SH, Adelstein JS, Cranford RE, et al.: The physician's responsibility toward hopelessly ill patients. *N Engl J Med* 1984, *319*:955-959.
39. Weinstein M, Fineberg H, et al.: *Clinical Decision Making*. Philadelphia, Pa.: W.B. Saunders, Co., 1980.
40. Buchanan A: Justice: A philosophical review. In Shelp EE (ed.): *Justice and Health Care*. Dodrecht, Holland: D. Reidel Publishing Co., 1981; pp. 3-21.

41. Mill JS: On the connection between justice and utility. In Bedaw H (ed.): *Justice and Equality*. Englewood Cliffs, N.J.: Prentice-Hall, Inc., 1971.

42. Cassell E: To justice, love, mercy: The inappropriateness of the concept of justice applied to bedside decisions. In Shelp EE (ed.): *Justice and Health Care*. Dodrecht, Holland: D. Reidel Publishing Company, 1981, pp. 75-82.

43. Rawls J: *A Theory of Justice*. Cambridge, Mass.: Howard University Press, 1971.

44. Wagner DP, Knaus WA, Draper EA: Statistical validation of a severity of illness measure. *Am J Pub Hlth* 1983, *73*:878-884.

45. Bartlett ET: Persons and the measurement of illness. *Philosophy in Context* 1984, *14*:60-69.

46. Nozick R: *Anarchy State and Utopia*. New York: Basic Books, 1974.

47. Office of Technology Assessment: *Medical Technology and Costs of the Medicare Program*. Washington, D.C.: U.S. Congress, OTA-H-227, 1984.

5 The Introduction of Major Organ Transplantation on the State Level: Ethical and Practical Considerations in the Development of Public Policy

David L. Jackson and George J. Annas

Medical science has sought to reverse the effects of major organ failure for centuries. Most recently, there has been increasing emphasis on surgical techniques to replace diseased organs with healthy ones.

The first corneal transplant to restore sight was performed in 1905 by Dr. Zirm, an Austrian ophthalmologist. It was not until 1954, however, that Merrill and his colleagues in Boston performed the first kidney transplant between identical twins[1] ; the first cadaveric kidney transplant was performed in 1962. In the late 1950s, Welch (liver) and Shumway (heart) began to perform transplantations of major organs in animals. The first series of human liver transplants was performed by Starzl in the 1960s.[2] Bernard performed the first human heart transplant in South Africa in 1967. Although the patient died 18 days after surgery from an infectious complication of immuno-suppressive therapy, normal cardiac function was temporarily restored.

Aggressive heart transplantation was largely abandoned after the dismal results obtained in the first 100 operations performed at 60 different centers around the world in 1968 and 1969. Cyclosporin, a new drug introduced in 1977, has the ability to suppress rejection response in a relatively selective manner, while "sparing" those components of the immune system that fight infection.[3] While there is still real concern about the potential long-range side effects of cyclosporin therapy, its introduction has been a dramatic step forward in transplantation technology.[4,5]

The number of patients undergoing both heart and liver transplants has increased dramatically since the introduction of cyclosporin. By 1984, more than 800 heart transplants and 500 liver transplants had been performed worldwide. The availability of more effective immunosuppressive therapy, improved surgical technique, stricter patient selection criteria, and increased postoperative support have enabled 80 percent of heart transplantation patients to survive at least one year with normal heart function; approximately 60 percent will be alive five years postsurgery.[6] Survival for liver transplantation patients is now approximately 65 percent at one year, almost double the percentage of one-year survival only three or four years ago.[7]

In the midst of this explosion of technological capabilities, extraordinary amounts of public attention have been focused on transplantation-related issues. The interest in organ transplantation far exceeds its relative importance in the overall health care system. In many respects, transplants are no different than other extreme and expensive technologies. On the other hand, the introduction of heart and liver transplants provides a unique opportunity to use the public's interest as a rationale for examining important values in medical care. The reasons for societal interest in organ transplantation are complex. Although the technique is clearly "life-saving," transplantation is extremely expensive and its use has provoked the first open professional and public discussion of the serious issue of health care rationing. Since denial of transplantation strictly for financial reasons seems to place a price on life, it directly challenges our society's belief that "necessary" health care services should not be available only to the wealthy. Finally, the media has been able to identify and publicize, often intensely and repetitively, individual stories of the crises that surround potential transplant recipients, thus maximizing public impact and attention to the issue.

The need to meet heart and liver transplantation expenses (ranging from $75,000 to over $250,000) has resulted in media and bipartisan political exploitation of the plights of individual patients and families.[8] Families have been literally forced to beg on television and in the newspapers for funds to place their loved ones on active waiting lists for transplantation. Instead of fostering the development of any rational and equitable transplant policy, these actions have perpetuated a "queen for a day" mentality.

These tragic spectacles are often intensified by the interplay between the media and political forces. For example, Medicaid's refusal to cover the cost of a proposed transplant for a Massachusetts child led to a bitter war of words in the media. When the patient's father declared that the governor of Massachusetts would be "responsible for the death of my daughter," the state agreed to Medicaid coverage. The patient's father lamented, "After working all my life, they made a panhandler out of me." In another case, a hospital initially refused to admit a transplant patient, even though the family had pledged over $180,000 in real estate assets to cover the costs. The hospital insisted on the delivery of $100,000 in "liquid assets" before the patient would be placed on the waiting list.

Over the past two years, there have been an increasing number of politically motivated "ambulance chasers" who have used the media to publicize individual cases. This was dramatically demonstrated in the case of an 11-month-old Texas infant who had progressive liver failure. Although the Texas Medicaid program had never before agreed to cover the costs of liver transplantation, intense political pressure resulted in the hurried passage of legislation authorizing the payment for this *one* patient. The full weight of the state and federal governments was mobilized behind this particular patient's situation. On his weekly national radio broadcast, President Reagan announced that an Air Force jet was available to transport any donor organ that became available for the infant. Sadly, no donor organ was found in time and the child died. No other patient in Texas, before or since, has been authorized for a liver transplant under Medicaid. In fact, not long after this incident, a lack of political and media attention resulted in the denial of transplant coverage by the Texas Medicaid program to a two-year-old with a similar medical condition. We believe an "applause meter" lacks the sophistication necessary in making such difficult resource allocation and social/medical/ethical decisions.

Although a federal Task Force on Organ Transplantation began studying broader issues in early 1985, recent federal policy has focused mainly on the issue of donor organ availability. The federal government has also established an independent group, the American Council on Transplantation, whose goals include increasing public and professional education, improving donor identification and referrals, encouraging multiple organ availability from each donor, and working to assure equitable access. This approach to transplantation policy development is based on the assumption that the key issues are: shortage of suitable donors; lack of public awareness of the value of organ donation; lack of trained specialists in organ retrieval and appropriate facilities; lack of knowledge about techniques to improve organ preservation during the time between retrieval and transplantation. This approach tends to minimize the inefficiencies and problems inherent in the development of a fragmented private sector response, as well as the gaps that can result from this approach.

Dr. Edward Brandt, the former Secretary of Health and Human Services, has stated that the nation needs more centers of transplantation excellence. By assuming that we want to maximize the number of transplants without any concern for how many are appropriate, this approach is similar to the concentration on organ donation in putting the "cart before the horse." We believe it is most appropriate to proceed cautiously until a clear picture of transplantation's reasonable role in the health care system emerges. We must develop effective responses to the complex ethical and social dimensions of this expensive, limited access health care service, thus keeping the growth of this technology proportionate to its potential benefits.

Social and Ethical Considerations in the Design of Public Policy

For the past 20 years, health care in the United States has focused on providing *quality* services to all those in need; prior to that time, the major policy issue was access. Health care costs have not been a high priority in either health planning or professional education. While rationing of limited health care services was rarely openly discussed, it was frequently implicit in the functioning of parts of the health care system, particularly in intensive care settings. Now cost containment has become a central concern.

The challenge in the development of organ transplantation policy is to achieve an appropriate balance among three often competing goals in health care: quality of services; equity of access; cost containment. In light of the fact that citizens may freely cross state lines to seek medical assistance and the need to seek potential organ donors from many states to obtain a match for an individual transplant candidate, a *national* policy on organ transplantation seems imperative. State and federal governments must work with the health care professions to develop a rational, equitable, and effective transplant system, including an organ procurement program and a reasonable and fair reimbursement policy. The policies developed by Massachusetts and Ohio can be helpful to other states and the federal government.

The Massachusetts Task Force on Organ Transplantation[9]

Commissioned in September, 1983, the Task Force was composed of citizens representing a broad spectrum of perspectives. Following more than a year of deliberations, including 15 public meetings, its report was presented in October, 1984. The report's basic premises are: Transplants are extreme and expensive procedures that do not cure disease, but replace a patient's underlying disease with a lifetime of immunosuppression. Introducing transplantation into the current cost-contained health care system threatens to displace other, higher priority health care services, including services to the Medicaid population and the poor. Therefore, transplants should not be performed at all unless they are done "on those who are likely to benefit from them, total cost is controlled and resources are not diverted from higher priority care."[9] The Task Force concluded that public regulation through the determination of need (DON) process would be ineffective if the burden of proving priorities was placed on the Department of Public Health. Accordingly, the Task Force recommended that any hospital applying to do transplants within the DON process should have the burden of demonstrating that "transplantation has a higher priority than any other currently available health service from which organ transplantation diverts funds and/or support systems."

With regard to the underlying issues of fairness and equity, the Task Force concluded that access to a transplant should be "independent of the individual's ability to pay for it." Thus, if heart and liver transplants are offered as part of the health care system, they should be part of the "minimum benefit package" to which all are entitled. The Task Force believed that intelligent and strong regulation would enable the fully allocated average-one-year costs to be decreased substantially in a health care system similar to that of Massachusetts—that is, a prospective total revenue hospital reimbursement system characterized by excess capacity. Thus, a limited number of transplants could be "squeezed into" the existing system without increasing capital plant or decreasing other "higher priority" medical care. The Task Force was only able to recommend a controlled, phased trial of transplantation because of the "slack in the system." The group concluded that, "If it turns out that liver and heart transplantation take resources away from higher priority medical interventions, and decrease their accessibility to the public, these procedures should not be performed." Since it may be difficult to determine which existing medical procedures have higher priority, the Task Force concluded that the burden of proving that any existing, currently performed procedure has lower priority than organ transplantation should be on the hospital which proposes, in its DON application, to decrease or eliminate that existing health care service in order to do transplants.

During Phase I, the Task Force recommended that heart and liver transplants be done within existing negotiated prospective hospital budgets; the only allowable exceptional costs would be for the organ itself and for new immunosuppressive drugs. Such an arrangement would severely limit any financial incentive to do transplants. Hospitals doing such work would have to obtain a DON and agree to certain basic conditions, such as collecting evaluative data on the costs, outcomes, and displacements caused by candidates who do and do not receive transplants. Such data would be made available to both the Department of Public Health and an independent evaluation group. In addition, hospitals would have to agree not to reduce free care or Medicaid care.

There is some remaining controversy over the experimental nature of heart and liver transplants, and a significant amount of research will have to be performed in Phase I. Accordingly, the Task Force recommended that all clinical protocols, organ procurement methods, patient selection criteria and procedures, organ matching and consent and confidentiality protocols be reviewed, approved, and monitored, either by the hospital's Institutional Review Board (IRB) or by a review board set up for this purpose by the Department of Public Health. This review process should focus on the consent procedure used by the hospital, as well as procedures used to withdraw consent and order the withholding of future treatment, if that is consistent with the patient's desires.

The Task Force also recommended that patient selection criteria be "public, fair, and equitable," with initial selection based on medical suitability criteria designed to maximize the probability of living for a significant period of time with a reasonable prospect for rehabilitation. Priority for transplantation within such a medically suitable group should be based primarily on a first-come, first-served basis, with consideration of organ match.

Even though the Task Force wanted to limit the number of transplants, it flatly rejected arbitrary, nonmedical criteria in the initial patient screening process. For example, although age can appropriately be taken into account as one possible factor that might influence survival and rehabilitation prospects, any specific age limit is an arbitrary excluder. Likewise, alcoholics should not be automatically excluded from liver transplantation; since their disease is largely undeserved and unpredictable, they should have an opportunity to be screened and selected. On the other hand, active alcoholism may be taken into account insofar as it might adversely affect their prospects for survival and rehabilitation—for example, inability to adhere to a required immunosuppression schedule.

Finally, the Massachusetts Task Force recommended that if more than one hospital was granted DON permission to undertake heart and liver transplantation, all hospitals involved should be required to work together in a "worthwhile" consortium, coordinating transplant services in such a way that all would operate like a single, integrated medical service. Any hospital granted DON approval should be able to demonstrate its ability to perform transplant surgery. It should agree to use a single set of patient selection and treatment protocols, work within a common organ procurement system, use a common format for data collection, and agree to joint publication of research results. Additionally, the Task Force recommended the establishment of formal programs for the interchange of residency staff and students, the development of a common training program, and the establishment of a central staff and organization with a record-keeping capability. The Task Force introduced the concept of a "worthwhile" consortium to distinguish between a meaningful, cooperative arrangement and an "on-paper only" agreement.

Although Massachusetts has been a leader in attempting to regulate the introduction of heart and liver transplantation, it is reasonable to argue that it has already failed. In Jaunary, 1984, the Massachusetts Department of Public Health awarded four certificates of need to hospitals that agreed in principle to work together as a "consortium" to offer liver transplants in the state. This consortium is now the second largest liver program in the United States in terms of patient volume, and the largest in terms of facilities and staff devoted to this procedure. In February, 1985, the Department approved four hospitals to do heart transplantation. At that meeting, consortium physicians argued successfully that all four hospitals should be approved in order to take maximum advantage of donor hearts as they become available in Boston, and to allow transplant surgeons at the sole hospital then doing heart transplants to better plan their vacations. Planning issues did not receive top priority at this meeting.

Both consortia are subject to several requirements: hospitals may not consider ability to pay or insurance status in patient selection, may not reduce Medicaid services as a trade-off for transplantation, and may not reduce free care; organ procurement, recipient selection, and confidentiality policies, as well as transplant protocols, including consent and withdrawal of consent policies, must be reviewed and approved by a consortium ethics committee.

The social and political pressures that compelled Boston's major hospitals to "work together" in order to achieve their "separate" goals of performing heart and liver transplants proved unstoppable at the health regulatory level. Accordingly, the success or failure of the attempted public policy intervention in the Massachusetts heart and liver transplant program must now be judged almost exclusively on the performance of the separate, but related, members of the Boston Center for Liver Transplantation, composed of Deaconess Hospital, Massachusetts General Hospital, Children's and New England Medical Center, and the Boston Center for Heart Transplantation. Each of these consortia was approved for an initial three-year period, as per the Task Force recommendation. Because of overlap, there are now a total of five Boston hospitals authorized to do heart and/or liver transplantation. Thus, Boston now has more hospitals performing or ready to perform these transplants than any other city in the world, and is the only city with more than two such hospitals.

The only way to prevent this unusual and unprecedented number of facilities from duplicating services and competing for patients and organs (thereby lowering patient selection criteria, and endangering survival rates and individual patients) is to enforce the "worthwhile" consortium requirement. The Department must make it clear that it is serious about conforming to the multiple conditions placed on the DON authorization and will monitor compliance vigorously. At the end of the three-year authorization phase, these DON conditions, as well as the results of the independent evaluation study, must be used as meaningful criteria in deciding the direction and magnitude of Phase II. While it is premature to pass judgment on the likely outcome of this social experiment in "forced cooperation," healthy skepticism seems appropriate.

Ohio Consortium for Nonrenal Major Organ Transplantation

When the Massachusetts Task Force was beginning its deliberations in December, 1983, a parallel but independent effort was initiated in Ohio. At the time, Ohio was in the midst of a seven-month moratorium on the review of all certificate of need projects in the health field. The legislation which established the moratorium specifically mandated that nonrenal organ transplantation (heart, liver, pancreas, heart/lung) programs required certificate of need review.[10] During this brief moratorium, the Ohio Department of Health initiated discussions with the three Ohio institutions that had filed formal notice of intent to initiate transplantation services over a six-month period. The Ohio Department of Health and these three institutions, the Cleveland Clinic

Foundation, Ohio State University Hospitals of Columbus, and University Hospitals of Cleveland, reached a philosophical and operational consensus regarding the critical issues of patient selection criteria, prioritization mechanisms, donor procurement, uniform treatment protocols, sharing of results, and appropriate collaborative research studies. There was also a broad consensus that the situation in Ohio presented a unique opportunity to introduce this expensive and limited access therapy without sacrificing institutional standards of medical excellence and technological evaluation or socially responsible and prudent public policy. A statewide Task Force was responsible for the development of specific criteria for certificate of need review of applications to join the consortium. Other critical ingredients were the open support of an involved and committed governor, Richard F. Celeste, and cooperation among the Departments of Insurance, Human Services, and Health.

All involved parties agreed that only institutions that had previously demonstrated both the resources for, and experience in, renal transplantation (more than 50 transplants per year) could be considered for consortium membership. All institutions would have to agree to abide by the operational and administrative guidelines established for the consortium. It was felt that there should not be more than four facilities/institutions involved during the initial three-year evaluation phase. Institutions seeking state approval for major solid organ transplantation programs would also have to be tertiary referral centers that support graduate medical education research programs. They must have demonstrated institutional commitment to transplantation by the 24-hour availability of *all* requisite medical and administrative personnel and facilities, including an adequate regional network for donor organ procurement. Adequate intensive care facilities with reverse isolation capabilities and adequate bed space for pre- and postoperative hospitalization without any added capital costs ("slack in the system," see above) must be available. Participating institutions would have to agree to share written patient management protocols, including specific protocols for immunosuppression maintenance and treatment of acute rejection. The consortium team would be responsible for establishing a uniform data collection and evaluation system.

Uniform Criteria for Patient Selection

Cooperative efforts that lead to a consistent, equitable, and practical patient selection process for transplantation must be based on medical suitability criteria, *not* on social value judgments. Uniform selection criteria specifically tailored to each organ are being established by the consortium. Recipient selection is nondiscriminatory with regard to race, sex, or economic considerations. Governor Richard F. Celeste, the Ohio Department of Human Services, and the Ohio Department of Health have agreed that the cost of heart, liver, and pancreas transplantation for any Medicaid-eligible individual selected by the consortium would be covered under the Ohio Medicaid program. In addition, those patients who become Medicaid-eligible because they expend a certain amount of financial resources in a given month or conform to the Medicaid provisions of Social Security disability, would have transplantation expenses covered through Medicaid. The Governor also mandated that the Medicaid program monitor the impact of reimbursement for major organ transplantation on the availability of resources for preventive and primary health care services. It is projected that the actual costs for the Medicaid transplant program will be financed out of savings in the general Ohio Medicaid program that result from new and innovative health care cost containment initiatives. Ohio was the fourth state in the nation to institute prospective reimbursement (diagnosis-related groups) for inpatient hospital services in the Medicaid program. Ohio has also placed a major emphasis on primary care management and health maintenance organizations for Medicaid clients. Limiting consortium institutions to those that have already established active renal transplant programs will lessen the marginal cost increase for each additional nonrenal major solid organ transplant patient. The commitment was made that Medicaid resources for basic and preventive care would never be decreased in order to support the transplant program.

Another innovative aspect of the Ohio program is the agreement of consortium physicians and institutions to contribute 25 percent of professional fees collected for transplant surgery and 25 percent of any institutional gifts from transplant recipients/families to help pay the immediate costs of transplants for those patients who are not eligible for Medicaid and lack sufficient private resources or insurance coverage. This fund will be dispersed by a committee, comprised of the CEOs of the consortium institutions and the Directors of the Ohio Departments of Health and Human Services.

The informed consent and review process at each of the consortium institutions has been evaluated for general consistency by the statewide Consortium Patient Selection Committee. This single committee is comprised of a representative from each of the cooperating consortium institutions, the Director of the Ohio Department of Health, a member of the clergy, and an attorney with an interest and background in medical ethics. Patients who have been recommended by an internal, broadly based institutional review committee are evaluated in terms of medical suitability by the statewide Patient Selection Committee; financial status is *not* considered in patient evaluation. The probability of benefit, chance for a significant period of survival, and rehabilitation potential are the major factors in patient selection. Patients who are considered excellent candidates are then placed on either the "urgent" or "semi-urgent" waiting list. Patients are considered "urgent" if, according to the best professional judgment, they have a high probability of death within less than two weeks. "Semi-urgent" patients are those who are not presently in danger of imminent death, but will have a very high probability of death within six months. Within the constraints of matching blood type, tissue histocompatability typing, and donor size, donor organs will be distributed on a "first-come, first-served" basis.

Uniform Criteria for Donor Selection, Organ Procurement, and Organ Distribution

The Ohio consortium agreed that organ procurement must be coordinated with the state's five established regional organ recovery agencies. Uniform criteria for donation of specific organs are being developed. General donor criteria include determination of donor brain death, as defined by the Harvard Medical School Criteria and the U.S. Collaborative Study of Cerebral Death.[9] Legal permission from the next of kin must be obtained, even in cases where the donor has granted prior approval through the Uniform Anatomical Gift Act.[11] In the case of unexplained death or death from other than natural causes, the coroner of the county in which the death occurred will be notified. Distribution of available donor organs will be based on uniform medical criteria, including red cell compatibility, a negative current cross match (for heart, heart/lung, and pancreas), the degree of donor-recipient histocompatibility matching, organ size compatibility, and urgency of medical situations. If all priority considerations are equally met by more than one patient, access to the donor organ will be determined by the time already spent on the waiting list.

Policies for efficient sharing of organ resources and communication among the five regional procurement agencies have been developed. Fair and reasonable organ acquisition charges will be developed and uniformly adhered to by all consortium institutions. These charges will be reimbursed as part of the transplantation expense. The consortium Patient Selection Committee will coordinate organ-sharing activities among the transplant services and organ recovery agencies, both inside and outside the state of Ohio.

Research and Data Sharing

Another important aspect of the Ohio consortium is the agreement among all the cooperating institutions and the Ohio Department of Health to participate actively in an ongoing, collaborative series of clinical, ethical, and socioeconomic studies. A nonprofit corporation has been established to operate the central data registry for all patients. Each of the four hospitals has pledged $20,000 toward the establishment of a consortium office. At the present time, a cooperative grant application involving all the institutions and the Ohio Department of Health is being prepared for review by major philanthropic foundations in Ohio. Each institution has agreed to enter all relevant data from the time of initial consortium evaluation until the patient's death. Analysis of all inpatient and outpatient care, readmission data, and long-term follow-up, emphasizing both long-term costs of health care services and the quality of life and level of rehabilitation, will be collected and analyzed. All transplanted patients and a cohort of matched controls who did not receive transplants will be included.

We do not mean to suggest that this consortium was formed without encountering any difficulties. At one point during the very intricate and complex negotiations between the Ohio Department of Health and the consortium institutions, significant political pressures jeopardized the success of the cooperative venture. A state legislator told the Director of Health that he had been informed of "a patient who needed a liver transplant, and the only reason it wasn't being done *today* was that the Director of Health wouldn't cut the bureaucratic red tape and permit the operation to go ahead immediately." The legislator had also been told by the patient's family that this was the patient's "only chance," and that one of the physicians at the hospital had told them that pressuring a legislator to intervene could change the situation.

We believe the facts of this case are instructive. The patient, who was an excellent candidate for a liver transplant, was rapidly deteriorating at the time of initial evaluation at one of the consortium hospitals. When apprised of that fact, the Director of the Ohio Department of Health made immediate contacts with other institutions outside Ohio and located one that was willing to place the patient on a priority list for liver transplantation as soon as a compatible donor organ became available—since there were none either in or out of Ohio. Unfortunately, the patient died before a donor liver became available.

When the substance of the conversation with the legislator was shared with the CEO at the consortium institution involved, forceful steps were taken to prevent recurrences of similar communications between staff, family, and political/media figures. The negotiations were rapidly completed and a review of the appropriate certificate of need applications expedited. Transplantation services were introduced at the Ohio consortium institutions without the media hype so common to new transplant programs, and with great care to protect patient confidentiality and privacy. This was accomplished without open interinstitutional competition to be "the first" to do a particular procedure. We believe that the development of innovative public policy must not be stampeded. We cannot afford to lose any of the rare opportunities to forge new directions in these complex areas.

The experience gained since the initiation of the Ohio consortium in July, 1984, can serve as an important role model for approaching the development of statewide, regional, and national programs in nonrenal major organ transplantation. We believe the collaborative approach used in Ohio enables the most effective and efficient use of the collective expertise of a number of nationally and internationally recognized medical institutions. This approach ensures equitable access to these procedures during the pilot phase, while heart and liver transplantation is undergoing rigorous, open, and full public evaluation. It is only by putting aside the territorial imperatives that have so often influenced the introduction of new technologies and treatments, and by entering into constructive public/private cooperative ventures, that we can successfully meet the challenges presented by the explosion in technological capability in the health care system.

REFERENCES

1. Murray JE, Merrill JP, Dammin GJ, et al.: Kidney transplantation in modified recipients. *Ann Surg* 1962, *156*:337-355.
2. Starzl TE, Porter KA, Putnam CW, et al.: Orthopic liver transplantation in 93 patients. *Surg, Gynecology, and Obstetrics* 1976, *142*:487-505.
3. Macek C: Cyclosporin's acceptance heralds new era in immunopharmacology. *JAMA* 1983, *250*:449-455.

4. Dummer JS, Hardy A, Poorsatter A, et al.: Early infections in kidney, heart and liver transplant recipients on cyclosporin. *Transplantation* 1983, *36*:259-267.

5. Keown PA, Stitter CR, Laupacis AL, et al.: The effects and side effects of cyclosporin: Relationship to drug pharmacokinetics. *Transplant Proc* 1982, *14*:659-661.

6. Pennoch JL, Oyer PE, Reitz BA, et al.: Cardiac transplantation in perspective for the future: Survival, complications, rehabilitation and cost. *J Thoracic Cardiac Surg* 1982, *83*:168-177.

7. Starzl TE, Iwatsuki S, Van Thiel DH, et al.: Evolution of liver transplantation. *Hepatology* 1982, *2*:614-636.

8. Annas GJ: Regulating heart and liver transplants in Massachusetts: An overview of the report of the Task Force on Organ Transplantation. *Law, Med, Hlth Care* 1985, *13*:4-7.

9. Annas GJ: Massachusetts Task Force on Organ Transplantation: Massachusetts Report of Health. 1984.

10. Section 1 (B) (2) of Sub. S.B. 269. 115th Ohio General Assembly, 1984.

11. Rivers SD: The uniform anatomical gift act. *JAMA* 1982, *248*:1452.

6   Critical Care Nursing

Barbara J. Daly

The highly technical, highly specialized, patient care units that we now term "critical care units" have developed over the past 30 years. Today's ultra-modern intensive care unit* is an outgrowth of a few units established prior to World War II for the care of postoperative patients who required close watching while awakening from general anesthesia. The polio epidemics of the 1950s spurred the realization that there are groups of patients with very acute illnesses who require a different, more intense kind of medical and nursing care than is generally available on the regular hospital wards, and that it is more efficient and effective to group these patients together. It became common to put such patients into recovery rooms, located next to operating room suites. The early trials with coronary care units confirmed the need for other specialized units, and "critical care" was off and running!

Any discussion of critical care today must include the major providers of continuous care—critical care nurses. Regardless of profession or specialty, all those involved in the care of critically ill patients interact with ICU nurses. Learning about this group of care providers is useful in daily interactions and in the anlaysis of the many complex issues described in the other chapters of this book, such as decision making and resource allocation. The purpose of this chapter is to provide the reader with a brief review of the history and status of critical

---

*In this chapter, the terms "intensive care unit (ICU)" and "critical care unit" will be used interchangeably.

care nursing, as well as a description of the issues related to the role of the critical care nurse.

TODAY'S REGISTERED NURSE

Demographics and Philosophy

Critical care nurses represent a portion of the registered nurse population. A brief description of the entire population thus provides useful background information.

The nursing profession as a whole is composed predominantly of females (97%), with a median age of 38 years. According to a 1980 survey, there are approximately 1.6 million nurses licensed to practice in the United States; 24 percent of these nurses are not employed in nursing.[1,2] Of those currently working, 70.8 percent are married; 46 percent are married and have children at home. Reflecting the dual roles required of working wives and mothers, 32 percent of employed nurses only work part-time. Two-thirds of all nurses were originally educated in hospital-based diploma programs. Seventeen percent graduated from a college or university-based Bachelor of Science in Nursing program, and an additional 5 percent later returned to school to obtain their B.S.N. Five percent of all nurses hold master's or doctoral degrees. Thirty-three percent of all admissions to basic nursing programs in 1979-80 were to B.S.N. programs. When compared to a 1970 survey, this study reflected increases in the number of registered nurses, the percent employed, the percent receiving a bachelor's degree as their initial educational preparation, and the percent of minority (including males) members. Decreases were shown in the average age and percent receiving their basic education in hospital-based programs.

Many of the challenges facing nurses today have their roots in these statistics. Nursing is a sex-segregated occupation. Unlike medicine, nursing loses a large number of its practitioners each year as women leave work to raise their families. In terms of educational preparation, nurses are a much more heterogeneous group than those in other health occupations; backgrounds of direct patient care providers range from a two-year community college education to a seven-year university-based program for the clinical specialist. This makes it difficult, to say the least, for others to develop appropriate expectations of nurses, which often causes conflict. It seems unlikely that these characteristics will change rapidly, although the identified trends are expected to continue.

Regardless of the practice setting, all nurses share elements of a common philosophy. Most of the significant contributions and conflicts of ICU nurses stem from this philosophical base.

The cornerstone of the nursing philosophy (if there can be said to be one philosophy) is caring, the raison d'être of the nurse. The word "nurse" stems from the Latin word for nurture; this origin provides us with the nurse's first obligation—to the patient—and is the source of one of the most persistent metaphors for nurse—that is, a mother substitute.[3,4] This image exists in the minds of the public and many other care providers, who expect the nurse/mother to embody all the positive characteristics associated with motherhood: caring, gentleness, and devotion. It also underlies many of the conflicts as others, particularly physicians and even some nurse administrators, expect subservience and acquiescence.

Kalisch and Kalisch conducted an exhaustive study of public media and confirmed the predominance of this image of the nurse in television and literature.[5,6] They found three basic portrayals: nurse as man's companion, man's destroyer, and man's mother or mother of his children. A content analysis of the personal attributes of nurses on television revealed that nurses rated high on obedience, permissiveness, and conformity; physicians scored high on sophistication, intelligence, rationality, and aggression. It was not until the 1960s that the media gained some recognition of nurses as real persons, with both positive and negative traits, who have some professional identity and assume responsibility for their own actions. Unfortunately, the 1970s brought a return to the use of nurse characters as sexual mascots for men, particularly physicians—stereotypes which were disparaging to both groups.

The abundance of definitions of nursing in the nursing literature is an indication of the degree to which this profession or occupation is in transition. All definitions, however, appear to have common elements. First is the notion of assisting, helping, ministering, or providing care; all of these actions are differentiated from curing or providing a specific technologic service. Thus, the basis of nursing activities is quite general and broad, and is not confined to a particular act or technique.

Next, all definitions refer to the recipients of care in an equally broad fashion: individuals, groups, families, peers—in fact, anyone who is experiencing a "broad range of health-illness phenomena."[7] There is generally a specific absence of reference to patients as sufferers of disease or seekers of certain services.

The last element, appearing more often in recent definitions, refers to the methodology used by the nurse to assist individuals, a specific art and science of nursing. This idea is in direct contrast to the "mother" image and notions of nursing as a natural female function. It is perhaps in critical care nursing that the nurse's goal of "caring for" is most obviously dependent upon the utilization of technical skills and basic science concepts. The American Association of Critical-Care Nurses (AACN) further defines critical care nursing as "the utilization of the nursing process (assessment, planning, implementation, and evaluation) in the prevention of or intervention in life-threatening situations."[8] At its most fundamental level, then, it can be said that all of nursing has a care, rather than cure, orientation, a wellness (prevention of disease or crisis)—in addition to illness—concern, and a whole person—rather than organ or subsystem—focus.

Further analysis of the philosophy of nursing must include reference to the nurse's role in the health care society, the source of the nurse's accountability. The hospital nurse today leads a somewhat schizophrenic existence. The institutional bureaucracy expects the allegiance of the nurse as an employee, the physician expects the loyalty of his handmaiden, and the nurse expects him/herself to be accountable to the patient. Each of these allegiances bears further discussion.

As an employee, the nurse certainly has contractual obligations to the hospital. This employee status is problematic in two regards. The hospital, like all organizations, imposes certain rules that reflect institutional values, such as growth, stability, and risk minimization.[9] These rules, however, may be in direct conflict with the nurse's perceptions of his/her obligations to the patient. Providing access to medical records or information about the patient's hospitalization is a common example of an activity that might present such a conflict. In addition to the dilemmas posed by the conflicts themselves, this state of divided loyalties encourages nurses to substitute hospital policies for action guides developed from individual reasoning. Consequently, "policy" is frequently cited as a reason for doing or not doing something.

Loyalty to the physician has long been considered one of the most essential qualities of the "good nurse," and is probably one of the most persistently disturbing issues to nurses today. The extent to which the nurse perceives an obligation, and the exact nature of that obligation, vary considerably with the nurse's education, experience, and practice location. It is an element of philosophy that has undergone tremendous change over the years. Consider the following two quotations:

In the segregation of this group of human commodities which constitutes the profession of nursing, there are four parties in interest: first, the public that it serves; second, the hospital system that it serves; third, the medical profession whose essential handmaiden it is, and fourth, the group of nursing women itself. . . . It [the medical profession] has been the habitual critic of her development, and very pertinently so because the physician is ultimately the only competent judge of the fitness of the nurse and the chief sufferer, held responsible to her employer, the patient, for her possible unfitness.[10]

This statement sets forth the American Medical Association's commitment to increasing the significance of nursing as a primary component in the delivery of *medical services.* . . . Professional nurses, by the nature of their education, are equipped to assume greater medical service responsibility *under the supervision of physicians.* . . . The nurse is the logical person *to support the physician* in the management and care of the patient [emphasis added].[11]

Unquestionably, the history of medicine and nursing reflects the origins of the nurse's role as a handmaiden who is under the control and guidance of the physician, has neither the ability nor the need to act independently, and owes allegiance to her master. Contrast this with the obligations of today's nurse set forth in the American Nurses Association Code for Nurses:

The nurse acts to safeguard the client and the public when health care and safety are affected by the incompetent, unethical, or illegal practice of any person.

The nurse assumes responsibility and accountability for individual nursing judgments and actions (American Nurses Association: Code for Nurses, 1976).

The interpretive statements published with the Code further emphasize the nurse's first and foremost responsibility—to the patient, not to the physician, with whom the nurse works in a collaborative, not dependent, fashion. The activities of the nurse are considered a primary and separate patient service. Although this service is obviously related to the work of the physician, the nurse is not considered only in the context of a physician's aide.

It may be argued that we have all come a long way from these historical origins. Yet, the existence of day-to-day conflict, reflected in numerous analyses in the literature and actual court litigation, speaks otherwise. As recently as 1977, a physician's complaint resulted in a nurse's license being revoked by the State Board of Nursing for "unprofessional conduct." At the patient's request, the nurse had provided the patient with objective information about alternatives to the cancer therapy recommended by the physician.[12]

Obviously, the philosophical ideals expressed here are not shared by all nurses. However, they are ideals and concepts to which all nurses are exposed in their education and socialization. As such, they may serve as background for a further examination of the critical care nursing role.

CURRENT STATUS OF CRITICAL CARE NURSING

The development of critical care nursing was a natural corollary to the growth of critical care units. The first specialty organization, like the first specialty units, was of coronary care nurses. As critical care broadened to include the care of patients who did not have cardiac diseases, the Association of Coronary Care Nurses expanded to become the American Association of Critical Care Nurses (AACN). By 1979, membership had grown from several hundred to over 39,000.[13]

More significant than the numerical growth of critical care nurses was the development of the science of critical care nursing. In 1975, the AACN's recognition of the need for a defined core body of knowledge resulted in the publication of the first *Core Curriculum for Critical Care Nursing*. The development of the certification exam occurred several years later. Today's critical care nurse considers him/herself a professional and a specialist.

As the numbers of critical care nurses have grown, increasing attention has been paid to the specialization of this branch of nursing. A particular focus has been comparisons between ICU and non-ICU nurses. As stated by Hay and Oken, the rationale is: "It stands to reason that nurses who operate special machines and perform special procedures for special patients must be special too!"[14]

Most surveys describe ICU nurses as younger than other nurses, with a slightly higher percent having a B.S.N. degree.[15-17] Grout's study of 1,238 ICU nurses revealed that the major reasons for choosing ICU nursing were the opportunity for learning, the intellectual challenge, and the opportunity to develop proficiency in nursing skills.[17] Although research has focused on the qualities or personality traits that differentiate ICU nurses from others, results have been equivocal.

In one of the earliest studies, Gentry found that ICU nurses reported more depression, hostility, and anxiety than non-ICU nurses. He identified situational stresses of the work environment of the critical care unit as significant variables.[18] On the other hand, Dear's study of 1,100 nurses found critical care nurses to be more highly satisfied with their work, with no differences in the level of perceived autonomy, locus of control, or turnover rates.[16] Looking specifically at stress tolerance, Maloney and Bartz reported that critical care nurses scored higher in alienation and external control, and were more likely to seek challenge.[19] However, another study by Maloney demonstrated that non-ICU nurses scored significantly higher than ICU nurses in both state and trait anxiety, job dissatisfaction, and reporting of personal and family problems.[20] Benton and White examined data on 565 nurses of various specialties (ICU, obstetrics, medicine, surgery, and pediatrics) and found that patient care itself was the job factor most important to satisfaction, followed by having an adequate number of personnel per shift; pay differential for experience, written job descriptions, and promotional opportunities were least important. The ICU group's rankings for these factors were the same as those of the total group.[21]

As outlined above, many of the comparisons of critical care nurses and other nurses have concentrated on measuring the stress to which the ICU nurse is subjected, the reactions of the nurse to stress, or the personality traits and defenses needed to cope with stress. This reflects a general perception of ICUs as stressful environments and a persistent, unsupported conviction that there must be some differences, some unique characteristics, that attract nurses to the ICU. This view has been encouraged by the recognition of the "burnout" phenomenon— that is, the disillusionment and emotional exhaustion associated with human service occupations which comes of personal surrender to overwhelming demands and external, unchanging realities.[22]

In his review of stress and intensive care nursing, Friedman cautions that the environmental demands that are perceived by one nurse as a "stressor" may represent a "satisfier" to another.[23] Nevertheless, certain factors do reappear in the literature as common or frequently reported stressors: conflict with other health care providers; inadequate staffing patterns; unresponsive nursing leadership; lack of recognition by physicians; lack of support in dealing with death and dying; dealing with families.

Eisendrath points out the likelihood of conflict arising from the similarities between many ICUs and family systems, in which the medical director is "father," head nurse is "mother," and the nursing and house staffs are "children."[24] This idea is consistent with the historical roots of the nurse-physician relationship. While it could provide an emotionally supportive base for young practitioners of both disciplines, it also leads to "sibling rivalry" and a repression of the growth of the "children."

In addition to recognizing that individuals vary in their perceptions and identifications of stressors, it should be noted that there may be significant differences among the various types of intensive care units. These differences may account for widely varying perceptions of stress and/or job satisfaction. For example, surgical intensive care units typically have a younger patient population with a shorter length of stay. The patients most often present with one or two major problems. The focus of care is to resolve or monitor those problems for a brief, defined, high-risk period of time. The frequent arrival of patients directly from the operating room provides a population that is most unstable and dependent upon caregivers for life-sustaining measures. Medical intensive care unit patients, on the other hand, tend to be older, have a higher mortality rate, and present with chronic diseases and multisystem problems requiring the use of more consultants. Variation among patients is great, ranging from the brief, one-day monitoring required by overdose patients to the prolonged, highly complex care required by septic, bone marrow transplant patients. Coronary care units have a patient population that is generally awake and alert, many of whom are experiencing their first major illness. While the focus of their care is on only one organ system, it requires in-depth investigation and intervention. The restful, quiet environment of the coronary unit provides a vivid contrast to the highly technologic focus of medical and surgical units.

The significance of these differences lies in the match between the individual nurse and the challenges and satisfiers presented by the particular environment. For example, the nurse who gains the greatest degree of satisfaction and reward from working overtime with patients and families, designing comprehensive care plans, and having the opportunity to see the fruition of his or her plans over weeks or months is likely to be dissatisfied with the environment of a surgical unit, and will find the constant, rapid turnover of patients stressful. The nurse who enjoys the short-term, highly defined, and intense relationships typical of the SICU, where priorities of care are well established, may perceive the slow progress of the MICU patient as a stressor.

Strategies proposed to deal with these stressors and prevent burnout primarily focus on interpersonal techniques, such as talking with others, group meetings, and role-playing sessions. Cook and Madrillo's work on perceived stress and situational supports confirms the importance of these interpersonal factors. In their study, the highest correlation with perceived situational support was positive coworker relationships.[25] After administering a Stress Audit to 1,800 nurses, Bailey, Steffen, and Grout also found that interpersonal staff relationships were among the three most important satisfiers.[26]

The Critical Care Team

The concept of multidisciplinary teams gained popularity in the 1970s. The increased complexity of illnesses and therapies required by critically ill patients mandated that planning, provision, and evaluation of care be extended beyond the primary doctor and nurse. Clinical pharmacists, dieticians, respiratory therapists, psychologists, social workers, and many others have become regular participants in critical care teams. In fact, most texts addressing management and organization of contemporary critical care units mention the need to have a team.

According to Adler and Shoemaker, in AACN's text on management, physicians and nurses originally formed teams in order to overcome political obstacles to the growth and development of intensive care units, and provide the support system necessary for the unit personnel.[27] Meltzer, one of the earliest proponents of coronary care units, called the team approach "the most distinguishing characteristic of the coronary care concept," referring to the improved communication, efficiency, and organization that resulted from this structure.[28] This concept has also gained popularity abroad. In describing England's "intensive therapy units," Ledingham also addresses the need for multidisciplinary activities and the regular involvement of ancillary staff, physiotherapists, and technicians necessitated by the diverse range of equipment used.[29] The National Institute of Health, in a Consensus Development Conference in 1983, defined critical care as "a multidisciplinary and multiprofessional medical/nursing field . . ."[30]

The question of whether this multidisciplinary group is truly a team has been addressed by Erde.[31] He points out that teams are generally understood to be democracies, yet the health care "team" rarely elects their leader. In addition to the physician's being self-appointed, patients expect him to be the captain. Also, women lack men's socialization to team behavior and are poorly prepared to operate as equal team members.

Erde begins his discussion with a definition of the term *team*, which includes the proviso that members share a common goal and a common set of norms. This definition in itself raises questions about the degree to which the health care team's goals and beliefs are truly the same. For example, the list below presents four beliefs held by many critical care nurses:

1. The nurse is an independent professional.
2. Care may be more important than cure.
3. The quality of life may be the most important outcome.
4. The nurse's primary responsibility is to the patient; all nursing actions must, therefore, be guided by the nurse's judgment of what is in the patient's best interest.

These are certainly basic rules, or norms, applicable to the practice of the critical care team; however, the extent to which these norms are recognized and accepted by all team members (even all nurses) is doubtful.

Contrary to the team notion, I believe critical care today is provided by a multidisciplinary group that interacts in a relatively undefined network of relationships, and has some degree of cohesiveness and identity. This cohesiveness is the product of the group's shared commitment to patient welfare, which members may or may not define in the same manner. The group identity is a function of both the shared commitment and the structure afforded by the organizational arrangement of duties, such as ICU medical director, head nurse, staff nurse, ICU social worker, and so on.

The formal organizational structure, informal distribution of work, and expectations of coworkers vary considerably from setting to setting. Major differences in norms may be observed by comparing the large specialty units found in major teaching hospitals with the small, mixed medical-surgical units of smaller community hospitals. Large, complex organizations typically have a wider variety of workers, each with a highly defined specialty. Since each member of the work group becomes quite expert in a narrow area, there is little overlapping of roles. Territorial concerns and tensions are not uncommon, as each member of the group struggles to protect his "turf." In contrast, the nurse working in a small hospital usually performs a multitude of roles and must be a generalist, equally skilled in caring for medical, surgical, coronary, and perhaps pediatric patients. While the nurse in some units has 24-hour access to IV, respiratory and physical therapists, laboratory and EKG technicians, transporters, and clerks, the community hospital nurse may have to assume all of these roles at different times.

The presence of house staff (residents, interns, and medical students) is also a significant variable in the development of group norms. Nurses who are accustomed to working with young student physicians, rather than primarily with older, senior, experienced physicians, are far more likely to adopt a questioning attitude and view physicians as less than omniscient. It is a curious paradox that nurses who work in a small community hospital ICU are often very independent because there is no physician present in the hospital during evening and night hours; yet, they are more likely to view the physician as the ultimate authority over all aspects of patient care, including nursing care.

There are several other characteristic differences between small community ICUs and those in medical centers that may be relevant to this discussion. As mentioned earlier, the relatively recent changes in nursing philosophy that advocate a more autonomous role for the nurse, with less emphasis on responsibility and accountability to the physician, are becoming more popular. It is the younger practitioners who are more likely to question and refute the norms of previous generations. The majority of new graduates seek employment in larger hospitals, particularly those affiliated with a university, because of the perceived challenges and learning opportunities. Thus, the nurses who are most likely to strongly reject the old norms and demand recognition for equal professional status are concentrated in the larger hospitals.

The nursing leadership provided in academic settings also supports the questioning of traditional relationships and role restructuring. As one would expect, the highest percentage of nurses with advanced academic preparation (master's and doctoral degrees) is found in university settings. These are the individuals who are the strongest proponents of the professionalization of nursing. The influence of their leadership and the organizational power of some nursing departments should not be underestimated. The young, inexperienced practitioner who is employed in this setting is exposed to a very different environment and very different role models.

In contrast, the ICU nurse who chooses a small town hospital often has limited access to professional nursing resources. He/she becomes a member of a work group that is older, more stable, and has traditional norms and values. As one nurse phrased it, "The physicians are our biggest resource. When we live, work, and socialize together in a small community, our relationship goes beyond the few minutes of professional contact in the ICU."[32]

The last variable that influences the operation of the "team" and the specific roles of members is the hierarchy within each specific unit. Units with consistent individuals in designated positions of leadership are more likely to form a stable team. The two most pivotal positions are those of physician director and head nurse. If there is no physician director, the physician-in-charge changes every month, or the physician director is not actively involved with the care of all patients on a daily basis, staff members are not likely to develop the kind of cohesive team described in the literature. The same is true of units in which the head nurse position is either vacant or filled by a nurse who does not accept the team concept.

These considerations are obviously generalizations, and many exceptions may be found. They are also not to be construed as determinants of the quality of care provided in any setting. Rather, they are intended to provide a description of some of the organizational factors that influence the critical care nurse's role and role relationships.

This variation in the nurse's role is evident in the specific tasks for which he/she is responsible and the nature of the nurse-patient relationship. Obviously, the nurse is responsible for providing what is generally accepted as "nursing care"—for example, monitoring patient status, administering treatments and medications, changing dressings, personal hygiene, discharge teaching, and so on. However, this description of tasks is not necessarily a full description of the nurse's role.

Aside from the educational preparation necessary to assume the tasks mentioned, there are other characteristics of the nursing role that enable the critical care nurse to perform a broader function. The two roles which have received the greatest attention are those of coordinator and advocate.

Developments in modern hospitals have created conditions in the intensive care unit that are conducive to having nurses assume different roles. The extensive increases in the amount and complexity of technology have left the consumer feeling that he is indeed a stranger in a strange land, ill-equipped to deal with this foreign environment. Advances in the breadth and depth of knowledge in the natural sciences have spurred an increase in specialization, thus increasing the fragmentation of care. Each organ and each disease entity is now managed by its own physician or paramedic, with no one looking after the owner. While the consumer movement of the 1980s is perhaps overdue, it has further widened the gap between the public's expectations and the ability of any one caregiver to meet all of the patient's biological, social, and emotional needs.

This gap has given rise to the notion that patients require someone to coordinate their care. Corless describes the coordinator's responsibilities as "ensuring that there are no gaps in care and that the patient receives the therapies which are required for his or her well-being."[3] Speaking of the need to restructure roles, Aiken describes the "continuing synthesis of the prescriptions of many physicians and professional surveillance of multiple diagnostic and treatment regimes."[34] In general, the coordinator is viewed as one who can put the pieces together, ensure continuity and thoroughness of care, and establish the priorities of care.

A closely related role is that of the advocate, a person who can assist the patient in exercising his or her rights. Annas specified four activities of the patient rights advocate:

1. guaranteeing that the patient has access to all medical records;
2. monitoring the quality of care;
3. gaining access to services or consultants;
4. participating in all discussions relating to patient care as the patient's representative.[35]

Other functions might include that of ombudsman—that is, someone to whom the patient can turn with questions or concerns, and lay counselor—that is, someone to assist the patient in evaluating decisions and resolving conflicts.

Those who believe the nurse should assume these roles point to the unique features of the nurse's educational preparation and relationship with the patient. As mentioned earlier, nurses are oriented towards caring for the whole person, rather than dealing with one subsystem. Their educational background prepares them for this focus. The Bachelor of Science in Nursing program educates generalists with equal preparation in the biological and social sciences. In addition, nurses are the only members of the health "team" who are continuous caregivers, present 24 hours a day. All other care—medical care, spiritual guidance, social service support, physical therapy—is episodic and transient; nursing care is provided from the first moment of hospitalization to the last. The recent growth of primary nursing, in which one nurse is expected to plan, direct, and evaluate all nursing care, has made the notion of the nurse as coordinator even more attractive.

Another characteristic that makes the nurse even more suitable for the coordinator and advocate roles is the peer relationship that is possible between nurse and patient. It is ironic that it is the public image of the nurse as a mother who performs a natural function in a warm and caring fashion—an image decried by nurses struggling to achieve recognition and professional status as scientists—that enables nurses to avoid what may be a crisis of alienation in medicine. Bergen, Lindenthal, and Thomas describe two current opinions about physicians. At worst, they are villains in a "drama of good guys vs. bad guys." At best, they are technicians who neglect the total patient and his psychological needs as a result of their necessary preoccupation with the biological realities of disease.[36] The patient's alienation from the physician is intensified by a "rule of silence" imposed on patients, who avoid confronting physicians and sharing their hopes, wishes, and needs. ". . . [I]f we do not speak about our values that can give and withhold other's authority over us, it is because we forswear speaking in favor of the ancient dream that by our becoming an object for another, the other will surely deliver us from suffering."[36] The patient expects no such deliverance from his nurse. Thus, he is free to unburden his worries and receive services which would never be demanded from the physician—for example, support, care coordination, and advocacy.

Issues and Conflicts

As members of the largest group of caregivers, nurses perform an essential function in administering direct care to acutely ill patients. They are, by and large, a well-educated group with increasing preparation at the university and postgraduate levels. Their defined body of knowledge is applied in a unique fashion. In addition, their qualifications should enable them to fulfill both the coordinator and advocate roles. Why, then, are these roles not legitimized as belonging to the nurse? The ideas of nurse as coordinator and nurse as advocate are so attractive and supportable, that there must be very fundamental and pervasive reasons why these roles have yet to be actualized to any great extent.

The concepts of rights and duties may serve as the basis for an explanation. Veatch describes duties of station—that is, the specific duties that accrue when one assumes a role, such as coordinator or advocate—as a kind of promising; one promises to fulfill the expectations that are inherent in the role.[37] In order for these duties to be legitimate, and for one to be obligated to fulfill the promise, one must have the *right* to fulfill the promise. Rights generally require the recognition or agreement of all parties involved. In this case, before the nurse can assume the duties of advocate or coordinator as part of the nursing role, other members of the health care establishment, such as physicians, hospital administrators, social workers, and so on, would have to accord to the nurse the right to be an advocate or coordinator. This is not done. Nurses—even critical care nurses—are generally accorded neither the autonomy nor the authority needed to enact these roles. Effectiveness in either role requires the ability to significantly affect the behavior and decisions of other care providers; this power, which is associated with professional status, has not yet been achieved by nurses.

Studies and descriptions of the reasons for the much-publicized nursing shortage of the late 1970s and early 1980s have repeatedly supported this description of the hospital hierarchy. Aiken, president of the American Academy of Nursing, stated that the shortage was mostly attributable to the fact that the hospital has become a less satisfying place for nurses. This arises from:

> the absence of appropriate organizational and managerial arrangements between nurses, physicians, and hospitals that clearly recognize the appropriate role of nurses in modern medical practice. . . . There are fundamental incompatibilities in the present social contract between hospitals, physicians, and today's professional nurses. . . . Despite the fact that hospitalized patients are more acutely ill than ever before, there has been little recognition of the importance of the nurse's role in the new level of clinical decision making required by these very sick patients.[38]

The American Hospital Association prepared an issue paper and distributed it to hospital executives to assist in addressing the problem. They stated: "Hospitals need to provide autonomy for nurses, foster positive attitudes of physicians toward collaborative practice, and enhance availability and quality of support services."[39] Frequent articles also appeared in the public media during this period. Most attributed the problem, as did a report in the *Wall Street Journal*, to the lack of respect from physicians, inadequate control over the content of nurses' work, poor working conditions, and inadequate pay for what nurses consider to be professional responsibility.[40]

After studying the historical development of nursing, Levi identified functional redundancy as the key reason for nursing's failure to be recognized as a profession.[41] She pointed out that all the jobs or tasks performed by nurses can also be performed by members of some other occupation. For example, many hospitals utilize monitor technicians to observe and assess data and functioning of cardiac and hemodynamic monitors. In some settings, respiratory therapists assume responsibility for mechanical ventilators and care of patients' airways. Pharmacy technicians may distribute medications. Licensed practical nurses provide physical care in many smaller community hospital ICUs, in place of registered nurses. Registered nurses claim that they provide higher quality of care, and that this functional distribution adds to fragmentation of care. This view is obviously not shared by many others. The fact that nurses lack a monopoly over significant skills, such as physicians possess, makes it unlikely that society at large, and other health care providers in particular, will accord to nurses the power and prestige necessary to make advocacy or coordinating a viable role.

An extremely important issue in examining the nurse's role is the categorization of nursing as a sex-segregated occupation. In addition to its psychosociological and economic influences, this factor impacts upon nurses' struggles to achieve autonomy.

Ashley, one of nursing's most outspoken critics of the current social order, views misogyny, the hatred of women, as a destructively pervasive characteristic of virtually all of human existence.[42] She discusses misogyny as an integral part of our society's patriarchal structure, and its effects on the health care culture. Describing the ancient origins of this patriarchy, she points to the genesis of woman as a secondary, derivative being who was the source of sin. Women's place in history has been reinforced as being weak, defective, and whole only when fulfilling the purpose of assisting or subjugating herself to man. The anti-female medical abuses criticized by feminists, such as the performing of unnecessary surgery and the excessive prescription of tranquilizers, are the inevitable result of an attitude that classifies women as sick by virtue of their sex. According to Ashley, these same misogynous myths are responsible for the fact that nurses have remained the servants of physicians. This is not seen as attributable to any aspect or characteristic of nurses or nursing; it is simply the result of its being an occupation in which women are the primary workers. In order to alter this state of affairs, nurses must stop being token instruments of physicians, and actively develop a separate, self-directing philosophy that is in accord with the goals and purposes of feminism.

While Ashley's view is perhaps more extreme than most, she is by no means alone in her accusation of female suppression. Lovell specifically accuses the male-dominated medical profession of conspiring to "use and abuse" women in their roles as wives and as nurses. She states, "If the physician, in his role as dominant of the dominants, is a 'man among men,' then the nurse is 'the perfect woman'."[43] Her central thesis is that women have historically been dominated and controlled in order to further the careers, finances, and personal goals of medical men. Like Ashley, she urges nurses to break loose from this imposed restraint.

Greenleaf considers the economic effects of belonging to a female occupation.[44] She presents clear data regarding the degree to which nurses suffer economically by failing to receive "equal pay for equal worth." For example, in the 1977 U.S. Department of Labor rating of job complexity, a factor used in salary determinations, the job of staff nurse in a medical setting was rated as less complex than those of a physician's assistant or laboratory technician in a veterinary service. Greenleaf also believes this undervaluing of nurses' work is directly attributable to an androcentric ideology that defines men's domain as the public sphere and man's work as essential and difficult; women's sphere is the home, and women's work is unimportant to the greater society.

Coordination and Advocacy as Inherent in the Nurse Role

The previous section has briefly reviewed some of the social norms and organizational characteristics that influence the role of the critical care nurse. Although the work group in most settings may be very cohesive, supportive, and efficient, it does not actually constitute a team in the strict sense. Characteristics of the specific unit and specific hospital may be significant determinants of how well the nurses and physicians work together.

In addition, explanations for the fact that the roles of coordinator and advocate are not formally assigned to, nor assumed by, nurses were discussed. These included a persistence of the historical image of nurses as handmaidens to physicians, prejudice and economic repression secondary to sex stereotyping, and lack of recognition as a profession, which is attributed to functional redundancy. Although important and relevant, these situational forces are not sufficient to counteract the persistent notions of nurses as coordinators and advocates. In fact, those experienced in critical care may well question why, given these factors, many nurses in many units *do* act as coordinators at times and *are able* to advocate effectively for some patients.

The answer to our dilemma may lie in a closer look at some of the other aspects of the critical care nurse's day-to-day responsibilities. For the purposes of our discussion, let us consider the care of a patient in an ICU in a large urban hospital. At the very least, the patient will have primary physicians, dieticians, laboratory technicians, and one or two allied professionals, such as a respiratory therapist and social worker, involved in his care. All of these individuals need to obtain information about the patient, have access to the patient, and transmit information back to the other caregivers. The gatekeeper or controller of these interactions has to be the nurse. The nurse at the bedside is the logical individual to answer questions about the patient, help plan a trip to x-ray, schedule a breathing treatment, and receive information intended for one of the other caregivers. Aside from simply being there to discuss plans with others, the nurse has the broadest data base from which to operate. It is the nurse who is there to observe the effects of the medication ordered by the physician, evaluate what time of day is best for a breathing treatment, know what preparations are necessary prior to a CAT scan, and know how the patient tolerated a new diet. If the patient has consultants involved in his care, it is the nurse who must integrate the consultants' orders and recommendations with the orders of the primary physician. Because the nurse is responsible for the "whole" patient, he or she is the person most likely to identify a need or problem that is not being addressed by anyone.

Coordination of these activities, plans, and communications is not really an optional activity. In fact, it is something that must be done if one is to get through the day! It is only a small transition from coordinating the activities of eight hours to coordinating the course of the patient's entire ICU stay. Experienced nurses quite naturally make this transition, resulting in an easier job for everyone else and better care for the patient. It is problematic only when the coordination has to be done very overtly and others must alter their plans in a significant fashion. Under such circumstances, the nurse's formal status and the lack of official recognition of the coordinator role are likely to produce conflict.

A similar analysis applies to the advocate role. The presence of nurses 24 hours a day and patients' willingness to talk with them about their concerns, hopes, and fears have previously been mentioned as factors supporting nurses' suitability for the advocacy role. Since the critical care nurse is literally at the bedside on a continuous basis, he or she cannot help but observe and participate in all of the patient's physiological and emotional reactions. It is the nurse who is available to help the patient who has been told that he must return to surgery, have an amputation, or give up his job because of his heart condition. It is the nurse with whom the patient talks when he refuses a treatment. It is the nurse who is at the bedside when the family arrives and asks, "How is he?" It is the nurse who implements orders and evaluates care when the patient cannot speak for himself and has no family.

The above-mentioned situations make it clear that one must be an advocate in order to provide nursing care. Unlike the surgeon, who operates for a specific pathology, the cardiologist, whose purpose is to prescribe medical treatment for heart disease, the internist, who cures or treats a specific disorder and its sequelae, *caring for the person* is the nurse's reason for existence. There is no way to do this without entering into the patient's world and assuming the patient's wishes, hopes, and fears. It is extremely difficult to respond to the patient who refuses surgery, states the medicine isn't helping, or says he doesn't want to live if he can't work, without being committed to working towards the patient's own goals.

Families expect nurses to intervene on behalf of patients. Perhaps one of the most difficult situations for the nurse-advocate to deal with is when the family approaches the nurse with questions and doubts about the appropriateness of continuing treatment or outright requests for the termination of life-support therapies. While the nurse may try to redirect the family's questions and concerns to the physician, the obligation to address expressed needs and wishes remains. The terrible, self-imposed burden of omniscience carried by the physician leaves him with the conviction that he already knows what is in the patient's best interest. Other caregivers, such as respiratory therapists or social workers, may be able to neatly identify such concerns as being outside of their purview. Nurses have no such avenues to relieve them from dealing with patient and family concerns; nor can they simply escape by leaving the situation.

A specific example of this all-too-common situation may further clarify the dilemma of the nurse advocate. Consider the case of a 70-year-old patient who has a history of chronic lung disease and metastatic prostate cancer. The patient is followed by a pulmonary specialist for his lung disease and an oncologist for his cancer. He came to the ICU when he developed a urinary tract infection which progressed to septic shock. He is intubated and on a respirator. An infectious disease specialist is the consultant advising on antibiotic regimens. The intensivist, or medical chief of the ICU, is directing his medical care in the unit.

The ICU nurse is likely to receive communication from the patient's wife and children that is based on their understanding of the prognosis and therapy of the illness, their understanding of what the physicians have said, and their questions, doubts, and satisfaction with the patient's care. In addition to communicating about matters related to the patient's illness and medical care, families also, over time, share information about other topics—for example, what the patient's life was like prior to the illness; the plans, goals, and hopes this illness has interrupted; identification of the decision makers in the family; past discussions regarding the patient's wishes for prolonged life support therapies; projections of what the patient would want.

Families do not often overtly ask the nurse to intervene in what they perceive as medical decisions. This probably reflects the public's view of the nurse as the physician's employee and helper. The nurse does, however, use the data communicated by the family to generate a diagnosis of patient/family problems and needs. Once these needs are identified, courses of action are indicated. In the same way that the nurse might determine that the patient is becoming dehydrated and take measures to correct this problem, the nurse must find a way to address patient or family distress—regardless of whether the family has overtly asked for nursing intervention.

There are many options potentially available to the nurse—for example, simply sharing the family's communication with others; getting answers from the physician to transmit back to the family; arranging meetings between physician and family; helping the family to ask their questions or raise their concerns with physicians or other caregivers; instituting a plan to enable consistency in the manner in which others interact with the family. Doing nothing is rarely acceptable. Repeated contact with the family, repeated questions and expressions of distress, and the reality of having to participate in care that is inadequate, unsatisfactory, or simply not wanted generate feelings which, in turn, provide the nurse with powerful motivations for advocacy attempts.

In order to fulfill the role of the nurse, a means of dealing with the perceived needs and wishes of patients and families must be found. As with the role of coordinator, the extent to which the nurse attempts to enact this role in a formal, overt manner, the skill with which it is performed, and the relationships established with other caregivers often determine whether the nurse will be successful or generate resentment in others and fail to accomplish the purpose.

SUMMARY AND CONCLUSIONS

This chapter has described critical care nurses as young, female, and educated in college or university settings. They are attracted to what may be an especially stressful setting by the challenges and opportunities for learning and developing their competencies. They share other nurses' susceptibilities to the negative effects of inadequate staffing, lack of pay for comparable worth, conflicts of loyalty between patient care and institutional goals, and lack of respect from physicians.

Like all nurses, the critical care nurse is oriented towards caring for the whole person and the wellness state. The uniqueness of the nursing role is derived from the unique combination of skills and abilities utilized in caring for patients 24 hours a day, rather than the specific tasks performed. All nurses are potentially capable of developing special relationships with their patients; in the ICU, this potential is enhanced by the patient's total dependence upon the nurse's caring and competence.

On the one hand, this special relationship contributes to the critical care nurse's attempts to act as advocate and coordinator. At the same time, the norms and values of the ICU environment prevent the nurse from gaining the formal rights necessary to fulfill these roles. The nurse can deal with this dilemma in several ways.

The nurse may attempt to deal with problems in an open and mature fashion, focusing on the patient's needs and confronting conflicts as they occur. This is clearly the most desirable approach, although it often precipitates additional stress. The nurse who perceives him/herself to be a competent professional, with appropriate goals based on identified patient needs and wishes, will not tolerate behavior on the part of others that denigrates the nurse's status or appears contrary to the patient's best interest. If the nurse disagrees with, or is concerned about, the care provided by others, he or she will intervene. Such an approach will obviously generate reactions from others, which will be based on their perceptions of the appropriateness of the nurse's intervention, the nurse's "proper" role in the unit, and the nurse's specific behaviors. This may result in everyone's gaining a better understanding of mutual goals, priorities, or points of difference, which may eventually produce a healthier working relationship. Or, it may result in heightened conflict and reinforced misperceptions. The fact that ICUs are staffed by young caregivers, who are not only struggling to establish their professional identities but are often not secure in their personal identities, makes this an all too frequent outcome.

The "doctor-nurse game" is another option for a nurse who is trying to achieve his/her goal. Stein coined this term to describe a mode of communication to which doctors and nurses are socialized.[4,5] In this variation on sex-based stereotypes, the nurse assumes a naive, unsophisticated demeanor in approaching the physician, the wise healer, who will assist in her plight—that is, will do what she wants for her patient. The object of the game is to have the nurse make a recommendation to the physician without appearing to do so. The physician is thus able to utilize the nurse as an expert consultant without actually asking advice, which would seriously threaten his image of omnipotence. This type of behavior is often the path of least resistance; it provides a quick way for the nurse to obtain the orders she needs for the patient, get a new IV started, or get the house officer to talk with the patient's family. However, it also demeans both parties, and reinforces a distorted image of the nurse as a helpless female and the physician as an omniscient being.

When facing a conflict, another appropriate option is to refer the problem to a higher authority. As members of the hospital's formal bureaucratic heirarchy, nurses are more likely to exercise this option than physicians, who may be more reluctant to appeal to others for help. The importance of having a supportive supervisor, and the deleterious effects of not having this resource available, are attested to by the stress studies mentioned earlier. Both Bailey[26] and Huckaby[46] found unresponsive nursing leadership and communication problems with supervisors to be among the most significant sources of stress. Inability or reluctance to appeal to higher authority is an unfortunate situation in that it eliminates an effective means of dealing with conflict. Referring disagreements to a higher level removes the issue from the bedside and assists in focusing on the issues themselves, rather than the personalities involved. Relocating the conflict frees staff nurses and physicians from interpersonal tensions that can hamper effective functioning, and is a valuable way to prevent disagreements from affecting patient care.

Another way for nurses to maximize their ability to control the situation is by utilizing their unlimited informal power. After a few years of experience in an ICU, the nurse becomes a system expert. He or she learns how to get "stat" lab results, which medications are stocked, the preferences and routines of senior attending physicians, and how the equipment works. In addition, the experienced nurse is quite knowledgeable about the usual effects of particular therapies, the usual course of a disease, recommended medication dosages, and other aspects of patient care that the young house officer has simply not yet had a chance to learn. Having this knowledge is a source of tremendous power for the nurse, enabling her to choose between helping the inexperienced physician or letting him flounder and learn the hard way. The nurse's choice is often influenced by the quality of previous interactions, the individual physician involved, professional security, and the other's willingness to request and receive help from a nurse.

The descriptions of these interactional styles are not meant to type-cast critical care nurses; they are meant to demonstrate how the issues discussed earlier in this chapter affect the relationships between the nurse and other caregivers. If there is a lesson to be learned from this analysis of critical care nursing, it is that the problems are more complex than they initially appear. The critical care nurse is a product of the history of nursing, the struggles of women in our society, the modern intensive care unit environment, and, most importantly, the conflicts and positive relationships with other care providers.

REFERENCES

1. Nurses today—A statistical portrait. *Am J Nurs* 1982, *82*:448-451.
2. Levine E, Moses EB: Registered nurses today: A statistical profile, in *Nursing in the 1980s—Crises, Opportunities, Challenges,* Aiken LH (ed.). Philadelphia, Pa.: J.B. Lippincott, 1982, pp. 475-495.
3. Winslow GR: From loyalty to advocacy: A new metaphor for nursing. *Hastings Ctr Rep* 1984, *14*:32-40.
4. Fagin C, Diers D: Nursing as a metaphor. *N Engl J Med* 1983, *309*:116-117.
5. Kalisch PA, Kalisch BJ: The image of nurses on prime time television. *Am J Nurs* 1982, *82*:264-270.
6. Kalisch PA, Kalisch BJ: The image of nurses in novels. *Am J Nurs* 1982, *82*: 1220-1224.
7. Greene JA: Science, nursing, and nursing science: A conceptual analysis. *Adv Nurs Sci* 1979, *2*:57-64.
8. Thierer J, Perhus S, McCracken MC, et al. (eds.): *Standards for Nursing Care of the Critically Ill.* Reston, Va., Reston, 1981.
9. Binder J: Value conflicts in health care organizations. *Nurs Econ* 1983, *1*: 114-119.
10. Beard RO: The trained nurse of the future. *JAMA* 1913, *61*:2149-2152.
11. AMA Committee on Nursing: Medicine and nursing in the 1970s: A position statement. *JAMA* 1970, *213*:1881-1883.
12. In *re Tuma.* Supreme Court of the State of Idaho. 1977 Case 12587.
13. Brault GL, Pflaum SS: Planning and development of a masters degree program in critical care. *Heart Lung* 1979, *8*:933-938.
14. Hay D, Oken D: The psychological stresses of intensive care nursing. *Psychosom Med* 1972, *34*:109-118.

15. Oskins SL: Identification of situational stressors and coping methods by intensive care nurses. *Heart Lung* 1979, *8*:953-960.
16. Dear MR, Weisman CS, Alexander CS, Chase GA: The effect of the intensive care nursing role on job satisfaction and turnover. *Heart Lung* 1982, *11*:560-565.
17. Grout JW, Steffen SM, Bailey JT: The stresses and satisfiers of the intensive care unit: A survey. *Crit Care Qtrly* 1981, *3*:35-45.
18. Gentry WD, Foster SB, Froehling S: Psychological response to situational stress in intensive and non-intensive nursing. *Heart Lung* 1972, *1*:793-796.
19. Maloney JP, Bartz C: Stress-tolerant people: Intensive care nurses compared with non-intensive care nurses. *Heart Lung* 1983, *12*:389-399.
20. Maloney JP: Job stress and its consequences in a group of intensive care and non-intensive care nurses. *Adv Nurs Sci* 1982, *4*:31-41.
21. Benton DA, White HC: Satisfaction of job factors for registered nurses. *J Nurs Admin* 1972, *2*:55-63.
22. Storlie FJ: Burnout: The elaboration of a concept. *Am J Nurs* 1979, *79*:2108-2111.
23. Friedman EH: Stress and intensive care nursing: A ten-year reappraisal. *Heart Lung* 1982, *11*:26-28.
24. Eisendrath SJ, Dunkle J: Psychological issues in intensive care unit staff. *Heart Lung* 1979, *8*:751-758.
25. Cook CB, Mandrillo M: Perceived stress and situational supports. *Nurs Mgmt* 1982, *13*:31-33.
26. Bailey JT, Steffen SM, Grout JW: The stress audit: Identifying the stressors of ICU nursing. *J Nurs Educ* 1980, *19*:15-25.
27. Adler DC, Shoemaker NJ (eds): *AACN Organization and Management of Critical-Care Facilities.* St. Louis, Mo.: C.V. Mosby, 1979, p. xii.
28. Meltzer LE, Pinneo R, Kitchell JR: *Intensive Coronary Care,* 3d ed. Bowie, Md.: Charles Press, 1977, p. 39.
29. Ledingham IM (ed): *Recent Advances in Intensive Therapy.* New York: Churchill Livingstone, 1977, p. 6.
30. National Institutes of Health: *Consensus Development Conference: Critical Care Medicine.* Washington, D.C.: U.S. Government Printing Office, 1983.
31. Erde EE: Notions of teams and team talk in health care: Implications for responsibilities. *Law, Med, Hlth Care* 1981, *9*:26-28.
32. Mullen A: Small-town critical care. *Dimensions Crit Care Nurs* 1982, *1*:212-214.
33. Corless IB: Physicians and nurses: Roles and responsibilities in caring for the critically ill patient. *Law, Med, Hlth Care* 1982, *10*:72-76.
34. Aiken LH (ed): *Nursing in the 1980s: Crises, Opportunities, Challenges.* Philadelphia, Pa.: J.B. Lippincott, 1982, p. 15.
35. Annas GJ, Healy JM: The patient rights advocate: Redefining the doctor-patient relationship in the hospital context, in Abrams N, Buckner MD (eds) *Medical Ethics.* Cambridge, Mass.: MIT Press, 1983.

36. Bergen BJ, Lindenthal JJ, Thomas CS: Alienation and medicine, in Bandman EL, Bandman B (eds), *Bioethics and Human Rights.* Philadelphia, Pa.: Little, Brown, and Co., 1978, p. 295.

37. Veatch RM: *A Theory of Medical Ethics.* New York: Basic Books, 1981.

38. Aiken LH: Nursing priorities for the 1980s: Hospitals and nursing homes. *Am J Nurs* 1981, *81*:325.

39. American Hospital Association: *Evolving Nursing Practice as it Affects Hospitals.* Discussion paper distributed to member hospitals. 1981.

40. Lublin JS: Critical condition: Severe nurse shortage forces some hospitals to close beds, units. *The Wall Street Journal,* July 18, 1980, pp. 1, 26.

41. Levi M: Functional redundancy and the process of professionalization: The case of registered nurses in the United States. *J Hlth Politics, Policy, Law* 1980, *5*:333-351.

42. Ashley JA: Power in structured misogyny: Implications for the politics of care. *Adv Nurs Sci* 1980, *2*:2-22.

43. Lovell MC: Silent but perfect "partners": Medicine's use and abuse of women. *Adv Nurs Sci* 1981, *3*:25-40.

44. Greenleaf NP: Sex-segregated occupations: Relevance for nursing. *Adv Nurs Sci* 1980, *2*:23-35.

45. Stein LI: The doctor-nurse game. *Arch Gen Psychiatry* 1967, *16*:699-703.

46. Huckabay LM, Jagla B: Nurses' stress factors in the intensive care unit. *J Nurs Admin* 1979, *9*:21-26.

7   Caring for Families
Joel E. Frader

INTRODUCTION

"I sat with him for 5-minute intervals, twice a day, in the cubicle bathed with that monstrous fluorescent light which gives everything white the dead waxen sheen of lilies."[1]

In *Heartsounds*, Martha Weinman Lear captures some of the complex reactions of family members to the intensive care unit (ICU): terror, reassurance, anger, confusion, misery, to name a few. Mrs. Lear's rage cannot fail to touch anyone who reads the story of her husband's long battle against severe heart disease. As she relates in her dramatic book, almost everything that befell her physician-husband became doubt-provoking, and doctors and hospitals do not receive gentle or sympathetic treatment. Ironically, Mrs. Lear barely mentions the indignity imposed upon her and her husband by his "isolation" in an ICU. She sees him for five minutes, two times a day! Perhaps his frightening appearance, pale and sick unto death, so upset her that more time with him would have been too much for her. Whatever the reason, Mrs. Lear did not protest. We must ask how such a visiting policy could exist. This query is part of a larger set of questions about the impact of the ICUs on the family, and that of the family on the ICU.

The existing health professions literature is nearly all critical. Physicians have not been especially concerned with the emotional needs of their critically ill *adult* patients. While psychiatric complications of cardiac *surgery* were hot topics in the 1960s,[2] and the "psychological hazards" to patients in *medical* coronary care units were recognized widely after Hackett, Cassem, and Wishnie's description,[3] the medical literature contains only sporadic discussions of the problems encountered by families of myocardial infarction (MI) victims. Despite the tremendous growth of interest in critical care, few papers about families of patients have appeared in professional medical journals oriented to the care of adults.

The nursing literature is far more extensive, but points out the problematic role of nursing in health care. Strauss, a medical sociologist, discussed ICUs in an issue of *Nursing Clinics of North America*.[4] He noted, "that the nurses were undertrained to care for family members and learned to devise various tactics . . . to minimize inconvenience to themselves and interference with their work." This approach may have extended to nursing academia. The nursing study by Brown reported that ten-minute visits by family members to a CCU were associated with increases in patients' systolic blood pressures and heart rates.[5] Though the physiologic changes were modest, the author touted their statistical significance and asserted that this "stress" was clinically important and "not conducive to good patient management." The article, which was accepted without much critical evaluation, seems to have served as post facto justification for already restrictive visiting policies. Nursing research and commentary has recently become more questioning of "accepted" practice, perhaps reflecting the drive toward a more independent status for nurses in the health care field.

The relative lack of medical and nursing interest in families is altogether different when families of critically ill children, especially newborns, are the focus of attention. Parents, of course, are necessary to the care of children. At the very least, doctors, nurses, and hospitals depend on parents for consent to treat children. More cynically, parents often pay the bills. But those who care for children have a fundamentally different outlook. Pediatric health care providers generally expect to join with parents in the common enterprise of helping to save dependent lives. Caution is in order though, because, as many have noted, even powerful cultural imperatives such as adults helping children may bow to the dictates of a technology-driven system of medical care.[6]

The rest of this chapter selectively reviews the literature on intensive care units and families, and recommends some ways to form beneficial and satisfying alliances with spouses, siblings, parents, and similar "significant others."

LITERATURE REVIEW

Adults

Klein and colleagues' study on "post myocardial infarction invalidism" was one of the first empirical studies of the impact of critical illness on the family.[7] The inordinate fears of some of the patients were apparently reinforced by wives who were plagued by uncertainty and inadequate medical information. Patients and wives believed that "the heart remained in a very fragile condition." This belief led to major changes in family roles, which resulted in some substantial marital conflict.

Wynn made a clear statement of concerns about relatives of coronary artery disease victims by commenting that there was "a disturbance of the whole family unit, whose suffering, indeed, may be seen as serious and more prolonged than that of the patient himself."[8] The wives of patients in Wynn's study "received inadequate moral support, guidance, reassurance and explanation from their husband's doctors." The consequence was undue fear and overprotective behavior by the wives. Adsett and Bruhn also recognized the importance of family support.[9] They reported the result of a trial of short-term group psychotherapy for wives of patients recovering from myocardial infarction. These women were noted to feel anxious, guilty, and depressed; compared to their husbands, however, they were relatively unable to deal openly with their feelings. Their anger and denial made the therapy experience less successful than the authors had hoped.

Wishnie, Hackett, and Cassem studied 18 families of convalescing MI patients.[10] Although "significant anxiety" was present in all of the families, the authors felt that the emotional response in 13 families was "disproportionate to the patient's current degree of disability." Families tried to coddle the heart attack victims, arousing resentment in the patients. The authors felt that the family disturbances "occurred even when the marriage and pre-morbid home life had been quite stable."

Zetterlund focused on the effects on the family of the acute, rather than the recovery, phase of the illness.[11] In a chapter of a nursing text, she reported the results of "an evaluation of visiting policies of intensive and coronary care units." Noting that the five minute per hour visitation practice had been recommended by a U.S. Public Health Service document published in 1962, Zetterlund commented that the restriction had "been of concern to some patients and families." She undertook a study that took advantage of differential enforcement of five-minute visiting policies in two coronary care units. Of 17 patients interviewed, 11 felt that five minutes was too short, five preferred the limitations, and one was noncommittal. Only one of nine family members accepted the limitation, one was ambivalent, and seven wanted longer visits. Zetterlund also measured patients' heart rates during visits and compared them to nonvisit resting rates. The observations were few and not clearly controlled, though the author felt justified in concluding "that visits longer than . . . desired by the patient" produced cardiac changes. In any case, the author wondered whether blanket restrictions were in the best interests of patients and families, and called for further study and debate on the matter.

Skelton and Dominian published an important paper which prospectively evaluated "psychological stress in wives of patients with myocardial infarction."[12] The study involved 65 wives of patients admitted to a British coronary care unit. The women reported initial "numbness and panic," with many having a feeling of "unreality." Also important in the acute phase of their husbands' illnesses were guilt, classic grief reactions, such as sleep and appetite disturbances, as well as psychosomatic symptoms.

A similar study in England was reported by Mayou, Williamson, and Foster.[13] Relatives of the MI patient found the hospital confusing and intimidating, and were especially frightened by the "gadgets and things." Anxiety prevented some family members from seeking desired information about their sick relatives, especially from the doctors. The authors suggested that simple measures like "written guidance" and clear lines of communication and responsibility would be beneficial. A later study of wives of MI victims emphasized that the fear of either death or the loss of the health of the mate predominated in the first hours and days of hospitalization.[14]

Epperson published a review of observations of 230 families of injured patients treated at the Maryland Institute for Emergency Medicine.[15] In her report, Epperson described the period of confusion attendant to the sudden, unanticipated trauma. Family members experienced anxiety, denial, anger, remorse, grief, and reconciliation in the "phases of recovery" following the accident. Effective intervention in the early hours emphasized "brief, accurate information" about the patient's status and treatment. Family members were also encouraged to express their feelings. As rage appeared over the next few days, relatives were helped by efforts to "focus on the real cause of their anger"—the patient. The accompanying guilt was relieved "only by open discussion." Sadness responded to quiet empathy. Reconciliation occurred when the social worker encouraged family members to focus on what they could and should do to facilitate the patient's rehabilitation.

In order to investigate the experience of relatives of critically ill patients, Molter conducted a descriptive study in two ICUs in teaching hospitals.[16] In highly structured interviews with 40 relatives of critically ill patients, she determined which "needs," out of a list of 45 generated by the investigator, were most important to family members. Examples included: "to feel there is hope"; "to visit any time"; "to talk about negative feelings such as guilt or anger." The most-often-cited needs involved hope, reassurance of care and concern for the patient by staff, and "adequate and honest" information about the patient. Frequent visiting was the tenth most important need. Nurses were most often identified as meeting family members' needs, though relatives turned to physicians for answers to questions about hope and prognosis. Similar results were obtained in later studies by Daley,[17] Stillwell,[18] and Mathis.[19]

Speedling spent six months observing in a nine-bed ICU in a community hospital.[20] He noted that the experience of critical care actually began in the emergency room lobby, where physicians announced the diagnosis (MI) and the need for the patient to be in the ICU. Shocked families requested little clarification, and "the physicians did not probe for questions or offer any assistance." When relatives arrived to see the patients in the ICU, "There was no systematic routine for introducing the family to the unit." Families were apparently viewed as "potentially disruptive," and the staff controlled relatives' behavior by ignoring them. Nothing about the organization of the unit welcomed or assisted families. The waiting area was uncomfortable, no privacy was available, physician rounds occurred before families were permitted to visit, and staff members "did not initiate communication with families." By the same token, Speedling felt relatives were emotionally unable to seek staff attention or were afraid the staff would punish the patients if the families were viewed as too demanding.

These family experiences, filled with deprivation and fear, contrasted with the patients' sense of staff attentiveness and concern. In turn, the patient-family differences created difficulties, largely with regard to prognosis and the rehabilitation process. Moreover, the ICU personnel never addressed these common conflicts. On the whole, the staff failed to involve and assist the families in treatment.

Recognition of the sorts of problems described by Speedling and others led to various interventions in the late 1970s. Atkinson, Stewart, and Gardner reported on their efforts in a university trauma unit.[21] They used an interdisciplinary team (ICU physicians, nurses, social workers, and a psychiatrist) in a structured family conference that usually took place "by the second hospital day." The meetings addressed "needs for information, emotional expression, usefulness, and a sense of communication with the staff." By involving the families and building a relationship with them, the authors felt the conferences improved family organization and coping, and thus assisted patient management. The family meetings and postconference staff meetings also facilitated a coordinated staff approach to patients and families, and helped to teach "the psychological care of the medically ill" to staff members.

Hodovanic and colleagues developed and described the impact of a family-oriented crisis intervention program for an MICU.[22] The nursing team used a standard format "to assess the psychosocial status of the patient," meet the family or contact relatives by phone, and convey specific information to the family about the patient's condition and treatment, as well as the visiting policy of the unit. A schedule was established for daily telephone contact from the patient's nurse to the family. Basic information about the medical team (nurses' and doctors' names) and the MICU environment was provided in written material, which also contained an explanation of the unit, the hospital, and common equipment and procedures employed in patient care. When considered appropriate, the nurse also escorted the family to the bedside for specific instruction and reassurance. The nurses also inquired about the adequacy of family resources to meet medical expenses, making social service referrals when appropriate. The structured nursing approach was supplemented by volunteers in the MICU waiting area during periods when family visiting was permitted. Volunteers provided information on logistics (lodging, food, parking, places to stay), communicated with the MICU staff as needed, and listened empathically to family members. Finally, a follow-up program for former patients and grieving families was established. Though the authors felt that their approach had improved care and family satisfaction, no formal evaluation was reported.

The attempts to respond to identified problems in family care have been neither long-term nor consistent. Indeed, the debate on visiting policies remains unsettled. Brown's finding that visiting caused physiologic stress to CCU patients was not challenged systematically until a 1982 study of a surgical ICU by Fuller and Foster.[23] Their nursing study looked at blood pressure, heart rate, and "vocal stress" (measured by "microtremor suppression" on audiotaped speech samples) in 28 SICU patients. Control strategies included the sampling of physiologic variables before, during, and after family visits, and two kinds of patient interactions with nurses. All interactions lasted 15 minutes. Neither the visits nor the nursing encounters had any statistically significant effect on the measured variables. The authors concluded that their "data do not support a reduction in patient visiting periods."

Kirchhoff reported on a national survey of ICU/CCU visiting policies for MI patients.[24] Smaller hospitals (under 200 beds) allowed visiting every one or two hours, while large hospitals tended to limit visiting to specified times—for example, 10:00 A.M., 2:00 P.M., 8:00 P.M. Visits were generally kept short, and often limited to immediate family members or only a few visitors. Nurses in these units "value and regularly impose the restrictions." The author correctly asks which visiting policy is best, as "no one has shown that visiting restrictions produce rest for the patient." Even this query begs other important unanswered questions, such as the meaning and value of "rest" for the critically ill patient. As Kirchhoff points out, long periods of isolation and separation after short visits may be more harmful, at least to some patients, than constant companionship.

Dunkel and Eisendraft addressed the institutional variables in ICU visiting policies.[25] Concerned with the effects families had on the staff, they observed in a unit after a policy change substantially increased visiting time. The new flexibility helped clarify both positive and negative reactions to families in the unit. The staff benefitted from the opportunity to build a trusting relationship with the patient through the visitors, especially if communication with the patient was limited. Families also provided staff with feedback when the patient could not. Visitors could provide otherwise unavailable personal histories for patients, thereby placing care in the context of the patients' lives outside of the ICU. Thus, a very elderly woman's "heroic" treatment was justified when her family provided information about her previous excellent health and independent life. Her acute, reversible condition was successfully treated with the help of this morale-building data. When patients did die, family members and staff were able to share grieving and facilitate mutual reintegration into daily activities.

On the negative side, Dunkel and Eisendraft reminded us that visitors may be critical and rejecting of the staff, undermining trust among family members, patients, and staff alike. This is especially trouble-some if the family has unrealistic expectations for the patient's survival or extent of recovery. The presence of visitors may also deter staff members from carrying out treatments, especially uncomfortable procedures. Such inhibition is especially likely if the staff member questions how beneficial the procedure is to the patient. Some nurses may dislike the pressure that results when colleagues develop strong attachments to families. Not every nurse felt able to live up to the expectations created by these special relationships. Finally, the authors pointed out that patient deaths may be more difficult to bear when staff members know the patients and families well. Responsibilities to family members and the related interpersonal burdens may be major reasons for promoting restrictive visiting policies in adult ICUs.

Children

Until the 1950s and 1960s, it was common for parents of children hospitalized in Western countries to endure even more restrictive visiting policies than those discussed above. Besides needing "rest," it was believed that illness-weakened little bodies could not tolerate the separation involved in parental comings and goings. A virtual revolution in child development theory and child-rearing practices in the post-World War II period generated sweeping changes in hospital pediatric policies. Families were not just permitted to visit on flexible schedules; they were literally invited to move in. Parental care units were established and beds were made available to mothers and fathers. In the 1970s, siblings, known as walking culture media carrying dread diseases, were sometimes permitted to visit their vulnerable brothers and sisters. By the time pediatric intensive care units were established, open access for parents was a nonissue in many respects. The ethos of pediatrics, at least in most tertiary care centers that house virtually all PICUs, made major restrictions on visiting unthinkable. Physical constraints often led to limitations on the number of family members at the bedside, and to loose restrictions on who could visit (parents, grandparents, siblings, and so on). Some units limit visiting during certain procedures—for example, lumbar puncture, cut-downs, although this practice varies. Most units also prefer to keep visitors out during extreme emergencies—for example, resuscitations, although the sudden, unexpected nature of these events frequently leaves some visitors staring from the sidelines.

Because pediatrics is necessarily family-oriented, the pediatric literature concerned with critical or terminal illness has long discussed the role of the family. Richmond and Waisman devoted a large portion of a paper generally concerned with psychological management for childhood malignancies to "the help which [the physician] may provide to the parents in their integration of a tragic event into their life experience."[26] The authors discussed family responses to these situations, echoing the themes already mentioned above with regard to families of sick adults (for example, shock, anxiety, need for information). Like other writers of pediatric literature, Richmond and Waisman emphasized the importance of parental guilt—that is, feelings of responsibility for the illness or, at least, feelings of responsibility for delay in seeking medical attention or for obtaining inappropriate care. The other major point in this early paper is that parents have considerable anxiety over separation from the ill child; this echoes the concern about isolation found in the adult literature.

As early as the mid-1950s, however, the pediatric response to such a family crisis was a straightforward recommendation for "the involvement of parents in the physical care of the child." "Parents," Richmond and Waisman said, "are very grateful for having had the opportunity to spend as much time with the child as possible."[26] The rationale behind our cultural decision that direct parental care of minor children in hospitals, especially ICUs, is acceptable and even desirable, while participation by spouses, children, or other loved ones in the care of adults is largely taboo, is an interesting and troubling issue.

During the 1950s and 1960s, several investigators conducted a series of empirical studies of parents of children with cancer and other fatal illnesses. Bozeman, Orbach, and Sutherland studied the mothers of 20 children with acute leukemia.[27] The authors identified 12 common psychological phenomena in these families:

1. initial denial of the (fatal) nature of the illness;
2. feelings of responsibility for the illness;
3. anger with the medical professionals;
4. intellectualization aimed at mastering the illness;
5. maintenance of hope despite realization of inevitable death;
6. distress with hospital organization and depersonalization;
7. despair in the face of staff usurpation of parental roles and/or limitation of access to the children;
8. reluctance to use family resources (especially the child's grandparents) for physical or emotional support;
9. increased use of previous friendships to meet emotional needs;
10. gratifying involvement with other parents in similar circumstances;

11. little comfort from religious beliefs or interactions with clergy;
12. frequent disturbances of eating, sleeping, and patterns of sibling care.

Natterson and Knudson reported on observations of 33 families of children with cancer.[28] They also noted initial denial and prominent anxiety. Early on, mothers tended to cling to their sick children and openly expressed their guilt. With time, these parents derived satisfaction from active participation in care and from relationships with other parents of cancer victims; in addition, they often developed an interest in the scientific aspects of cancer. As the deaths of the children approached, many mothers withdrew somewhat from their ill child and turned to other members of their own families and to helping other families cope. An important observation is that when the interval between diagnosis and death was less than four months, maternal reactions were more likely to be overtly tense and anxious, even hysterical.

In three papers published over a five-year period, Solnit and Green discussed the psychological management of childhood deaths.[29-31] While the first paper was prescriptive, rather than a discussion of experience or data, it explicitly raised some of the most important and debated issues in family care: truthtelling; the difficulties of medical uncertainty; medical ethnocentrism regarding grief; physician discomfort with strong emotions; informing siblings about the death of a brother or sister; obtaining autopsy permission; and other topics.[29] In the second piece, the authors reviewed the literature on "the child's reaction to his own imminent death and the manner in which he can be helped to cope."[30] Though much of that material may have been supplanted by contemporary work in child development, the authors reminded us of the importance and strength of the fears of separation and pain for ill and dying children. This knowledge has obvious value in counseling families.

The last of these papers described a "vulnerable child syndrome," in which parental expectations or fears of the child's premature death "react with a disturbance in psycho-social development."[31] The paper dealt with more than 50 children in three groups seen over six years. The largest category included the parents of 25 of the children, who had been told by the physician "that the child was going to die, was likely to die, or would not live long." Although all of the children recovered, their parents regarded them as "vulnerable to serious illness or accident and destined to die during childhood," whether or not a realistic threat to life continued. Some of the mothers became seriously depressed or suffered recurrent "nightmares about losing their child"; both parents and children had sleep problems. Later, "pathologic separation difficulties" developed. Psychosomatic complaints and school phobias or underachievement in school were frequent. The parents became "overprotective, overly indulgent, and oversolicitous" of children who were infantile, unruly, and even abusive of their mothers. Thus, even when serious threats to the life of a child had been long overcome, they impinged on family relationships and the development of healthy independence in the children. The authors cautioned physicians to use the term "critically ill" judiciously and to strive to emphasize recovery when it is apparent, rather than dwell on the prior seriousness of an illness.

Another trio of papers, written by Friedman and colleagues, appeared in the 1960s.[32-34] One reported the results of interviews and inpatient clinical observations of parents of 27 children whose malignancies were treated at the National Cancer Institute (NCI).[32] Additional data came from parent questionnaires about daily activities and nurses' observations on a separate ward at the NCI where the parents stayed. Although initial "shock" was universal, overt denial was not seen in this group. Again considerable, though transient, guilt was expressed by virtually all parents. These parents had "an insatiable need for information," often revealing their anxiety or other turmoil in the search for intellectual mastery of their child's disease. As in Bozeman's study, the parents resented the relative importance of the professionals in the lives of their children. There were also major conflicts with grandparents and inconsistent solace from religious beliefs or practices. The parents achieved some relief from stress by increasing their physical activity and establishing relationships with other parents of cancer-stricken children. When death approached, these parents verbalized their wishes to share pleasant experiences with the children, and their desire for the pain to be over for all concerned. The parents gradually withdrew from the dying children to attend to others and return to a more normal life.

In the second 1963 paper, Friedman and coworkers used urinary corticosteroid secretion to gauge stress of the parents of the NIC-hospitalized children.[33] Elevations of hormonal secretions were noted at the time of the child's first admission to the NCI and at times of subsequent medical crises. Overall, the data "revealed a remarkable stability of adrenal cortical function," which was interpreted by the research team as an indication of physiologic adaptation to chronic stress. Also noteworthy was their impression that the hormonal modulation did not occur when events occurred too rapidly for parents to mobilize psychological defenses. The final paper in the series is prescriptive, telling physicians how to care for families with a child who has cancer.[34] Here Friedman reminded us that anticipatory grief behavior, with the parents trying to assist others prior to the death of their child, may be easily misinterpreted by the staff as abandonment. Yet, medical professionals should support this tacit acceptance of death and the implication of impending relief from suffering.

The middle 1960s saw the publication of numerous papers by pediatricians advising their colleagues on approaches to dying children and their families. Although the authors clearly had considerable experience, few of these papers reported any systematic collection or analysis of information gathered during the care of critically ill children. Howell, for example, provided much previously unwritten common sense about the value of informing both parents together of a fatal diagnosis, the importance of privacy, pitfalls of predicting length of survival, and so on.[35] In a similar discussion, Evans emphasized shielding the child from the fear of death.[36] This approach was different from that of many writers and markedly at odds with the attitudes of Vernick and Karon, the authors of one of the only studies of children's reactions to actual or impending death on a cancer ward.[37] What is important here is the paternalistic nature of the debate. With the exception of the few researchers in the field, the authoritative writers of the day did not consider the possibility that medical staff and families, not to mention families on their own, could collaboratively decide on the best way to deal with each particular child's needs.

Two papers published in the late 1960s reported on retrospective studies of families who had experienced childhood fatalities. Martin, Lawrie, and Wilkinson in London interviewed parents of children who had died of thermal injury.[38] Of note was that some of the parents had been advised "that it might spare their feelings if they did not see the child . . . [and] such advice now seems very questionable." The parents' belief that they had not given their children adequate support accentuated their grief and guilt. Because parents blamed one another for the accident which caused the death, counseling aimed at this issue might have been helpful.

Binger and others interviewed the parents of 20 children who had died of leukemia during a two-year period.[39] These families recalled some reaction patterns that differed from those observed in the earlier prospective studies. Prominent in the memories of a few was the withdrawal of hospital staff as the child's death approached. Also, "the fathers found many ways to absent themselves from painful involvement with their troubled families." Like other groups, these authors felt that a short course of illness was associated with greater family turmoil than situations in which the children lived longer and the family had time for adaptation.

The literature on families of children beyond the newborn period who are actually in intensive care units first appeared in the 1970s. In a report of his observations as a psychiatric consultant to a pediatric intensive therapy unit (ITU) during a six-month interval, May remarked that the works of many of the authors reviewed above revealed much that was similar to his ITU experiences.[40] Nominal visiting restrictions for parents (15 minutes per hour) were not enforced, and parents could be found at the bedside at any time. Nurse-patient interactions were noted to be humane and ordinary—for example, children were held and rocked, families were casually instructed about the goings-on—actions that occur "without loss of professional nursing identity or skill." May believed that "the whole family must be treated, rather than just the sick child." This was easily accomplished because parents readily recognized the superior care in the ITU, and because the parents needed "to minimize and deny their fear, to minimize the danger of their child's condition." Frequent communication between staff and parents and among staff members reduced inconsistency and parental anxiety. May concluded that parents "do have the need to be involved in their own child's care." Jay published a nursing article urging ICU nurses to engage parents with their children during the crisis.[41]

In 1979, Frader published the results of an ethnographic study of a large PICU.[6] The paper focused on the difficulties for staff working in such environments. Important for purposes of this chapter was the documentation of the commonly observed phenomenon that the physicians in the unit concentrated their attention on technical care. The human aspects of child or family care were rarely discussed. Psychosocial and ethical concerns arose only when "scientific" medicine had little else to offer. In a follow-up paper, Frader and Bosk examined the actual language of PICU rounds.[42] Using audiotaped, transcribed data, they found that the physicians rarely mentioned patients' families. Most references to parents came during presentations of medical histories or "planning for patient discharges." Only seven of 19 discrete references to parents were made during discussions of treatment alternatives. Those discussions that did mention parents were those which occurred "when the physicians are no longer comfortable acting on scientific grounds."

At about the same time, others involved in pediatric intensive care were expressing their concern about family coping, especially when a poor prognosis had been proffered by the medical staff. Waller and others discussed "the Cassandra Prophecy"—that is, dire outcomes were predicted for four critically ill children and their parents responded with "hostile denial."[43] The bad prognosis itself was seen by the families as a sign that the staff could not or would not do everything possible to save the patients. The parental reactions angered the staff and frustrated their attempts to rationalize care. The authors suggested that the difficulties were partly due to the extreme pain caused by hearing that the child would die of a condition that the parents did not usually associate with death. Because of the illnesses' sudden onset and the patients' rapid deterioration, and because the medical conditions made relatively little sense to them, the families did not behave like the previously studied parents of cancer patients. Perhaps the physicians used prognostic statements to defend against responsibility for the deaths; the illnesses were so overwhelming that the doctors felt that they could do nothing to help. The doctors also sought to avoid the pain of uncertainty. Interestingly, the authors believed that the conflicts had been less black and white than the physicians appreciated at the time. Parents hinted to the PICU social workers that their denial was not complete, and the social service personnel escaped inclusion in the angry confrontations.

The experience led Waller and colleagues to suggest that "prognosis is probably best given to parents, and best heard by them, at those times that they request it, with appropriate attention to our inability to see with certainty into the future." The authors acknowledged that even though the parents may not always ask, the staff feels the parents must be informed. They advised honesty in such cases, tempered with a promise to do everything possible to prevent the predicted poor outcome. Waller and colleagues also urged: 1. involvement of others on the PICU team (social workers, psychiatrists) to assist staff and parents in their relationships; 2. "additional emotional support" for parents; 3. reflection by staff members on their own feelings and behaviors in these difficult situations; 4. occasional recourse to the courts for conflict resolution.

Green's accompanying editorial went even further.[44] He reminded readers to attend to parental comforts, including their needs for a place to sleep, food, continuity of communication and care of the child, current information about treatment and procedures, and prospective preparation for stressful events, such as the initiation of a brain death protocol.

Rothstein discussed "Psychological Stress in Families of Children in a Pediatric Intensive Care Unit."[45] From his own work as a pediatric intensivist, he noted that parents were initially shocked—that is, disbelieving and feeling helpless. These reactions were sometimes exacerbated by the physical appearance of the child. Guilt was common as parents sought to understand what had happened and why. With stabilization, the family began to anticipate the adverse effects of the condition and its treatment. As they waited, parents became demanding of staff, expressing impatience or rage. Transfer of the child out of the ICU occasioned the same anxious feelings that were observed with adult patients and their families.

Woolston has described the PICU "as a community comprised of several sub-groups, including the staff, patients, families and the physical setting."[46] Reiterating what others have said, he also pointed out that parents, in identifying and sharing experiences with families of other PICU patients, could become competitive, thus increasing tension and guilt in the waiting room.

Woolston urged the staff to consider families' past experiences with crises and loss. A parent with "important losses is much more vulnerable to disorganization in response to the child's PICU hospitalization." Failure to appreciate such personal histories can lead to misunderstandings and staff-parent conflict. Also, the author argued, each illness or stress has its own course or story, with a beginning, middle, and end. These sequences may be experienced differently by each sub-group in the PICU community. "A lack of synchrony among sub-units of the community or a lack of appreciation for the developmental aspect of reactions leads to many communication problems."[46]

To counter the pitfalls he described, Woolston recommended several interventions: "regular staff meetings with a group facilitator"; maintenance of strong hierarchical leadership in the PICU; creation of an interdisciplinary team (doctors, nurses, social workers, child life specialists, and child psychiatrists) to work with patients, families, and staff. The author also cautioned against paternalistic intervention. Parents must give their consent to, and be participants in, what happens to their child. "Although staff members may feel that parents have no right to have information withheld from children, the solution should be to understand and, it is hoped, to change the parental attitude, rather than disregard or override their decision."[46]

The literature on pediatric intensive care as reviewed above reflects three themes. First, critical or life-threatening illness in a family member has a definite, often predictable, impact on the family. Second, the critical illness of a child evokes a special set of responses from family members and professional caregivers (witness the visiting policies). Third, the difficulties attendant to life-threatening illness in children are often more complex because they involve delicate issues of law and morality. Parents ordinarily have the responsibility to decide on matters of medical care in situations where "autonomous" adults would decide for themselves.

Neonatal Intensive Care

As in the other areas surveyed, much of the literature on families of critically ill newborns is anecdotal and normative. The advice offered in these prescriptive papers is generally not different enough from what we have already reviewed or from the recommendations based on actual investigation to justify inclusion at this point. This section focuses largely upon published research on family responses to life-threatening illnesses or deaths of newborns.

Kennell, Slyter, and Klaus examined the mourning responses of mothers who had physical contact with their fatally ill newborns, compared to the reactions of mothers who only had visual contact with their babies.[47] Contrary to general expectations, they found that physical contact was not "unduly upsetting," and that the mothers' grief was remarkably similar "to that described with the deaths of other close family members." On the basis of their findings, Kennell and coauthors recommended that hospitals abandon "protective . . . routines to discourage mothers from having contact with premature and sick newborn infants. . . ." That recommendation coincided with a wider call in the early 1970s for increasing postnatal mother-infant contact to improve "bonding" and possibly reduce pathologic reactions to separation, including child abuse.

In a highly controversial paper, Duff and Campbell reviewed decisions to discontinue life support for critically ill newborns.[48] Their retrospective analysis led them to conclude that parents could and should actively participate in such decision making: "if families regardless of background are heard sympathetically and at length and are given information and answers to their questions in words they understand, the problems of their children as well as the expected benefits and limits of any proposed care can be understood clearly in practically all instances.''

Benfield, Leib, and Reuter studied attitudes, feelings, and behavior of parents whose critically ill newborn infants were referred to their tertiary care NICU.[49] Their paper discussed 101 families with infants who survived, and where it was possible for parents to fill out a questionnaire the day the baby was discharged from the NICU. These parents experienced reactions similar to those described when infants did not survive. Mothers generally had experienced greater worry, symptoms, and sadness (anticipatory grief) than did fathers. The fathers, on the other hand, had to shuttle between the infants' and the mothers' hospitals, often encountering frustrating bureaucratic obstacles. The investigators concluded that there was a need for a social service support program to begin early in the infant's hospital course.

Benfield, Leib, and Vollman[50] returned to the questions raised by Duff and Campbell. In follow-up conferences with 50 sets of parents of infants who had died in their NICU, the authors administered a questionnaire about parental grief. They compared the responses of two groups of parents: those whose babies had received "uninterrupted care" and those who had joined with the physicians in a decision to withdraw respiratory support for their hopelessly ill infants. There were no statistical differences in the overall grief experienced by the two groups. The parents who had participated in a decision to limit care had lower scores on some individual items—for example, irritability. Benfield and colleagues noted that the babies whose respiratory support had been limited had survived longer, and that the additional time may have permitted their parents to resolve their grief more easily. In any case, the authors concluded that parental participation in decisions to withdraw life support was practical and not psychologically harmful.

Rowe and others conducted a retrospective interview study of mothers who had experienced a perinatal death ten to 22 months prior to the survey.[51] None of the mothers cited physicians as a source of support during their grieving, and some criticized their doctors for not contacting them with autopsy results. There had been no follow-up in half the cases, and four out of 13 of these mothers were judged to have an inadequate understanding of the cause of death and the risk of recurrence of fatal illness with another child. Dissatisfaction about

the death was common (19 of 26), and was related to lack of understanding and lack of follow-up. The authors recommended a program
of follow-up coordinated by a social worker. The same authors evaluated their follow-up program and published their results in 1979.
Seventy-six percent of the families chose to have follow-up with a
physician. Over half returned to the tertiary care center for a meeting
with the infant's medical team. Parents least likely to use follow-up
were teenagers, the unmarried, those without telephones, or the un-
employed.

In more recent work on families experiencing the death of a critically ill infant, attention has turned to the value of staff anticipation
of death. In "The Application of Hospice Concepts to Neonatal Care,"
Whitfield and colleagues reviewed their experience with an NICU hospice program.[52] They concluded that the establishment of a private
"Family Room" within the unit facilitated a shift from "rescue" to
palliative care with greater parental involvement. Postmortem follow-
up improved from 60 to 90 percent after the hospice approach was
instituted. Harmon, Glicken, and Siegel, from the same institution as
Whitfield, described the reactions of 38 mothers whose infants died
in their NICU.[53] Half of the deaths occurred prior to the hospice program implementation and half after it began. The hospice program
improved communication with parents about autopsy results, and generally increased staff follow-up. The nursing staff discussed funeral
arrangements with families more frequently after the start of the hospice program.

A British group reported on their experience with NICU deaths
when parents had not been exposed to an official, organized approach.[54] Eleven of the 12 families questioned expressed the view
that they had "wanted to participate more in the care of their baby."
Postmortem contact with families was felt to be inadequate, autopsy
results and recurrence risks had not been consistently discussed with
parents, lasting memories had not been provided for with photographs
and other tangible mementoes, and the families felt there had been in-
sufficient opportunity or encouragement to touch their babies before
or after death. The authors developed and recommended a systematic
approach to neonatal deaths.

For babies who survive, debate continues on the best approach to
family support. Minde and coworkers reported on their efforts to intervene with families in order to reduce stress and perhaps improve
parental caretaking.[55] They organized self-help groups for parents of
NICU patients. The group meetings occurred weekly over 7-12-week

periods. Parental satisfaction and parenting behaviors were measured and compared with the same measures taken on a control group of patients. The authors concluded that the group experience improved family satisfaction with the NICU and increased parental visiting and parent-infant interaction. The parents who attended the groups also seemed more comfortable with their babies. Subsequently, a paper from two British NICUs also reported improved family satisfaction from attendance at parent meetings.[56] The authors noted, however, that single parents, those with language difficulties, and parents of infants who "were likely to be handicapped or die nearly always stayed away."

Yu, Jamieson, and Astbury recounted their observations of 20 parental pairs given unrestricted access to their infants in intensive care nurseries.[57] Noting that NICU visiting restrictions or rigid policies designed to limit infection tended to minimize contact between parents and sick newborns, the authors undertook a study of parental attitudes and reactions when the family members determined the extent of their own involvement. Parents and other family members were oriented to the unit, permitted to stay as long as they wished, and were allowed to participate in care, including stimulation for apnea or the provision of physiotherapy. Parents were also allowed to stay for all procedures, with the exception of extreme emergencies, such as intubations or resuscitations.

The investigators found no change in infection rates with the new policy. Thirty-four of 38 respondents to the questionnaire were pleased with their involvement. Two admitted to being uncomfortable or anxious, and two did not answer the question about enjoyment. Five of the parents indicated concern that their contact could cause harm, seven were uncertain about the effects, and 27 believed their infants "enjoyed the contact and felt more loved and secure as a result." Most of the group felt that they would have objected to a more restricted visiting policy. Schwab reported that sibling visits to an NICU were not harmful to infants or older children and that the families had a "uniformly favorable" response.[58] Another controlled study by Maloney and others also reported sibling enjoyment of visits to an NICU, with some improvement in sibling behavior and no adverse effects on infants or older children.[59]

In a literature review, Klaus and Kennell remarked that studies of parent-infant interactions showed that "mothers who become involved, interested, and anxious about their infants will have an easier time when the infant is taken home."[60] Moreover, there was evidence of an important element of reciprocity in mother-infant interactions—that is, each responded to the other. These studies seemed to reveal that infants, much of the time, determined the pace and quality of the interaction. When mothers were asked to deliberately increase their own activity, infant attention to the mothers decreased. Klaus and Kennell believed that such data suggested a need for caution in the trend to increase external stimulation for sick and/or premature babies.

Jones conducted an "Environmental Analysis of Neonatal Intensive Care" and noted a major difficulty with modern regionalized newborn medicine.[61] There was an inverse correlation between parental visiting time and the distance between the hospital and the parents' home. When distances were over 50 miles, the parents of only one of ten infants visited at all. Three of these long-distance babies became wards of the state during the study. Piecuch recognized the problem of separation secondary to transport to a tertiary care center, and reported improved nursery staff-mother contact when a videophone link permitted mothers to view their infants in the distant NICU.[62] The problem of distance also came up in a study by Smith and Baum.[63] These authors documented that for several populations of British families, 25 percent had serious financial problems that limited the parents' ability to visit their infant in a regional NICU. Few resources were available to assist families in overcoming these mile and dollar obstacles.

The manner in which NICU staff members relate to parents depends upon more than the staff's evaluation of the family as people. According to an ethnography of several ICUs done by Bogdan, Brown, and Foster, the way in which the staff think about the babies also helps determine their approach to the parents.[64] That is, the personnel categorize the infants ("baby" as opposed to "nonviable") and behave with the parents in ways "appropriate" to their child's category. The authors stated that "what exactly is expected of a parent who is thought of as a good parent varies depending on the status of the child." Also, "good" parents ask questions, accept medical uncertainty, are grateful and give positive feedback to the staff, observe NICU rules, visit frequently, touch the baby when visiting, call often, and are most frequently middle or upper middle class. "Not so good" parents can't or won't understand the babies' condition (because of intellectual or psychological limits), don't visit or call often enough, leave the nursery quickly or don't touch the infant enough, and have resources too limited to provide what the staff believes the child should have. Bogdan and colleagues felt these characterizations of parents were "based on limited knowledge derived mainly from short observations, limited conversations or second-hand reporting of incidents and information."

Despite an ideology extolling the virtue of communicating with families, the NICU staffs observed by Bogdan, Brown, and Foster had an unsystematic, idiosyncratic approach.[64] Few staff members had had any formal training in interviewing or counseling. Parent communication was not subject to scrutiny or review, as were medical aspects of infant care. And, unlike the process of technical medical care, overt prejudices and inadequate information influenced family care.

The question of how the experience of having a critically ill infant influences parental perceptions of their baby and subsequent parenting behavior returns to the literature frequently. Philipp studied 37 mothers and 26 fathers of NICU patients.[65] She compared these parents to previously studied other parents "from a presumed normal population." Philipp found no differences in the two samples in parental perceptions of their children, and concluded that there was no evidence for a long-term disruptive effect of serious newborn illness. Clearly, the definitive word on the lasting effects, if any, of NICU hospitalization on family well-being has not yet been written.

The literature on family involvement in clinical and ethical decisions is too extensive and diffuse to be reviewed usefully in this chapter. Watchko provided a helpful conceptual summary of the arguments of the "two schools of thought regarding participation in decision making on critically ill infants."[66] One view is that decisions about life support are too difficult to be made by individuals, especially parents who are emotionally overwrought and whose interests may conflict with those of their baby, especially if the child is likely to survive with significant handicaps. Those holding this view believe that interdisciplinary committees of impartial experts and lay people will provide formal protection (due process) for the infants and "logical moral reasoning." The alternative approach assumes that our pluralistic society can and should tolerate a wide range of options for families and infants. In the absence of a clear social mandate on the care of critically ill infants, it is the families, in conjunction with professional counsel, who should make the decisions. After all, it is argued, the families will experience the greatest impact of commitments for or against life support. Moreover, emotionally distant committee members cannot appreciate the complexities with which families must cope. Finally, the society has not provided extensive systems of financial or social supports for families who must care for severely disabled infants. Without such resources, no one should require families to accept life-saving treatment for their children.

Clearly this debate, too, will continue for some time. It now becomes our task to recommend an approach to families and other loved ones of the critically ill.

Providing Family Care

This section of the chapter draws on the challenges, problems, and proposed solutions identified in the works already reviewed. The ideas also spring from the advice and counsel provided by other commentators. Although specific citations will be used where appropriate, the reader should remember that many of the concepts and particular suggestions in the literature overlap, and attribution to individual sources would be misleading.

Not long ago, a medical historian recommended an eighteenth century physician's approach to providing comfort to the absent father of a burned child.[6][7] Dr. John Warren's words of 1792 might well "still serve as a standard." Dr. Warren wrote to the faraway father, "I thought it not improper to relieve you of the anxiety which might possibly be given you in this way by informing you of the facts myself." A perusal of the literature reviewed above truly suggests Dr. Warren's wisdom. Families need, want, and deserve immediate information, delivered by someone directly involved, most preferably the physician in charge. Research and experience teach us that those who care about our critically ill patients want to know what is going on, what is likely to go on, how they may participate, and how the lines of communication work. For proof, each of us need only ask how we would want to be treated if our spouse or child or parent were receiving treatment in an intensive care unit.

How should those running and working in intensive care units respond to these needs? Two thoughts should be kept in mind. First, our ICUs are now organized around the needs of the staff and, to some extent, patients, not families. Second, no prescription can be written for every organizational contingency. Each unit should develop and maintain some *system* for dealing directly with the patients's families and other visitors. Family care requires the same attention as fluids and electrolyte balance, cardiovascular integrity, and nutrition. No intensivist should tolerate haphazard communication with families, any more than he or she would accept sloppy management of respiratory failure. The benefits of successful staff-family interactions are obvious. As one commentator put it, "Failure to interact appropriately with families may lead to heightened anxiety and fear, misunderstandings, mistrust, hostility, failure to obtain important information about the patient, and even lawsuits."[6][8] The fact that we do not insist upon the same degree of rigor in interpersonal matters in the ICU as we require with respect to technical matters reflects our values and discomfort with our feelings. If, for the sake of maintaining clinical "objectivity," physicians and nurses must divorce themselves from affective communication with families, then medical personnel must willingly and graciously cede these responsibilities to social workers, psychologists, and others prepared to assume the tasks.

GENERAL CONSIDERATIONS

It may be helpful to review, in general terms, how families respond to a relative's ICU hospitalization, at least when the situation has not been anticipated (as in elective surgery with routine postoperative ICU management). Initially, there is a sense of shock and loss. This first period may precipitate a number of emotional reactions, including denial, guilt, and depression, with its components of sadness and anger. Frequently, one may observe regression, especially in such situations as the NICU hospitalization of the preterm infant of not fully mature parents. Eventually, one expects to see acceptance of the reality of the illness and its possible consequences. As family members accept what is happening, they move to reestablish a relationship with the patient, perhaps one based on radically altered perceptions about the loved one's future. This new relationship may require planning based on the changed needs, if any, imposed by the medical condition which brought the patient to the ICU.

In the shifting, often uncertain context of critical illness, it is impossible to predict the timing of the evolution of the family's response. The variables are too many, the contingencies too complex. A patient's rapid recovery may moot the entire question of family reaction. Generational and educational differences or preexisting turmoil within the family may cause some relatives to react quite differently from others. Social and cultural differences between family and staff may, unwittingly, cause substantial miscommunication and conflict. Staff members working with the family must, therefore, make a difficult, but essential, effort to monitor their own responses to the situation. Such self-consciousness can avert inappropriate imposition of staff members' values and preferences on an already stressed family system. When there is doubt about family members' wishes or behavior, perhaps the best response is tactful inquiry aimed at confirming or refuting the presence of a perceived problem. Similarly, if communication with the family is going poorly, the staff should explore other approaches and/ or employ other individuals. Not all styles of interaction mesh well. Most importantly, the staff members should remember the simple device of asking the family what they believe to be wrong and what they think will best help them.

The nature of the system used to assist families should fit with the style of the ICU's resources. Different units have had success with different approaches. ICUs with a primary nurse system may choose to have the primary nurse greet the family and provide basic information about the patient and the unit. Other units employ nurse clinicians whose major responsibility is to assist families and provide liaison with the medical and nursing staff. Some units have social workers who do most of the work with families. Team approaches have also been successful.

Supplements to in-depth work with individual families may include volunteers to listen sympathetically and answer general questions, written materials on diseases commonly treated in the unit and the methods and devices the staff employ in their therapy, and formal or informal group sessions with family members. These latter may be general and informational or more intimate and therapeutic. Several ICUs have developed written reminders to ensure that staff give family care, especially when a change in the patient's status takes place. When the patient goes to the operating room, "graduates" to another nursing unit, requires resuscitation, or dies, part of the routine involves contacting the family. A written protocol covering essential elements of the interaction might be available to the staff member talking with the family. One British group included such items as "offered time to be with and hold baby" and "grief reaction advice" on its check list.[54]

ICU directors will also have to educate the doctors who care for patients in their units, if only on defensive grounds. The social science literature on malpractice sends a clear message that skill in communication with patients and families, rather than technical expertise, is a key determinant of the frequency of lawsuits. Highly sophisticated specialists cannot expect their reputation or academic reward to substitute for time and effort spent in answering questions and conveying concern. House officers should be schooled in interviewing and counseling distressed families. If attending physicians cannot or will not serve as effective, compassionate role models and teachers, training directors should insist that representatives from behavioral sciences (liaison psychiatry, psychology, social work) provide didactic instruction, monitor practice, and give feedback to residents.

Policies About Visitors

No published data provide substantive support for restricted visiting. Some of the research in NICUs and extensive experience in pediatric and neonatal ICUs support the value, at least to parents, of unrestricted visiting. Older children and adults can often speak for themselves, and it is not clear why such self-determination should not guide who visits when; general guidelines should be used to provide some structure—for example, no more than two visitors at the bedside, normal sleeping hours observed if appropriate to the patient's condition, and so on. Visiting during procedures can be negotiated, depending upon the patient's level of comfort, the visitor, and person or persons performing the task. Some patients, especially children, may be so calmed by the sight or touch of a loved one during a noxious procedure as to require no other sedation or restraint. Even novice staff members usually welcome such assistance.

As mentioned repeatedly in the literature, actual family involvement in care may free ICU staff for other activities, can provide visitors with something to do while maintaining a vigil, and may allow family members to feel they are contributing usefully to the patient's treatment. The latter function may be especially helpful when guilt feelings are strong. Moreover, the high level of surveillance in an ICU might well permit family members to learn tasks they will need to perform at home (tracheostomy care, for example) while still in the safest possible environment. Those who bristle at the vision of families invading their units must assume the responsibility for demonstrating that limiting visiting is in the best interest of patients.

There may be times when visiting may be seen as excessive. The staff needs to find out whether family members have an alternative place to stay. Do financial constraints make commuting impossible or hotel or boarding house costs out of reach? Perhaps the family believes a close relative is expected to be on hand at all times. More importantly, visitors may feel an obligation to stay against their own wishes. Such families need to be given permission to leave, and a genuine assurance that they will be contacted regularly and in emergencies.

It should go without saying that provisions for the personal comfort and privacy of visitors are extremely important. Pleasant waiting areas with access to information about the patient, such as a telephone link or intercom to the ICU, are especially helpful. Also important are reminders of the real world: televisions, clocks, calendars, windows, and such. At minimum, there should be information about services such as food, shelter, laundry, stores, religious services or clergy availability, financial counseling, and the like. These could be provided on bulletin boards, in brochures, by volunteers and/or patient service representatives. Ideally, there should be sleeping and ample bathroom facilities, including showers. These latter are particularly valuable in regional tertiary care centers.

Family privacy is so often disregarded that one wonders if the notion has been abandoned by the critical care community. A separate place, beyond the eyes and ears of fellow vigil holders and other staff alike, should be available for staff consultation with families and for family members to hold meetings among themselves. Public announcements of "turns for the worse" or death may protect staff members from the pain of dealing directly with family anguish; in the long run, however, such maneuvers can correctly be seen as cruel and almost always unnecessary.

Family Counseling

It is impossible to stress too strongly the crucial element of success with families: information. Relatives and friends want to know the diagnosis, the meaning of the diagnosis, the treatment, and the consequences of disease and treatment. (Professionals must be careful, of course, about the persons authorized by patients or parents to receive information. Confidentiality is a necessary element of a trusting relationship.) Family members frequently want this information repeatedly, knowing full well nothing has changed since the last time the data were sought and reiterated. Perseverance and saintly patience are required. It must be admitted that there are hazards lurking in the seemingly innocent acts of explanation, reply, and recitation. Family members may hang on differences in intonation or wording between one encounter and another. Answers that two professionals might consider equivalent may be seen by anxious loved ones as inconsistent, contradictory, or evidence of staff confusion and incompetence. The inevitability of such difficulties should be acknowledged to families at the earliest possible moment. When particular families seem to thrive on identifying and using minor differences to divide the staff, the number of people exchanging information should be minimized. In addition, the staff should emphasize communication with and through the physician and nurse most directly responsible for the patient's care. It may also be helpful to negotiate with a large family to appoint a principal spokesperson. Retreat into silence by the staff when a family is challenging or demanding only invites conflict escalation.

Such problems in the flow of information and sentiment bring up another set of concerns that bridge the psychosocial and moral dilemmas of working with families in intensive care units. These may be loosely lumped under the category of "continuity." Part of the problem is caused by the family's troubles identifying who is in charge and who provides overall coordination of the patient's care. In the private practice setting, this difficulty arises when one partner or associate makes rounds or consults at one time and other colleagues come at other times. At the very least, families (not to mention patients) deserve an explanation of how the doctors arrange their time and coordinate their efforts. In academic centers, house officers have nights on-call and often leave the ICU the following morning, while family may not have met any of the other physicians. Rotations end, attendings go "off-service," and nurses have schedules that do not conform to family expectations. Sadly, medical professionals often view themselves as interchangeable parts, assuming their persons or personalities have no meaning or value to patients and families. To the extent possible, families should have the systems explained and reassurance given that someone is indeed overseeing what may appear to be highly fragmented, mechanistic attention to the patient. The staff, on the other hand, must grapple with the consequences of such inconstancy and acknowledge the depersonalization entailed.

The other part of this issue arises when an adult patient becomes incompetent and cannot provide continuity in decision making for him- or herself. (This is not meant to dismiss the philosophical and practical problems associated with minors or others who have always been legally viewed as incompetent. Those considerable difficulties go beyond the scope of this chapter.) There is little problem in handling the common situations where the staff is confronted with a need for emergency action and the patient cannot consent. Ethically and legally, one presumes the value of treatment to the patient and provides it. The problem comes when, in the course of treatment which has been generally but not specifically consented to, the patient loses his or her ability to consider and express valid opinions about continued efforts. Medical custom has been to rely on the next of kin for proxy consent and direction. While such practice should continue, problems may surface.

First, the spouse or other relative may indicate a direction of treatment contrary to what the staff believes the patient would have wished. Second, strong conflict about the course of treatment may exist within the patient's close family. Third, one high court has indicated that, at least in the state of jurisdiction, no legal authority for family decision making exists in the absence of a separate petition for guardianship by a relative. (See the New Jersey Supreme Court's decision in the *Conroy* case.[69] For a contrary view, see the Court of Appeals of the State of California decision in the *Barber-Nejdl* murder prosecution.)[70]

These concerns are raised here to alert ICU staff members to what may become increasing involvement with the legal system. More importantly, contingency planning should become part of comprehensive patient and family counseling. Patients should be urged to provide "living wills" or establish a durable power of attorney. Families and patients should consider who should assume decision-making responsibility if the patient cannot. The families should think specifically about the extent of technologic intervention desired if quality of life (in the patient's terms) becomes compromised. Of course, all of these points assume that the patient and family should be an integral part of the medical decision making.

The message here is that patient and family autonomy must, as a rule, be respected, with appropriate caveats.[71] The staff must fight the tendency of medical professionals to be somewhat paternalistic and authoritarian, resist the natural tendency to ethnocentrism which causes the staff to overlook the values and desires of families from different backgrounds, and constantly search their own hearts and minds for evidence that feelings may be interfering with effective work with families. Examples of these behaviors include: 1. staff imposition of its judgment that a neurologically damaged child would only burden a family, when the parents see the child's survival as a welcome miracle; 2. glib advice to families to consult with clergy, rely on an extended family, or turn to a primary care physician when disappointment with God, intrafamilial conflict, or blame for misdiagnosis or mistreatment (whether justified or not) loom large; 3. staff assumption that screaming or head banging represent emotional disturbance, rather than a culturally approved reaction; 4. bland reassurance to parents that they can "always have another child."

Along these same lines, other authors[46,72-73] have warned that the constant exposure to crisis may blunt the ability of the ICU staff to respond empathically. In addition, they have reminded us that the behavior of the families may reflect the actions and emotions of the staff. If the staff is overworked, rushed, and angry, visitors may well respond with impatience, increased demands, and anxiety. When the staff has suffered a bad stretch of frequent or unexpected deaths, family members may react with excessive sadness or fear of deaths of their loved ones.

All of these potential pitfalls require staff members to constantly assess the impact of their interactions on the families and to solicit feedback from family members. Do the visitors really understand why the monitor alarms (a lead has become disconnected), or that the evident paralysis is pharmacologic, not a permanent consequence of injury or therapeutic misadventure? Have the doctors and nurses overwhelmed the family with jargon or condescendingly oversimplified their explanations? Do the parents of the 850 gram infant understand they can call any time or request the nurse to phone them long distance at two or three specified times a day?

It is the author's belief and experience that careful but exhausting attention to details of family care will yield great reward. Guiding relatives over the emotional roller coaster attendant to critical illness can provide the kind of interpersonal reward many of us sought when entering the health professions. Humanizing the experience for families may rehumanize technologic medicine for us.

REFERENCES

1. Lear MW: *Heartsounds.* New York: Pocket Books, 1981:31.
2. Kornfeld DS, Zimberg S, Malm J: Psychiatric complications of open-heart surgery. *N Engl J Med* 1965, *273*:287-292.
3. Hackett TP, Cassem NH, Wishnie HA: The coronary-care unit—An appraisal of its psychologic hazards. *N Engl J Med* 1968, *279*:1365-1370.
4. Strauss A: The intensive care unit: Its characteristics and social relationships. *Nurs Clin North Am* 1968, *3*:7-15.
5. Brown AJ: Effect of family visits on the blood pressure and heart rate on patients in the coronary-care unit. *Heart Lung* 1976, *5*:291-296.
6. Frader JE: Difficulties in providing intensive care. *Pediatrics* 1979, *64*:10-16.
7. Klein RF, Dean A, Willson LM, Bogdonoff MD: The physician and postmyocardial infarction invalidism. *JAMA* 1965, *194*:123-128.
8. Wynn A: Unwarranted emotional distress in men with ischaemic heart disease-Melbourne. *Med J Aust* 1967, *2*:847-851.
9. Adsett CA, Bruhn JG: Short-term group psychotherapy for post-myocardial infarction patients and their wives. *Can Med Assoc J* 1968, *99*:577-584.
10. Wishnie HA, Hackett TP, Cassem NH: Psychological hazards of convalescence following myocardial infarction. *JAMA* 1971, *215*:1292-1296.

11. Zetterlùnd JE: An evaluation of visiting policies for intensive and coronary care units. In: Duffy M, Anderson EH, Bergersen BS, Lohr M, Rose MH, eds. *Current Concepts in Clinical Nursing.* Vol. III. Saint Louis, MO: CV Mosby Co, 1971:326-325.

12. Skelton M, Dominian J: Psychological stress in wives of patients with myocardial infarction. *Br Med J* 1973, *2*:101-103.

13. Mayou R, Williamson B, Foster A: Attitudes and advice after myocardial infarction. *Br Med J* 1976, *1*:1577-1579.

14. Bedsworth JA, Molen MT: Psychological stress in spouses of patients with myocardial infarction. *Heart Lung* 1982, *11*:450-456.

15. Epperson MM: Families in sudden crisis: Process and intervention in a critical care center. *Soc Work Health Care* 1977, *2*:265-273.

16. Molter NC: Needs of relatives of critically ill patients: a descriptive study. *Heart Lung* 1979, *8*:332-339.

17. Daley L: The perceived immediate needs of families with relatives in the intensive care setting. *Heart Lung* 1984, *13*:231-237.

18. Stillwell SB: Importance of visiting needs as perceived by family members of patients in the intensive care unit. *Heart Lung* 1984, *13*:238-242.

19. Mathis M: Personal needs of family members of critically ill patients with and without acute brain injury. *J Neurosurg Nurs* 1984, *16*:36-44.

20. Speedling EJ: Social structure and social behavior in an intensive care unit: patient-family perspectives. *Soc Work Health Care* 1980, *6*:1-22.

21. Atkinson JH, Stewart N, Gardner D: The family meeting in critical care settings. *J Trauma* 1980, *20*:43-46.

22. Hodovanic BH, Reardon D, Reese W, Hedges B: Family crisis intervention program in the medical intensive care unit. *Heart Lung* 1984, *13*:243-249.

23. Fuller BF, Foster GM: The effects of family/friend visits vs. staff interaction on stress/arousal of surgical intensive care patients. *Heart Lung* 1982, *11*:457-463.

24. Kirchhoff KT: Visiting policies for patients with myocardial infarction: A national survey. *Heart Lung* 1982, *11*:571-576.

25. Dunkel J, Eisendrath S: Families in the intensive care unit: Their effect on staff. *Heart Lung* 1983, *12*:258-261.

26. Richmond JB, Waisman HA: Psychologic aspects of management of children with malignant diseases. *Am J Dis Child* 1955, *89*:42-47.

27. Bozeman MF, Orbach CE, Sutherland AM: Psychological impact of cancer and its treatment: III. The adaptation of mothers to the threatened loss of their children through leukemia: part I. *Cancer* 1955, *8*:1-19.

28. Natterson JM, Knudson AG: Observations concerning fear of death in fatally ill children and their mothers. *Psychosom Med* 1960, *XXII*:456-465.

29. Solnit AJ, Green M: Psychological considerations in the management of deaths on pediatric hospital services: 1. The doctor and the child's family. *Pediatrics* 1959, *24*:106-112.

30. Solnit AJ, Green M: The pediatric management of the dying child: part II. The child's reaction to the fear of dying. In: Solnit A, Provence SA, eds. *Modern Perspectives in Child Development.* New York: International Press, 1963:217-228.

31. Green M, Solnit AJ: Reactions to the threatened loss of a child: A vulnerable child syndrome. *Pediatrics* 1964, *34*:58-56.

32. Friedman SB, Chodoff P, Mason JW, Hamburg DA: Behavioral observations on parents anticipating the death of a child. *Pediatrics* 1963, *32*:610-624.

33. Friedman SB, Mason JW, Hamburg DA: Urinary 17-hydroxycorticosteroid levels in parents of children with neoplastic disease: A study of chronic psychological stress. *Psychosom Med* 1963, *15*:364-76.

34. Friedman SB: Care of the family of the child with cancer. *Pediatrics* 1967, *40*:498-507.

35. Howell DA: A child dies. *Pediatr Surg* 1966, *1*:2-7.

36. Evans AE, Edin S: If a child must die. *N Engl J Med* 1968, *278*:138-142.

37. Vernick J, Karon M: Who's afraid of death on a leukemia ward? *Amer J Dis Child* 1965, *109*:393-397.

38. Martin HL, Lawrie JH, Wilkinson AW: The family of the fatally burned child. *Lancet* 1968, *2*:628-629.

39. Binger CM, Ablin AR, Feuerstein RC, Kushner JH, Zoger S, Mikkelsen C: Childhood leukemia: Emotional impact on patient and family. *N Engl J Med* 1969, *280*:414-418.

40. May JG: A psychiatric study of a pediatric intensive therapy unit. *Clin Pediatr* 1972, *11*:76-82.

41. Jay SS: Pediatric intensive care: Involving parents in the care of their child. *Matern Child Nurs J* 1977, *6*:195-203.

42. Frader JE, Bosk CL: Parent talk at intensive care rounds. *Soc Sci Med* 1981, *15E*:267-274.

43. Waller DA, Tordos D, Cassem NH, Anderten A: Coping with poor prognosis in the pediatric intensive care unit. *Am J Dis Child* 1979, *133*:1121-1125.

44. Green M: Parent care in the intensive care unit. *Am J Dis Child* 1979, *133*:1119-1120.

45. Rothstein P: Psychological stress in families of children in a pediatric intensive care unit. *Pediatr Clin North Am* 1980, *27*:613-620.

46. Woolston JL: Psychiatric aspects of a pediatric intensive care unit. *Yale J of Biol Med* 1984, *57*:97-110.

47. Kennell JH, Slyter H, Klaus MH: The mourning response of parents to the death of a newborn infant. *N Engl J Med* 1970, *293*:344-349.

48. Duff RS, Campbell GM: Moral and ethical dilemmas in the special-care nursery. *N Engl J Med* 1973, *289*:890-894.

49. Benfield DG, Leib SA, Reuter J: Grief response of parents after referral of the critically ill newborn to a regional center. *N Engl J Med* 1976, *295*:287-288.

50. Benfield DG, Leib SA, Vollman JH: Grief response of parents to neonatal death and parent participation in deciding care. *Pediatrics* 1978, *62*:171-177.

51. Rowe J, Clyman R, Green C, Mikkelsen C, Haight J, Ataide L: Follow-up of families who experience a perinatal death. *Pediatrics* 1978, *62*:166-170.

52. Whitfield JM, Siegel RE, Glicken AD, Harmon RJ, Powers LK, Goldson EJ: The application of hospice concepts to neonatal care. *Am J Dis Child* 1982, *136*:421-424.

53. Harmon RJ, Glicken AD, Siegel RE: Neonatal loss in the intensive care nursery: Effects of maternal grieving and a program for intervention. *J Am Aca Child Psychiatry* 1984, *23*:68-71.

54. White MP, Reynolds B, Evans TJ: Handling of death in special care nurseries and parental grief. *Br Med J* 1984, *289*:167-169.

55. Minde K, Shosenberg N, Marton P, Thompson J, Ripley J, Burns S: Self-help groups in a premature nursery—A controlled evaluation. *J Pediatr* 1980, *96*:933-940.

56. Dammers J, Harpin V: Parents' meetings in two neonatal units: a way of increasing support for parents. *Br Med J* 1982, *285*:863-865.

57. Yu VYH, Jamieson J, Astbury J: Parents' reactions to unrestricted parental contact with infants in the intensive care nursery. *Med J Aust* 1981, *1*:294-296.

58. Schwab F, Tolbert B, Bagnato S, Maisels MJ: Sibling visiting in a neonatal intensive care unit. *Pediatrics* 1983, *71*:835-838.

59. Maloney MJ, Ballard JL, Hollister L, Shank M: A prospective, controlled study of scheduled sibling visits to a newborn intensive care unit. *J Am Acad Child Psychiatry* 1983, *22*:565-570.

60. Klaus M, Kennell J: Interventions in the premature nursery: impact on development. *Pediatr Clin North Am* 1982, *29*:1263-1273.

61. Jones CL: Environmental analysis of neonatal intensive care. *J Nervous Mental Disease* 1982, *170*:130-142.

62. Piecuch RE, Roth RS, Clyman RI, Sniderman SH, Riedel PH, Ballard RA: Videophone use improves maternal interest in transported infants. *Crit Care Med* 1983, *11*:655-656.

63. Smith MA, Baum JD: Costs of visiting babies in special care baby units. *Arch Dis Child* 1983, *58*:56-59.

64. Bogdan R, Brown MA, Foster SB: Be honest but not cruel: Staff/parent communication on a neonatal unit. *Human Organization* 1982, *41*:6-16.

65. Philipp C: Parental perceptions of children who were hospitalized in neonatal intensive care units. *Child Psychiatry Hum Dev* 1983, *14*:76-86.

66. Watchko JF: Decision making on critically ill infants by parents. *Am J Dis Child* 1983, *137*:795-798.

67. Waserman M: Relieving parental anxiety: John Warren's 1792 letter to the father of a burned child. *N Engl J Med* 1978, *299*:135-136.

68. Gardner D, Stewart N: Staff involvement with families of patients in critical-care units. *Heart Lung* 1978, 7:105-110.
69. In re *Conroy*, 486 A 2d, 1209 (N.J. 1985).
70. *Barber* v. *Superior Court*, 147 CA3d, 1006 (Calif. 1983).
71. Jackson DL, Youngner SJ: Patient autonomy and 'death with dignity': Some clinical caveats. *N Engl J Med* 1979, *301*:404-408.
72. Kachoris PJ: Psychodynamic considerations in the neonatal ICU. *Crit Care Med* 1977, *5*:62-65.
73. Brody EB, Klein H: The intensive care nursery as a small society. *Paediatrician* 1980, *9*:169-181.

Index

coronary care, 128, 130, 149-50, 151-53, 154-55

costs, 112; and decision making, 32, 37; of ICUs, 89-91, 94, 95-96; of neonatal intensive care, 72; of organ transplantation, 113-14, 118. *See also* reimbursement

counseling, 174-77

courts, 61, 70, 176. *See also* legal issues

CPR, 18, 23, 30; patient decision against, 25-26; success rate of, 17; unique characteristics of, 15-17. *See also* DNR orders

cranial hemorrhage, 77

critical care medicine: association with institutions, 6; growing sector of economy, 4; team approach to, 5, 131-36; technology and, 2, 3. *See also* intensive care units; medical profession; neonatal intensive care; nurses

Cummins R.O., Prehospital cardiopulmonary resuscitation, 16

cyclosporin, 109-10

death, 15-16, 29, 31, 35-36, 158-60, 165-66. *See also* DNR orders; termination of treatment

decision making: broad input, 70; families involved in, 164-65, 169-70, 176; inhibiting, 41; in neonatal intensive care (*see* neonatal intensive care); nurses involved in, 27-28; patients and, 24, 37; and rationing of ICUs, 97-98; technology and, 3; and termination of treatment, 36-37; uncertainty of, 22; and values, 7, 98. *See also* DNR orders

Department of Health and Human Services, 67

determination of needs process. *See* DON process

diagnostic-related groups. *See* DRGs

dialysis, 93

DNR orders, 15; and abandonment, 29-32; confusion regarding, 20-21; documentation and specification of, 18-22, 26; in ICUs, 29-30, 88; involvement of health professionals, 27-28; legal consequences of, 21; and nonmedical values, 30-32; patient and family involvement in, 23-27; review of, 29; for viable patients, 30. *See also* CPR; termination of treatment

doctors. *See* physicians

documentation, of DNR orders, 18-22

donors. *See* organ transplantation, donor selection.

do not resuscitate (DNR) orders. *See* DNR orders

DON process, 113-16. *See also* needs assessment

Down's syndrome, 66-67

DRGs, 94, 96, 105

Duff, R.S., Moral and ethical dilemmas, 164-65

Dunkel, J., Families in the intensive care unit, 155-56

economic interests, 74. *See also* costs

economy, 4

education, 4; of nurses, 124, 128, 135

egalitarianism, 102-3, 113, 114

elderly, 88-89

end-stage renal disease programs. *See* ESRD programs

England. *See* Great Britain

Epperson, M.M., Families in sudden crisis,

equity, 102-3, 113, 114

Erde, E.E., Notions of teams and team talk in health care, 131-32

ESRD programs, 92, 93

ethics, 98, 112. *See also* moral reasoning; values

ethnography, 168-69

euthanasia, 53, 57-58, 65, 74. *See also* DNR orders; mercy killing; termination of treatment

Evans, A.L., The do-not-resuscitate order in teaching hospitals, 23

families: of adult patients, 151-56; care of, 170-73; of coronary care patients, 149-53; counseling, 174-77; involvement in DNR orders, 23-27; medical profession and, 155-56, 161-62, 165-66, 176-77; and neonatal intensive care, 69, 72, 164-70; nurses and, 141-42, 150, 154, 156; and organ transplantation, 110-11; of pediatric patients, 150, 156-64. relationships, 159; and termination of treatment, 40-41. *See also* parents

fathers, 161. *See also* families

feminism, 138

follow-up, 165-66

Frader, J.E., 161-62

[neonatal intensive care]
72; parents and, 159, 164-70; priority principle, 79-81; prolongation of life in, 73-76; and quality of life, 76-78, 81-82; and the right to die, 76-78; termination of treatment in, criteria for, 72-73; termination of treatment in, historical context, 64-68; termination of treatment in, who should decide, 68-71; visitation, 167-68, 173. *See also* infants; intensive care units
New Jersey Supreme Court, 61
NICU. *See* neonatal intensive care
no-code orders, 18-19, 20, 22. *See also* DNR orders
nurses, 18-19; as coordinators and advocates, 134-42; current status of, 128-42; defined, 125; demographics of, 124, 128; education of, 124, 128, 135; effects of misogyny on, 138-39; and families, 141-42, 150, 154, 156; informal powers of, 144-45; involved in decision making, 27-28, 41; issues and conflicts, 136-39; lack of autonomy, 137; media images of, 125; and other health professionals, 137-38; and patients, 126-27, 132, 140-41, 161; philosophy of, 125-28; and physicians, 126-28, 143-44; and the prolongation of life, 73-74; roles of, 126-27, 134-37; sex segregation of, 124, 138, 144; stress and, 128-31; variable group norms for, 132-34
nursing homes, 89
nutrition, 78

obesity, 16-17
Ohio, organ transplantation in, 116-21
optimal care, 79
organ transplantation, 2, 118; cost of, 113-14, 118; donor selection, 119-20; duplicated service, 116; history of, 109-10; in Massachusetts, 113-16; media and, 110, 121; Medicaid and, 110-11, 118; in Ohio, 116-21; organ procurement and distribution, 119-20; patient selection, 114-15, 117-19; politics and, 110-11, 120; research and data sharing, 120-21; review of, 114, 116-17; social and ethnical considerations, 112; survival rate, 110
oxygen supplementation, 64

pain, 56, 76. *See also* suffering
painkillers, 53
pancreas transplantation, 118. *See also* organ transplantation,
paramedics, 16
parents, rights of, 66, 68. *See also* families
paternalism, 24, 59-60, 160, 163-64, 176
patients: alienation of, 136; autonomy of, 37-38, 40, 59, 66, 78; communication with, 24-25, 40; competence of, 39-40, 55-56, 175-76; influence on, 40-41; interests of, 72, 77; involvement in DNR orders, 23-27; nurses and, 126-27, 132, 140-41, 161; rights of, 52; and termination of treatment, 54
patriarchy, 138
pediatrics, 150, 156-64. *See also* neonatal intensive care
personal histories, 163. *See also* documentation
Philipp, C., Parental perceptions of children, 169
physicians: and nurses, 126-28, 129-30, 143-44; and patients, 52, 57-58, 68, 70-71, 101. *See also* medical profession
PICU. *See* pediatrics
Pius XII, 43
policy, public. *See* public policy
politics, 110-11, 120
postindustrial society, 1-8
premature birth, 69-70, 72, 80-81. *See also* neonatal intensive care
"premium baby" mentality, 66
prenatal care, 92-93
President's Commission for the Study of Ethical Problems in Medicine and Biomedical and Behavioral Research, 22, 29, 36, 61, 71
preventive medicine, 92, 96
primitive intuition, 51-52
priority principle, 79-81
privacy, 174
private investment, 94
professional associations, 5-6
prognosis, 90, 162
progress notes. *See* documentation
prolongation of life, 35-36, 41, 42-43, 59; in neonatal intensive care, 72-73; in neonatal intensive care, in the interest of infants, 74-76; in neonatal intensive care, in the interest of others, 73-74
prospective payment. *See* DRGs

Contributors

George J. Annas, J.D., M.P.H.
Utley Professor of Health Law
Boston University School of Medicine
Chief, Health Law Section
Boston University School of Public Health
80 East Concord Street
Boston, Massachusetts 02118

Marilyn Bennett
Department of Philosophy
University of Minnesota
Minneapolis, Minnesota 55455

Claudia J. Coulton, Ph.D.
Professor and Chairman of Doctoral Program
School of Applied Social Sciences
Case Western Reserve University
2035 Abington Road
Cleveland, Ohio 44106

Barbara J. Daly, R.N., M.S.N., F.A.A.N.
Assistant Director of Medical/Surgical Nursing
University Hospitals
2074 Abington Road
Cleveland, Ohio 44106

Joel E. Frader, M.D.
Assistant Professor of Pediatrics
University of Pittsburgh School of Medicine
125 De Soto Street
Pittsburgh, Pennsylvania 15213

David L. Jackson, M.D., Ph.D.
Former Director of Ohio Department of Health
1591 Fishinger Road
Upper Arlington, Ohio 43221

William A. Knaus, M.D.
Director of ICU Research
Co-Director of ICU
Associate Professor of Anesthesiology
George Washington University Medical Center
2300 K Street, N.W.
Washington, D.C. 20037

Mary B. Mahowald, Ph.D.
Associate Professor of Medical Ethics
(appointments in Departments of Pediatrics, Reproductive
Biology, Medicine, Philosophy)
Co-Director of Center for Biomedical Ethics
Case Western Reserve University School of Medicine
2119 Abington Road
Cleveland, Ohio 44106

David Mayo, Ph.D.
Associate Professor of Philosophy
University of Minnesota
Department of Philosophy and Humanities
Duluth, Minnesota 55812

Stuart Youngner, M.D.
Associate Professor of Psychiatry and Medicine
Case Western Reserve University School of Medicine
Cleveland, Ohio 44106